MY INDIANA
101 MORE
PLACES TO SEE

MY INDIANA
101 MORE
PLACES TO SEE

Text and Photos by
EARL L. CONN

INDIANA HISTORICAL SOCIETY PRESS
INDIANAPOLIS 2009

Printed in China
This book is a publication of the
Indiana Historical Society Press
450 West Ohio Street
Indianapolis, Indiana 46202-3269 USA
www.indianahistory.org

The paper in this publication meets the minimum requirements of
American National Standard for Information Sciences—Permanence
of Paper for Printed Library Materials, ANSI Z39.48-1984.

ISBN 978-0-87195-276-9

To my dearest wife, Christina, who has been
and continues to be my support
and guiding star in all that I do

Table of Contents

SOUTH CENTRAL

SOUTH

Preface

First, I want to thank readers who purchased—and, hopefully, enjoyed—my previous book, *My Indiana: 101 Places to See.* My understanding from the Indiana Historical Society Press is that the first printing sold out and a second printing also has done well. I am deeply gratified it found such favor with readers.

This second book, *My Indiana: 101 More Places to See*, seemed a likely writing and publishing decision. Once again, this book is based on my travel articles that have appeared in Indiana newspapers.

Let me note a few differences readers might observe in the two books.

My conversational writing style has continued to evolve as evidenced by a number of the articles in this book. "Essays" might be a term that could describe them more accurately than articles or travel columns.

I have included a wider variety of places in this book. To see what I was including, I divided each place selected into categories: parks, courthouses, art, cities, etc. I found I had fourteen such categories. The "biggies," as you will find, are museums, parks, history, tours, and cities. It is an eclectic group and sets this book apart from most travel books—for better or for worse.

Many other elements remain the same.

Again, I divided Indiana into the six areas following the format of the Indiana Department of Commerce: North, East, Central, West, South Central, and South with a similar number of places within each. Each section is preceded by a map locating its sites. In organizing each section, its list most often moves geographically from west to east as the first book did, except where a grouping of two or more numbers in the same general region seemed logical.

You will also again find that places you know well have been included. Also some "back in the corners" spots that perhaps you don't know as well, or, perhaps, haven't even heard about. Hopefully, they are interesting, too.

All of the photographs in the book are ones taken by me when I visited each site. I still use a 35 mm. film camera, although I have a new digital one. Don't ask me why I stay with film; I just do.

And, once again, I know how easily mistakes can be made, especially when many facts, figures, directions, etc., are used. Each article has been examined by knowledgeable sources at the site for any factual errors or significant omissions. In addition, I have revised and updated some and given each my own editing as has the Indiana Historical Society Press. Nevertheless, I accept the responsibility for whatever errors might exist.

Beyond errors, remember that things change. It's always a good idea when traveling to first call or go to the Web site to make certain about a location and that its hours still are correct.

And a note about our state.

Indiana continues to amaze me. Others tell me it still amazes them as well. No doubt, similar examples could be found in every state. Still, it seems, just when you think you have heard everything, yet another place, another happening, or another oddity pops up that makes a trip there more than worthwhile.

Finally, thank you again for the first book's reception. I hope you find this one equally readable and helpful.

Earl L. Conn
Muncie, Indiana
January 2009

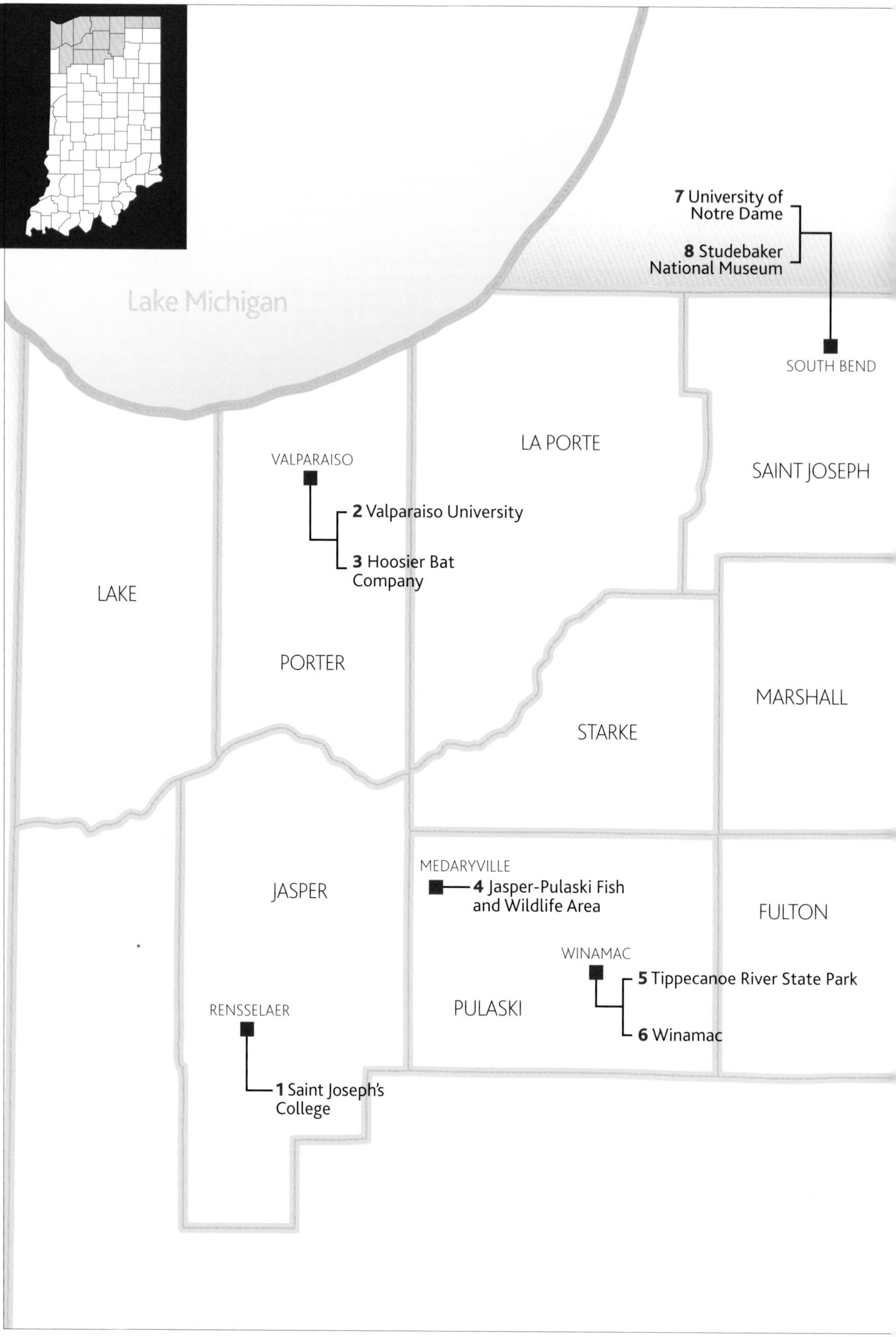

NORTH

Lake Michigan

7 University of Notre Dame

8 Studebaker National Museum

SOUTH BEND

LA PORTE

SAINT JOSEPH

VALPARAISO

2 Valparaiso University

3 Hoosier Bat Company

LAKE

PORTER

STARKE

MARSHALL

MEDARYVILLE

4 Jasper-Pulaski Fish and Wildlife Area

JASPER

FULTON

WINAMAC

5 Tippecanoe River State Park

RENSSELAER

PULASKI

6 Winamac

1 Saint Joseph's College

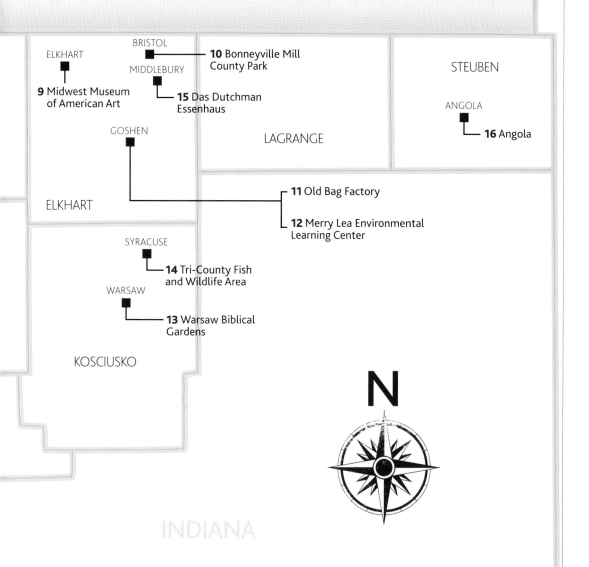

MICHIGAN

OHIO

BRISTOL

ELKHART

10 Bonneyville Mill County Park

MIDDLEBURY

STEUBEN

9 Midwest Museum of American Art

15 Das Dutchman Essenhaus

ANGOLA

GOSHEN

LAGRANGE

16 Angola

ELKHART

11 Old Bag Factory

12 Merry Lea Environmental Learning Center

SYRACUSE

14 Tri-County Fish and Wildlife Area

WARSAW

13 Warsaw Biblical Gardens

KOSCIUSKO

N

INDIANA

HALLECK STUDENT CENTER. It provides a focus for student activities on the campus at Rensselaer.

SAINT JOSEPH'S CHAPEL. The identifying landmark on the Saint Joseph's College campus in northwestern Indiana.

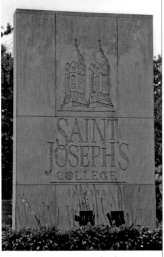

COLLEGE ENTRANCE. This large stone marks the entrance to Saint Joseph's College in northwestern Indiana.

Saint Joseph's College, Rensselaer

RENSSELAER—It's one of those scenes replicated across Indiana—across the whole United States, for that matter—and yet each in its own way has its own distinctive character, its own special something—or several somethings—that sets it aside from the rest.

I'm speaking of college and university campuses, especially the smaller schools that dot the land—in the relatively small state of Indiana, more than thirty of them. Over the years, I have visited most of them, and—I suppose it's the romantic in me—but I find something very special and endearing about each one. Take, for instance, Saint Joseph's College on the south side of Rensselaer in northwestern Indiana.

As I have noted elsewhere about campus visits, most of them, quite naturally, are made by prospective students and their parents to "check it out." Nothing can quite give you the "feel" of a campus compared to actually being there. But every campus I have seen also has welcomed the visitor who shows up simply to look around.

In Saint Joseph's case, I stopped by the Admissions Office's Welcome Center, located in Schwietermann Hall, and chatted with the receptionist. She told me visitors can call ahead for an escorted tour or just show up and use a campus map to conduct their own tour. Also remember, since the college is located in Jasper County, one of six northwestern Indiana counties on central, or Chicago, time, it's one hour earlier than most of the rest of the state. (I told the receptionist I was surprised to find her still working at 5:30. Of course, it wasn't 5:30; it was 4:30 p.m.)

What's special about Saint Joseph's College? One must be careful in making judgments at all, let alone from a rather brief time on campus. Still, I would note a few.

Although I'm a no-frills Quaker by preference, I still find much about Catholicism to be of great interest. So, I found myself fascinated by the beautiful Saint Joseph's Chapel and its twin spires as well as the Lourdes Grotto and Stations of the Cross. The chapel perhaps is even more inspiring when seen across the reflecting pond as you enter the campus on

LOURDES GROTTO. A frequently visited place on the Saint Joseph's College campus, along with the adjoining Stations of the Cross walkway.

Father Gross Road. And just to walk along the path to the Grotto following the Stations of the Cross gives a sense of quiet and peace not felt too many places on this earth today.

I suspect that the Halleck Student Center is the hub of the campus. It houses practically all of the student services and administrators of that area, the college store, ballroom, dining room, snack bar, and lounge.

Athletics always have been important at Saint Joseph's. The northern portion of the campus is devoted to baseball, football, track and field, tennis, basketball, volleyball, and a recreation center. Soccer and softball are a bit removed, over on the southwest side of the campus.

It's less necessary to plan your visit when the students are not on campus at these smaller schools. You'll probably find a parking spot without great difficulty. As I observed earlier, it's one of Indiana's smaller campuses—about 180 acres. You can see everything in a fairly short period of time.

Maybe that only adds to its charm.

IF YOU GO

GETTING THERE: The college is just south of Rensselaer on U.S. 231.

INFORMATION: Call (800) 447–8781, or go to http://www .saintjoe.edu/.

FEES: None.

THE VICTORY BELL. It rings following Valparaiso University football and basketball wins. It stands in front of the university's Student Union Building.

BELL TOWER. The Brandt Campanile—bell tower—stands adjacent to the Chapel of the Resurrection on the Valparaiso University campus.

Valparaiso University, Valparaiso

VALPARAISO—Every college or university has that one place that must be seen. Often it's the landmark for which the campus is best known. The Chapel of the Resurrection has long filled that assignment on the Valparaiso University campus. Dedicated in 1959, the university's centennial year, it dominates the view as visitors swing onto the campus off heavily traveled U.S. 30 in northwestern Indiana.

University publications declare it to be the heart of the campus. That wasn't hard to believe during my visit there. People poured in and out of the main entrance. Small groups were meeting here, there, and everywhere. In the main chapel, with seating for two thousand, there were numbers of people, most of them appearing to be busy about various tasks.

The facts about the chapel, termed one of the largest collegiate chapels in the world, are impressive. Cost—$7.5 million in 1950s dollars. Chancel height—98 feet of limestone, ending in a nine-point-star roof. Nave length—193 feet. Organ—4 manuals, 101 ranks. Freestanding Brandt Campanile—140 feet with 12 bronze bells cast in Holland, the largest weighing 8½ tons.

But it's the stained-glass windows of the chapel that especially catch the visitor's eye. The three windows—sometimes called "sermons in color"—are the creation window, the redemption window, and the sanctification window. Their panels, thirty in all, depict much about the Christian message as well as the church's outward role. The thirtieth window is Martin Luther's coat of arms with the torch of the university.

Originally founded in 1859 as Valparaiso Male and Female College, it was one of the first coeducational institutions in the United States. It was purchased in 1925 by the Lutheran University Association, which operates it today.

Awe-inspiring? Absolutely. But the campus, of course, is more than the chapel.

Nearby is the Center for the Arts, home of the Brauer Museum of Art, which periodically hosts special exhibitions and includes more than two thousand pieces of art. Its public showings are free.

VALPARAISO UNIVERSITY. Chapel of the Resurrection is a highlight for any visitor to the northern Indiana university campus.

IF YOU GO

Next to the chapel is the Christopher Center for Library and Information Resources, a $33-million project that opened in 2004. Immediately off U.S. 30 is the astronomical observatory with its sixteen-inch, computer-controlled reflecting telescope that, according to the university, is used in NASA-supported research.

Another new building is Kallay-Christopher Hall, a 16,830-square-foot structure opened in 2005 that houses the department of geography and meteorology. It's touted as a "state-of-the-art learning environment." Harre Union, part of a $74-million project, opened in January 2009.

It doesn't take all that long, however, to tour the four thousand-student campus, regularly ranked for the quality of its programs by *U.S. News and World Report* and as a "best value." A telephone call to University Relations can make arrangements for a campus student-led tour that will last from one-half to three-quarters of an hour. A chapel tour lasts half an hour. Bus tours also are welcome, beginning at the Student Union Building.

GETTING THERE: The university is immediately to the north off U.S. 30 as you enter the Valparaiso area from the east.

INFORMATION: For tours, call University Relations at (219) 464–5114. For information about exhibitions at Brauer Museum of Art, call (219) 464–5365. Visitors can park either at the student union or at the administration building.

FEES: None

HERE IT IS. Debbie Cook holds one of the three-piece wood bats, patented by her husband, David Cook. It's made of ash in the handle, hickory in the hitting area, and maple on the barrel end and has proven to be more durable than regular ash bats.

ONLY AUTOMATED PART. Lathe at the Hoosier Bat Company that trims wood into bat shape in baseball bat production at the Valparaiso company.

Hoosier Bat Company, Valparaiso

VALPARAISO—When you're watching a baseball game, either at the field or on television, and you see the hitter at the plate cocking his bat as he gets ready for the next pitch, take a look at the bat about midway between his hands and the end of the barrel. If you can see three painted rings going around the bat—and you will for about thirty-five to forty major leaguers—you can take a little Hoosier pride in what you see. That player is swinging a Hoosier Bat Company piece of hardwood produced at a Valparaiso business, which sends out about fifty thousand a year all around the world.

"We also sell them to several hundred minor leaguers, colleges, and high schools, as well as in Germany, Japan, Canada, Australia, Mexico—and we're working on other countries," says Debbie Cook, Hoosier Bat co-owner along with her husband, David Cook, a former New York Yankee scout.

Because of its proximity to Chicago, big purchasers have been the Cubs and White Sox. Two of the best-known Hoosier Bat Company hitters have been the recently retired home-run hitter Sammy Sosa and former White Sox slugger Frank Thomas. Major league teams pay for their players' bats, and Cook says Thomas usually has ordered four dozen at one time. The typical player orders a half dozen or dozen. "We usually do one or two first so the players can try to get the bats just the way they want them," Debbie says.

Those rings around the bat are painted one-by-one by hand by two Hoosier Bat employees—one of whom has "been doing it for a long time—and they get them straight." It's part of the basically hand-operated bat producing process, the only automated step being the lathe that turns a piece of lumber into a bat shape before hand sanding.

Since bat weight is critical to hitters, each bat is frequently inspected and weighed. The first time is when the wood comes in. Calculations are made for each model about how much wood will come off from the lathe with sanding and how much should be added through lacquer—black, natural, hickory, burnt orange—and sealing.

YES, THIS WILL BE A BAT. Blocks of ash, hickory, and maple will be "finger-locked" to produce the Hoosier Bat Company's patented bat. Sammy Sosa used one for two years in batting practice before the handle broke.

The special bat of the company is the three-piece patented bat not used in major league games but often part of batting practice. David designed the bat with its ash handle, hickory in the hitting area, and maple on the barrel end. It's held together by "finger-joint" cuts resembling interlocked fingers. "Like a weld," Debbie calls it. She says the bat's durability is in the barrel because it doesn't peel like an ash bat.

"Sammy Sosa used one for two years in batting practice before he finally broke the handle," she says. "If it had been a solid ash, after one round (of batting) the wood already would have started peeling. It's just the nature of the wood," Debbie explained.

Not surprising, the price of the bats goes up over time. At last check, they were selling for forty dollars for solid ash and fifty-five dollars for the three-piece bat.

Bats are produced year-round. "We do a good Christmas business. We do little retail here but mostly ship out our bats," says Debbie. The company has been in its present building since 1998.

IF YOU GO

GETTING THERE: On U.S. 30 in Valparaiso, take the Indiana 49 exit north to the Indiana 2 exit. Turn left off the ramp and at Silhavy Road turn right. At the next light, turn right again onto Evans Avenue to the Hoosier Bat Company at 4511 E. Evans. From Interstate 94, take the Valparaiso exit south to Indiana 49. Exit at Indiana 2 and turn right. At Silhavy Road, turn right, and then right again onto Evans at the next stoplight.

INFORMATION: Call first at (800) 228–3787, or go to http://www.hoosierbat.com/.

FEES: None.

HEADING SOUTH. Going toward Georgia and Florida for their fall migration, these sandhill cranes leave the Jasper–Pulaski Fish and Wildlife Area in northwestern Indiana.

SUNRISE. The sun is just breaking over this observation tower at the Jasper–Pulaski Fish and Wildlife Area near Medaryville. The migrations of sandhill cranes can be seen from the observation tower at dawn and dusk.

Jasper–Pulaski Fish and Wildlife Area, Medaryville

MEDARYVILLE—There's a cliché in sports about "taking one for the team": a basketball player takes a charge so he can shoot free throws, a baseball hitter is hit by a pitch so he can get on base to start a rally. To see the sandhill cranes, I felt as though I had taken one—or two or three—for readers. Let me explain.

For years I had heard about the sandhill cranes and their migrations to and from the South in the late fall and spring and about one of their major stopping sites—sometimes for weeks—at the Jasper–Pulaski Fish and Wildlife Area in northwestern Indiana. The area is a remnant of the huge Grand Kankakee Marsh that once covered perhaps as much as a half million acres. Now about thirty thousand acres remain of which slightly more than eight thousand are in this state fish and wildlife area.

The birds nest for the summer in the Great Lakes region and lower Canada before departing in the autumn for their winter homes in Georgia and Florida. Each journey takes somewhere around a month. Then they do the return trip in the spring.

When I talked to state personnel, I was told to come in early November to mid-December when the big migrations came through, heading south: "Fewer in October and late December," I was told, "although there still are several thousand in October and the weather is nicer."

But to report about the cranes and get that information to the readers so they might have time to make the trip, I needed to go when, in fact, I wouldn't see as much. So, that was taking one.

The best time to see the cranes in the sky is near dusk, as they are coming in to roost in the nearby wetlands for the night, and around daybreak, when they may be taking off on the next leg of the journey. This is not the easiest trip from eastern Indiana, especially at this time of the year when nightfall seems to come so quickly.

When I arrived, I took a few photos that I thought probably wouldn't be any good because it was too dark—they weren't— and realized my only hope to get better photos was to stay at

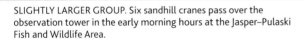

SLIGHTLY LARGER GROUP. Six sandhill cranes pass over the observation tower in the early morning hours at the Jasper–Pulaski Fish and Wildlife Area.

some motel overnight and go back out at daybreak. That was taking a second one.

The next morning, I was at the observation stand well before daybreak, after getting up before 6 a.m. In the chilly morning air, I set up a folding chair and waited. That may or may not be called a third one.

In the predawn light the cranes, mostly in groups of two or three, began to rise from the area and fly off to the south. As they prepared to leave, they were "gabbing," as one of the wildlife personnel called it. This "socializing" goes on as they feed on field grains and bugs.

Sandhill cranes have a seven-foot wingspan and stand about four feet tall. "Majestic" is a term often used to describe them as they take off and land. While they migrate, they search for air currents so they can glide. When they stay here, they are more likely to flap their wings during their daily feeding flights into surrounding fields. Using binoculars to watch—which I didn't think about—also would have been a good idea, although spotting scopes are provided at the observation area.

IF YOU GO

GETTING THERE: From U.S. 421, turn west to Indiana 143. Turn north to the entrance to the area. Once on the entrance road, do not turn at the main entrance but proceed to the next and turn right to the observation tower parking area.

INFORMATION: Call (219) 843–4841. Go to http://www.dnr.IN.gov/fishwild and to the Site Index for the Jasper–Pulaski Fish and Wildlife Area for more information, for a sandhill crane video, and for sounds of the cranes.

FEES: None.

ONE TRAIL. A summer view at Tippecanoe River State Park, north of Winamac.

TIPPECANOE RIVER STATE PARK. The park's nature center is on the right. A park shelter is at the left.

Tippecanoe River State Park, Winamac

WINAMAC—Indiana state park users tend to divide themselves into two groups. One likes the outdoors—hiking, biking, fishing—but they also appreciate the creature comforts of life, so they tend to opt for state parks featuring lodges, cabins, and swimming pools. The second group prefers the more rustic experience—group camping, toilets, hot water, and showers are sufficient. Tippecanoe River State Park mostly is an example of the latter, with one additional activity not found at all state parks.

First, there's camping. It seems as if about everyone in Indiana has "gone camping" at some time or the other. This family campground has 112 class A campsites with a few adapted for the physically handicapped. A youth tent area for up to 120 persons, divided into four units, occupies part of the north portion of the park, just south of the sandhill nature preserve.

Second, a horsemen's camp—fifty-six sites primitive in nature—and day use area are located at the south end of the property. Six horse trails, some of them paralleling hiking trails, range from .8 of a mile to 3.5 miles in length.

Third would be the hiking trails. All ten of them are easy to moderate in terrain. They extend from a short one-half-mile trail up to two 3.5-mile trails that cover much of the northern part of the property.

Fourth, while there's no swimming permitted in the river, there is a boat ramp available for launching of private boats. No launch fee is required. There's even a small, ten-site canoe camp—tents only—with a launch into the river.

Picnicking? You bet. Tables, grills, playground equipment and playing fields, toilet facilities, and shelter houses are all there with shelters reserved by inquiring at the park office.

One facility not found at all state parks, however, is the Potawatomi Group Camp for organized youth groups under adult supervision and other groups. Its buildings offer a 160 capacity for summers and a 120 capacity for winters, along with kitchen facilities, available from mid-April to mid-October.

The Tippecanoe River basically forms the eastern border of the state park property. To the west, across U.S. 35, is the Winamac Fish and Wildlife Area.

TIPPECANOE RIVER. The river flows through the state park named after it. It helps form the eastern boundary of the park.

This part of Indiana was inhabited by the Potawatomi during the 1600s and 1700s. French fur traders were the early explorers, using the river for navigation. After the Native Americans were forcibly removed in the 1830s, this part of Indiana was open for settlement.

Because of the land's high sand content, it is not suitable for agriculture. The federal government owned more than seven thousand acres before transferring it to Indiana in 1943, creating the fish and wildlife area and the state park. Most of the existing facilities were built during the Great Depression years of the 1930s by the Works Progress Administration—another long-lasting benefit from the WPA.

IF YOU GO

GETTING THERE: Located to the west of U.S. 35 north of Winamac.

INFORMATION: Call (574) 946–3213. The park's address is 4200N U.S. 35.

FEES: Admission charged.

MEMORIAL BRIDGE. The "Swinging Bridge" is a pedestrian walkway across the Tippecanoe River at Winamac.

COURTHOUSE. Completed in 1895, the Pulaski County Courthouse continues to dominate the downtown business district in Winamac.

THE TEACHER. Shows a Native American teaching a youngster the art of river fishing, such as might have occurred on the Tippecanoe River.

Winamac

WINAMAC—It's a story repeated in county after county across Indiana.

First, the men who governed Pulaski County met in the log home of John Pearson, one of the county commissioners of "Winnemack." Then, in the 1840s, they ordered a frame courthouse constructed. That was followed in 1862 by a brick courthouse. Finally, in 1895, a limestone, Romanesque-style courthouse was completed.

That's the point at which paths of this story diverge. In some cases, those courthouses still stand. In others, these limestone buildings have been replaced by more modern structures.

The courthouse in Winamac, county seat for the government of Pulaski County, is an example of the former. The Bedford limestone building with a central clock tower remains as the center of the downtown district. Its clock tower still can be seen for blocks away. While some functions have been moved to other buildings, the courts and much of the rest of county government remain there.

Those readers with longer memories will recall that the courthouse was the site of the famous Ford Pinto trial in 1980. According to *Indiana: A New Historical Guide*, the fuel tank of a Pinto exploded in a crash, killing three teenagers. Ford Motor Company was sued for reckless homicide, and the trial, which attracted national attention, lasted for ten weeks. Ford eventually was found innocent.

Not too far from the courthouse is another structure for which the town perhaps is even better known, at least locally. It is the Memorial Bridge—usually referred to as the "Swinging Bridge"—a footbridge that crosses the Tippecanoe River.

The bridge, constructed in 1923 as a memorial to Pulaski County soldiers and sailors, is two hundred feet in length with a four-foot walking space. It's a steel-cable suspension bridge and can swing as one walks across it. I'm not sure, but it may be the only public pedestrian bridge across the Tippecanoe.

On the east side of the river is the town park on a nearly forty-acre horseshoe bend in the river. It is the site of the Pulaski County 4-H Fair and other local events as well as a walk-

HISTORICAL MUSEUM. The Pulaski County building is behind the public library in Winamac.

ing trail. Back on the west side of the river is the Pulaski County Historical Society Museum, located behind the Pulaski County Public Library. Housed in a Quonset-type building, it includes numerous artifacts contributed over the years.

Another city feature is the recent—2002—bronze sculpture, *The Teacher*, showing an adult Native American demonstrating the art of river fishing to a Native American child. The inscription says it "honors the Potawatomi and Miami tribes who fished the Tippecanoe River." The sculpture by Casey Eskridge was funded by the historical society and the Arrow Head County Resource Conservation and Development Area.

Yet another place to attract visitors is the Winamac–Pulaski County Chamber of Commerce and Railroad Depot Museum. It is open five days a week.

Pulaski County is named for Casmir Pulaski, a Polish volunteer in the Revolutionary War, who was mortally wounded leading a colonial cavalry charge during the Battle of Savannah.

IF YOU GO

GETTING THERE: Winamac is located in northwestern Indiana at the crossroads of U.S. 35 and Indiana 14.

INFORMATION: The historical museum is open only for special local events and by arrangement. For other information and tours call the Railroad Depot Museum at (574) 946–7600. To reach Memorial Bridge, turn on Main Street from U.S. 35 toward the river and follow it down the hill to the Winamac town park.

INSIDE THE GOLDEN DOME. This photo looks up to the inside of the Golden Dome where Vatican artist Luigi Gregori painted this scene in the late 1800s. Read the essay to learn about the missing eyebrow.

STORIED STADIUM. The Notre Dame home of the Fighting Irish was built in 1930. It had a $50 million restoration and expansion in 1997.

THE GROTTO. This smaller version on the Notre Dame campus of the Grotto of Our Lady of Lourdes in France attracts students and visitors who light candles and pray. For what two events is it most attended? The essay has the answer.

University of Notre Dame, Notre Dame

NOTRE DAME—Where do the universities find these excellent young men and women to show visitors around the campus? I asked myself that question as Aaron Briggs, a Corning, New York, Notre Dame sophomore at the time, explained the Notre Dame campus to me and another visitor. What a great job he did.

I already had spent an hour or so walking around the campus. I usually prefer to see the site I'm visiting as any other tourist would see it. But Notre Dame certainly was an exception. I learned so much from Aaron that I would never have known otherwise. While he took pride in telling us about the campus features, two buildings in particular seem to bring out his best descriptive powers.

One was the Basilica of the Sacred Heart. What a magnificent structure! It's awe inspiring in its beauty and in its aura of reverence. Aaron told us it took twenty-three years to build and was finally completed in 1892. It has, he said, the largest collection of nineteenth-century French stained glass in the world. It also has the fourteen Stations of the Cross, frescoes, and murals, all painted in the late 1800s by Vatican portrait artist Luigi Gregori.

It was while Gregori was working there that the Main Building, today's campus administration building, burned in 1879. Father Edward Sorin, Notre Dame's founder, was not detoured, however. He immediately set upon a rebuilding program, one feature of which is a series of twelve Christopher Columbus corridor murals, also painted by Gregori.

In addition, Gregori painted the scene inside the twenty-three-karat gold leaf Golden Dome, arguably the best-known college building in America. So the story goes, according to Aaron, Gregori realized after he finished—and the scaffolding on which he had worked had been dismantled—that he had left an eyebrow off one angel. Hanging over an upper floor railing, he used a brush attached to a fishing pole to paint the missing eyebrow. Today, Aaron said, no one knows which eyebrow.

The building underwent a $58 million renovation from 1997 to 1999. Individual floor tiles—there must be millions

FROM MAIN BUILDING'S STEPS. Looking south from the steps of the Main Building, the Golden Dome, through the main quadrangle toward Notre Dame Avenue.

of them—were removed and cleaned, for example. The fifth floor, not in use for fifty years, was restored. The 144,000-square-foot building's 4.35 million outside bricks were cleaned and repaired.

Nearby is the Grotto of Our Lady of Lourdes, a down-sized replica of the famed shrine at Lourdes, France. It's a popular place for prayers. Aaron wondered if we could guess the two times it is most used. We did. (Answers at the end of the essay.)

Of course, there's also Notre Dame Stadium, home of the Fighting Irish, a truly legendary football palace. It had its own $50 million restoration and expansion in 1997. It now seats 80,225.

Those two times when most students light candles and pray at the Grotto of Our Lady of Lourdes? Before final exams and before home football games—especially against Michigan.

That dateline that begins this article is correct. Notre Dame has its own post office. Father Sorin was no fool; he knew in the 1840s that the United States maintained roads to its post offices.

IF YOU GO

GETTING THERE: In South Bend, stay on Indiana 933, Michigan Street. Turn east at Angela Avenue at the edge of the campus. Go to Notre Dame Avenue at the first traffic light and turn left. The visitors center is the first building on your left.

INFORMATION: The Eck Visitors Center's telephone number is (574) 631–5726. Next door to the center is the campus bookstore with a coffee shop. The visitors center's Web site is http://www.nd.edu/visitors. The center is open 8 a.m. to 5 p.m. Monday through Saturday and 10 a.m. to 5 p.m. Sunday. Tours are given during the academic year at 11 a.m. and 3 p.m.

LINCOLN CARRIAGE. This carriage was the one in which the president rode to Ford's Theater the night of his assassination. It was purchased by a Westfield, New York, doctor and sold to Clement Studebaker in 1890. It had been a gift to Lincoln from the people of New York City.

UNUSUAL FOR MUSEUMS. Vehicles stored at the Studebaker National Museum are placed in "visible storage" on the ground floor, with units rotated off the ramps for display on the main and upper floors.

THE NEW STUDEBAKER NATIONAL MUSEUM. Located in South Bend, it is adjacent to the Center for History, west of downtown.

Studebaker National Museum, South Bend

SOUTH BEND—If South Bend couldn't claim to have north-central Indiana's top historical facilities in the past, it would seem to certainly have those bragging rights now.

A nearly $10-million three-story building housing the Studebaker National Museum, next to Copshaholm, the elegant former home of Joseph D. Oliver, and the Center for History, has created a three-unit complex that provides visitors a wide range of views of the area's history, dating back to the days of Native Americans and early French trappers. That's in addition to downtown's national College Football Hall of Fame as well as the rich history associated with the University of Notre Dame, sitting on the city's north side.

The Studebaker National Museum is the latest jewel in the crown. It opened in late 2005 after residing in its "temporary" headquarters inside a former car dealership in near downtown since 1983.

Studebakers were manufactured in South Bend until 1963, although production continued until 1966 at the Hamilton, Ontario, plant. It had survived transportation trends from horses and buggies and wagons through gasoline engines during a history of more than one hundred years.

The Studebaker National Museum's three floors are divided with military trucks and vehicles on the lower level along with a "visible storage" of cars not currently on display, the main floor showing Studebaker's early years as well as historic carriages, and the upper level for more modern cars.

The "visible storage" is unusual for automotive museums, where vehicles not on current display usually are unavailable for viewing. This museum's storage is on a series of lifts open to the room so they may at least be seen.

Included among the special acquisitions on the main floor is the carriage in which President Abraham Lincoln rode to Ford's Theater the night of his assassination. Clement Studebaker bought it from a Westfield, New York, doctor, who had purchased it earlier.

Speed fans will be interested in the 1927 Commander that David Abbott "Ab" Jenkins drove from New York City to San

CHAMPION. Of all Studebaker designs, the 1950 Champion convertible with its bullet nose, inspired by the World War II P-38 fighter plane, probably was the best known. Actually, the design was only used for 1950 and 1951 models.

Francisco, driving the 3,302 miles in 77 hours and 40 minutes. The Commander cost $1,595.

Other automotive favorites include the 1963 Avanti, Studebaker's final effort to capture a part of the American market; the 1950 Champion convertible with its bullet nose, inspired by the World War II P-38 fighter plane and the best known of all Studebaker designs; and a 1966 Cruiser, the last car built by Studebaker.

While gasoline-powered vehicles dominate the museum's displays, a feature is a Studebaker 1876 Centennial Wagon that received a gold medal at the Philadelphia exposition that year. Horse-drawn vehicles make up one-fourth of the collection.

The entrance to the Center for History also serves the new Studebaker museum as well as the bookstore and gift shop, restrooms, and auditorium.

Funding for the $9.6 million structure came from a $5 million pledge from the city with the museum expected to raise a similar amount. Construction began in July 2004.

IF YOU GO

GETTING THERE: The easiest route to the museum is to go west on Washington Street off U.S. 31 Business and south on Chapin Street to the corner of Chapin and Thomas streets. The museum is on the northwest corner. Parking is available at the entrance to the Center for History.

INFORMATION: Call toll-free (888) 391–5600 or visit http://www.studebakermuseum.org/. Hours are Monday through Saturday 10 a.m. to 5 p.m. and Sunday noon to 3 p.m. Closed New Year's Day, Easter, Thanksgiving, Christmas Eve, and Christmas Day.

FEES: Admission charged.

ROCKWELL EXHIBIT. Famed American painter Norman Rockwell's "Four Freedoms" *Saturday Evening Post* covers are on display at the museum, including, left, "freedom of speech" and, to its right, "freedom from want."

Midwest Museum of American Art, Elkhart

ELKHART— It's hardly an original thought, but it really is a small world. When I walked into the Midwest Museum of American Art and handed my card to the woman behind the counter at the entrance, she said, "I know who you are. I've read your column."

Turns out she is Jane Burns, one of the trustees and founders of the museum. More to the point for those in the Muncie area, where I live, however, she is the mother of Jennifer Abrell, a Muncie lawyer who is also a museum trustee. So I didn't have to do a lot of explanation about why I was there.

"There" is an interesting story. Outside, the museum looks like a bank. Of course, that's because it was a bank. Burns also explained that shortly after the museum obtained the bank building, a project was started to take out the vault. It was going to be a major job, though, so it was left in place. Now it's one of the features of the art museum with part of the permanent exhibit displayed inside the open vault!

The museum's purpose is to showcase nineteenth- and twentieth-century American art. The museum brochure explains "this is a time of enormous and accelerated change in America" so the trustees' goal is to "preserve and celebrate our cultural heritage." The museum's more than 3,200 works go from nineteenth-century American Impressionism to twentieth-century Primitives.

That includes the work of Norman Rockwell. One of the features of American art on the second floor is a series of numbered lithographs by Rockwell, whose *Saturday Evening Post* covers captured the imagination of the nation for years. In all, Rockwell painted more than three hundred covers for the *Post*.

Included in the display are Rockwell's well-known works that popularized the four freedoms for which the Allies fought during World War II—freedom of speech, freedom from want, freedom of worship, and freedom from fear.

Rockwell also is featured in the exhibit that greets the visitor at the door. Another painting in the entryway display is by J. C. Leyendecker, who was Rockwell's predecessor with the *Post*.

LOOKS LIKE A BANK, DOESN'T IT? That's because it was a bank before it became the Midwest Museum of American Art in Elkhart. Part of the permanent exhibit is in the vault.

There's a painting by Grandma Moses, the New England artist who started her career late in her 101-year life. John Singer Sargent is represented with a drawing and Edward Moran with a pastel.

The twenty-five thousand-square-foot facility has seven galleries, which show permanent and traveling exhibits. Up to twenty-five thousand persons come to the museum each year, many of them schoolchildren. Docents provide tours for all age groups.

The museum is more than its displays, however. Hands-on workshops for elementary students in the summer include printmaking, drawing, watercolor, ceramics, sculpture, and collage. Other classes, workshops, lectures, and films for children and adults are offered throughout the year. The museum also sponsors bus trips to other museums for special exhibitions.

The museum offers free noontime talks every Thursday, often accompanied by films and free admission on Sunday afternoons, called "Free Family Day."

IF YOU GO

GETTING THERE: The museum is located at 429 S. Main Street in downtown Elkhart.

INFORMATION: Call (574) 293–6660. The Web site is http://midwestmuseum.us/. The museum is open Tuesday through Friday from 11 a.m. to 5 p.m. and Saturday and Sunday from 1 to 4 p.m. Closed Monday and holidays.

FEES: Admission charged, but free admission on Sunday.

DAHLIAS. Grown by the Elkhart Dahlia Society in the Bonneyville Mill Trail Garden at the county park, they are across the river from the mill.

GRINDING FLOUR. Craig Kirkwood operates the smaller grinding stone while filling a flour sack at the Bonneyville Mill near Bristol.

Bonneyville Mill County Park, Bristol

BRISTOL—Craig Kirkwood, assistant mill manager, was busy when I stopped by Bonneyville Mill. A customer had ordered fifty pounds of wheat flour and was waiting while Kirkwood was grinding it on the smaller of two grinding stones at the mill.

"The larger turbine isn't working, so I can't use the bigger grinding stone," he said. "Right now, I'm grinding both wheat and corn flour on this smaller one. That's in addition to the rye and buckwheat we also mill." He explained that he and John Jenney, mill manager, were hoping a grant would come through to fund repairs and maintenance for both turbines.

For the layperson such as myself, of course, it doesn't matter which grind stone is used. The interest comes from watching the process and walking through the old mill, the central feature of the Bonneyville Mill County Park.

The mill is called the oldest continuously operated gristmill in Indiana, started in the 1830s by Edward Bonney on the Little Elkhart River. Bonney had dreams of a major metropolis growing up around his gristmill and a sawmill. When the area was bypassed by the railroads and a proposed canal ended up only proposed, any possible glory days for Bonney's dreams were over.

In one fashion or another, the mill continued operation through the 1950s. Finally, in 1968 the Elkhart County Chapter of Michiana Watershed purchased the mill, giving it to the Elkhart County Park and Recreation Board the following year.

The park board makes certain the mill continues in its old-fashioned ways, grinding flour every day from May through October.

The mill has four floors, with the third floor of the mill originally used for storing grain. The water behind the flume wall is seven feet deep and is channeled into the mill by a small dam south of the mill.

The mill has a steady stream of visitors. The week I was there, those signing in included travelers from Arizona, California, Illinois, Michigan, South Carolina, Texas, and, of course, Indiana.

BONNEYVILLE MILL. The mill lies across the Little Elkhart River in Bonneyville Mill County Park in Elkhart County. The mill has been in operation since the 1830s.

While the mill is the major attraction at the park, local visitors enjoy much more. One beauty spot is the Bonneyville Mill Trail Garden, operated by the Elkhart Dahlia Society. The garden is just across the canal from the mill, and the dahlias were in full bloom at the time of my visit.

Second would be the park itself, with its 223 acres, providing five miles of hiking trails, fishing in the Little Elkhart River, playgrounds, and wintertime cross-country skiing and sledding hills. In addition, there are picnic tables spread throughout the park along with five shelters with tables, grills, water, and restrooms.

The park lies 2 ½ miles southeast of Bristol. Other nearby tourist spots are historic Middlebury and the Das Dutchman Essenhaus restaurant, only a few miles to the southeast.

Park hours are January, November, and December, 9 a.m. to 6 p.m.; February and October, 8 a.m. to 7 p.m.; March and September, 8 a.m. to 8 p.m.; April and August, 8 a.m. to 9 p.m.; and May, June, and July, 8 a.m. to 10 p.m.

IF YOU GO

GETTING THERE: From Indiana 120 east of Bristol, turn south on County Road 131 about a mile to the mill.

INFORMATION: The mill is open daily from May through October. Hours are 10 a.m. to 5 p.m. Telephone number at the mill is (574) 825–9324. For more information about the park or to make reservations for tours, call the Elkhart County Park and Recreation Department at (574) 535–6458. The department's Web site is http://www.elkhartcounty parks.org/.

FEES: None.

OLD TROLLEY LINE. An example of the trolley line still remains at the Old Bag Factory. At one time, the line ran to the southern part of Goshen.

ORIGINAL SWITCH PANELS. The panels controlled the power for the Goshen trolley system from this building from 1896 to 1929 and are on display in the front lobby of the Old Bag Factory. They were made of copper, slate, and marble with power generated at the east end of the building, using coal for fuel.

Old Bag Factory, Goshen

GOSHEN—"Retired factories back on the job" was the headline for an article a couple of years ago in the *Indiana Preservationist* magazine, recounting how former Hoosier factories are being converted today for other uses—a number of them into shops and galleries. One that has been around for more than twenty years—and, so, one of the earlier conversions and a longtime destination for northern Indiana shoppers—is Goshen's Old Bag Factory.

I visited there twice in the years before the *Preservationist* article came out, once just to check it out and a second time looking for a quilt for my daughter-in-law. I was there again recently on a reporting trip through northern Indiana.

The Old Bag Factory is a four-story brick building that originally manufactured Cosmos Buttermilk Soap and served as the terminus for a city trolley system, developed by Goshen entrepreneur J. J. Burns. The trolley system was a three-mile line that stretched from the factory, where electric power was generated, to Kercher Road on Goshen's south side. Rails ran through the center of the city's brick streets with power supplied by overhead wires.

According to information about the trolley, it was said to be the envy of many an Indiana town in those days near the beginning of the twentieth century. Every one of these Hoosier cities was trying to find a way to separate itself from the rest with some innovation or claim to fame—in Goshen's case an electric trolley line. It ran until the 1930s.

In the early 1900s the Chicago-Detroit Bag Company moved in as the manufacturing unit of the building. Then in the 1920s the Chase Bag Company took over the operation and continued until 1982. Two years later, Larion and Nancy Swartzendruber began the task of changing the deserted factory building into shops.

As elsewhere with other such Indiana projects, it was no simple task. The *Preservationist* article said Swartzendruber did much of the work himself, which included refinishing floors, fixing windows, reinforcing wood, and putting in new electrical, heating, and fire safety systems.

OLD BAG FACTORY. Looking at the main entrance from the east. Other "outside" shops are to the left.

While much work needed to be done, the building's nearly eighty thousand square feet allowed numerous options for merchants, whose shops quickly began to attract a steady stream of visitors to Goshen.

Swartzendruber's Furniture Galleries remains the centerpiece of the Old Bag Factory. At last count, fourteen artisans, antique shops, gift and specialty stores, an art gallery, and a café make up the merchants in the facility and its "outside" buildings.

Concerts, performed on the Old Bag Factory's third floor in the LVD Concert Hall, are another feature of the Old Bag Factory. Folk, Celtic, blues, bluegrass, and country musicians have been performing there since 2003.

A dinner-theater package is possible with meals in the first-floor Trolley Café starting at 5 p.m. Doors open at 6:30 with the program itself beginning at 7 p.m.

The Old Bag Factory has seen some transition through the years. Stores have come and gone. Still, shoppers come from all over America, Canada, and beyond to visit the shops, purchase a unique gift, enjoy a pleasant lunch, and simply enjoy a little quiet time.

IF YOU GO

GETTING THERE: On U.S. 33 in Goshen, watch for the intersection with Chicago Avenue. A sign directs you north to the Old Bag Factory at the intersection of Chicago and Indiana avenues. (Look for the tall smokestack.)

INFORMATION: Hours, Monday through Friday 9 a.m. to 5 p.m.; Saturday 9 a.m. to 4 p.m.; closed Sunday and holidays. Trolley Café open Monday through Saturday 8 a.m. to 2:45 p.m. For dinner-theater packages, call (574) 534–3881. Old Bag Factory's Web site is http://www.oldbagfactory.com/, and its telephone number is (574) 534–2502.

FEES: None.

SUNFLOWER HULLS. Cabinet doors made of compressed sunflower hulls are one "sustainable feature" of the kitchen in a Rieth Village cottage at Merry Lea Environmental Learning Center.

WIND GENERATOR. Merry Lea's ten-kilowatt wind generator that helps provide energy for the Rieth Village "ecological field station" operated by Goshen College. At times, the center can even sell some energy to the local electrical supplier.

Merry Lea Environmental Learning Center, Goshen

GOSHEN—Just about everybody knows the world is using energy resources at an alarming rate. Many would agree that being energy efficient probably should come before worrying about developing new sources of energy—or at least be on the agenda along with finding new sources. But very few, I would guess, think about the cost of energy and the use of resources needed for the delivery of products from one place to another, including transporting energy-saving products.

So when designers of the present three cottages of Rieth Village at the Merry Lea Environmental Learning Center near Goshen "built green," they not only used wood for the buildings' exteriors and ceilings, but they also chose a wood—Indiana tulip poplar—that could be milled nearby, transported for only a short distance, and required almost no maintenance.

"Think about the energy that would be used in purchasing wood from California, for instance, and then shipping it to Indiana—plus we knew the forest these tulip poplar trees came from and that the wood on the exterior of our buildings will never need any coating whatsoever so long as they are under a good roof, which they are," says Luke Gascho, Merry Lea executive director. Actually, he makes the case for energy efficiency first and then looking for new sources, believing that enormous amounts of energy would be saved through better efficiency.

Merry Lea is a 1,150-acre preserve, administered by Goshen College, that contains a diverse group of Indiana ecosystems—a complex of wetlands, bogs, lakeshores, upland and lowland forests, prairies, and meadows. Its mission is to provide a natural sanctuary for plants and animals, offer environmental education—thousands of students come through annually—and make available a setting to "benefit the human body and spirit while not exploiting the land or excessively disturbing its ecosystems."

Rieth Village is an "ecological field station" for Goshen undergraduate programs with two cottages providing housing for up to thirty-two students.

I visited Merry Lea's Rieth Village to look at its use of alternate energy derived from wind power to generate electricity,

TOTAL SAVINGS. Tulip poplar wood siding for this Rieth Village building was harvested from a nearby forest, saving transportation energy and requiring less maintenance.

or, as they are called nationally, "small wind electric systems." I should have realized there would be much more to the story than that.

A 10-kilowatt wind generator; solar water heaters and ground heat pumps; photovoltaic panels producing 4.8-kilowatts; energy efficient appliances and light fixtures; windows aligned for good day lighting; and no outside light pollution are among many other "sustainable features" of Rieth Village.

Some measure of the village's success is indicated by the recently awarded Platinum LEED (Leadership in Energy and Environmental Design) designation by the Indiana chapter of the U.S. Green Building Council, one of only forty-two such awards in the entire nation.

The name, Merry Lea? Donors Mary Jane and Lee Rieth didn't want the complex named for them, so a friend came up with the homonyms of Merry—meaning happy—and Lea—meaning meadow.

IF YOU GO

GETTING THERE: Take U.S. 33 to Wolf Lake, midway between Goshen and Fort Wayne. Turn south on Indiana 109 and then right on CR 200 S. Rieth Village will be on your left in one-half mile.

INFORMATION: Call (260) 799–5869 or go to http://www.goshen.edu/merrylea. Rieth Village is open 8 a.m. to 4 p.m., Monday through Friday, as is Merry Lea's Learning Center. Guided tours for ten or more people may be available if you call in advance.

FEES: None.

Warsaw Biblical Gardens, Warsaw

EVANGELIST'S HOME. The home of well-known evangelist Billy Sunday sits atop this hill at Winona Lake. Close by are shops of the Village at Winona Lake.

FLOWING BROOK. Water is precious in biblical lands, as illustrated by this flowing brook in the Warsaw Biblical Gardens.

A HIGHLIGHT. This grape arbor is the highlight of the orchard section of the Warsaw Biblical Gardens, dedicated in 1991.

WARSAW—In these days of ever-escalating gasoline prices, it's a good idea if you can tie together several places to go during one trip, especially if they are close to each other.

One such possibility would be to combine a visit to the Warsaw Biblical Gardens and nearby shopping at the Village at Winona at Winona Lake, which offers an expanding shopping center specializing in arts and crafts. If you like to walk and browse, maybe take some time for coffee or a good meal, then you're going to love shopping at the Village.

First, though, consider stopping at the Warsaw Biblical Gardens.

The Biblical Gardens, said to be one of only a few in the United States, came about because of the work of a single woman. After Warsaw's Levin and Sons scrap yards closed in 1981, the area was cleared and remained open parkland until Saralee Levin had the idea of creating a biblical gardens—one where plants, trees, flowers, and herbs mentioned in the Old and New Testaments could be studied, grown, and admired. Several years later, with private donations of more than $600,000 and the support of the Warsaw Community Development Corporation, the gardens were formally dedicated on June 23, 1991.

The gardens contain more than 110 species, representing the diversity of climates found in Israel. Gardens' literature reports that most of the plantings can be sustained in the midwestern climate; others are replanted annually or are "wintered elsewhere."

The gardens include a "gathering area" near the entrance and a "sitting area," meant to be especially conducive to meditating, in addition to the six specific biblical areas: herbs and crops, desert, brook, forest, orchard, and meadow. The planners consulted biblical authorities in deciding upon appropriate garden creations.

None of the areas is large, of course, gathered as they are in less than an acre of land. The meadow is in the middle of the gardens. A flowing brook passes through several environments, while a dry brook is related to the desert. A grape arbor

THE GARDENS OF CENTRAL PARK. These park gardens are located near the Biblical Gardens in Warsaw, just north of downtown.

is the centerpiece of the orchard. The forest has large shade trees and plants. The herbs and crops section contains more than thirty varieties of mostly useful plants, many used for medicinal purposes.

Then, only a few miles southeast of U.S. 30 is Winona Lake with its long-standing religious history and part of the impetus for the Biblical Gardens. One of its most famous residents was Billy Sunday, the early 1900s evangelist. It is estimated that, without the aid of radio, television, or speaker systems, he preached to more than one hundred million people. Now a museum, the house, together with a nearby visitors center, comprise the Billy Sunday Home Museum and Visitors Center.

Nearby is the Village at Winona with about twenty artsy, craftsy shops plus nooklike eating places, including the Boat House restaurant, which is well known throughout the state.

A good time to plan a visit is in late spring when the Biblical Gardens have more color. (In the autumn the meadows and grasses are the highlights.)

IF YOU GO

GETTING THERE: In Warsaw on U.S. 15 north of downtown, turn west into Central Park and right to the Biblical Gardens at the corner of Canal Street and Indiana 15. Go east on U.S. 30 to the Center Street exit and then south to Argonne Road to Winona Lake.

INFORMATION: Call (574) 267–6419 for information about the Biblical Gardens, the Web site is http://www.warsawbiblical gardens.org/; (800) 800–6090 for the Kosciusko County Convention and Visitors Bureau, http://www.koscvb.org/. Hours are dawn to dusk, April 15 to October 15; tours can be scheduled between May 15 to September 15. The Web site for Winona is www.villageatwinona.com/ or call (574) 268–9888.

FEES: None, but donations accepted.

TARGET PRACTICE. Takes place at the ten-yard range at the Tri-County Fish and Wildlife Area near North Webster. Other ranges go up to one hundred yards.

Tri-County Fish and Wildlife Area, Syracuse

SYRACUSE—It was one of those warm, lazy days of late summer when I stopped by the Tri-County Fish and Wildlife Area. Since it was a Wednesday, most outdoorsmen who might otherwise have been there probably were at work, so the area appeared largely deserted.

Actually, other than state workers, I found only one person who was using the ten-yard target range for pistol practice. In between rounds, he told me that he was a regular and he had never seen it that empty. A few days previously, he said, target shooters were in line waiting to use the various ranges.

Tri-County Fish and Wildlife Area—it's referred to in state parlance as "the property"—is located east of Indiana 13 between North Webster and Syracuse. Property literature says the 3,546 acres include 650 acres of lakes and wetlands. The deepest of its ten natural lakes is seventy-five feet.

The whole idea of its extensive wetlands, lakes, and ponds is to provide habitat for migratory waterfowl, furbearers, shorebirds, and fish as well as a setting for people interested in many outdoor activities, which do not include swimming or camping.

Established in 1951, the property is one of the older fish and wildlife areas in Indiana. By 1953 the property had been formally opened. In 1963 a dam constructed at the outlet of six of the property lakes created Flatbelly Marsh, a substantial marsh area that covers much of the northwest part of the property.

Nine boat ramps serve those interested in fishing, although all fishing areas are closed during waterfowl seasons. No gas-powered motors are allowed, only electric. Shoreline fishing is available on Goldeneye and Bass ponds and at nearby Wawasee Family Fishing Area.

Hunting includes woodland game, upland game, and furbearers. (If you're wondering what that means, a generic card to be completed at the end of a hunt lists rabbits, quail, squirrels, doves, pheasants, grouse, woodcocks, snipe, and crows and, at night, raccoons, red and gray foxes, coyotes, and opossums.) Recent cards had been completed by persons from South Bend, Goshen, Syracuse, Elkhart, Logansport,

FORTY-FIVE-ACRE SPEAR LAKE. Located near the center of the Tri-County Fish and Wildlife Area, where only electric motors are allowed on the property.

IF YOU GO

Pierceton, and Albion and others who simply listed Kosciusko County.

A daily check-in is required. Hunting seasons and bag limits apply, and current hunting regulations are available at the property office. The office is located near the intersection of 850 East and 850 North, just to the east of Indiana 13 between North Webster and Syracuse.

To be honest with you, I am not an outdoorsman. But I know those who are hunters and fishermen and there's nothing they love more than doing what I have described above.

GETTING THERE: North of North Webster on Indiana 13, go to 900 N and turn east to the tee and then south on 850 E. Travel one-half mile. The office is on the left.

INFORMATION: Call (574) 834–4461 for information. Check with the office for property hours, fishing and hunting times, rules, permits, and limits.

FEES: No admission charge.

OLD WITH THE NEW. The older thirty-three-room inn has been "blended" with a new fifty-six-room inn and conference center at Das Dutchman Essenhaus at Middlebury.

NOW THEY'RE SHOPS. Yoder farm buildings have been converted into shops as part of the Das Dutchman Essenhaus complex at Middlebury.

Das Dutchman Essenhaus, Middlebury

MIDDLEBURY—Perhaps it's been a while since you were in northern Indiana and stopped to eat at Das Dutchman Essenhaus, located on U.S. 20 south of Middlebury. When another trip takes you to that area, you won't find that the restaurant has changed all that much. However, you may notice some significant changes in the rest of the complex—started in 1971 by Bob and Sue Miller.

Essenhaus Inn and Conference Center has been expanded and enlarged. The original inn, with thirty-three uniquely designed rooms, along with a three-story atrium and a conference room for small meetings—the conference room a replica of a one-room schoolhouse—remains the same as when it originally opened.

What has been added is a 60,000-square-foot addition, creating an inn and conference center. It contains fifty-six more guest rooms—some three-room suites and other suites with kitchenettes, an indoor pool, game room, exercise room, outdoor patio, and 4,000 square feet of meeting space in three rooms with a capacity of 450 (theater style) or 300 (dining style at round tables).

The inn and conference center literature speaks of "suites with outdoor balconies and beautiful view of our manicured grounds," and indeed they are. A seasonal carriage ride, which includes a drive through a covered bridge on the east side of the property, is one way to enjoy them. Plus, there's an eighteen-hole miniature golf course and bicycle rentals.

Naturally, having the Essenhaus Village Shops only a few feet away doesn't hurt. Specializing in unique gift items, the shops include: Dutch Country Gifts, the Clothesline, the Cabin, the Corn Crib, the Quilt Shop, and Olde Tyme Country Oak. The buildings were originally farm buildings on the Tobias Yoder farmstead.

For many visitors, though, the Essenhaus Amish-style restaurant still is the feature attraction. It's a really big operation, seating up to 1,100 customers.

Signed photographs on its walls show famous customers, ranging from Jimmy and Rosalyn Carter to Bobby Knight.

DAS DUTCHMAN ESSENHAUS. The Middlebury restaurant includes several dining rooms and also houses the bakery and gift items.

IF YOU GO

During my last visit to the restaurant, I started with a sandwich and salad because I definitely wanted to save room for pie, even though the menu goes on and on—more than twenty different dinner items, multiple sandwiches, children's specialties, soups, and family-style dining options.

If you're there for breakfast, Essenhaus has "traditional breakfasts," or you can opt for the "thresher's breakfast"—a seventeen-item buffet option.

My pie selection took some serious thought. The menu and the home-style bakery offer had thirty choices! Only pie for dessert? Oh, no. The menu includes numerous other dessert selections, too. I finally settled on a pie I had never eaten—never heard of: raisin cream made sugar free with Splenda.

Was it good? My next stop was the bakery to buy one to take home.

Amish-style "country cooking" also can be catered. Plus, there's a wholesale food store, Essenhaus Foods. For my waistline, it's probably just as well that I don't live too close.

GETTING THERE: The Essenhaus complex is one mile west on U.S. 20 from its intersection with Indiana 13 near Middlebury.

INFORMATION: Telephone toll-free (800) 455–9471, or go to http://www.essenhaus.com/. Restaurant and bakery hours are Monday through Thursday 6 a.m. to 8 p.m. and Friday and Saturday 6 a.m. to 9 p.m. Closed Sundays. Shop summer hours are Monday through Saturday 9 a.m. to 8 p.m. Call about winter hours as they are subject to change. The inn is always open.

CIVIL WAR VETERANS HONORED. This granite monument at Angola's town square honors Steuben County's soldiers who fought in the Civil War.

LAMENT FOR THEIR DEAD. At the base of the granite shaft commemorating Steuben County's Civil War dead is this oft-repeated remembrance: "On fame's eternal camping ground, their silent tents are spread. And glory guards with solemn round, the bivouac of the dead."

Angola

ANGOLA—Sooner or later when you're at an Indiana state park, you're going to want to go into town. You're lucky if you're at Pokagon State Park because that means you can go into Angola. Not that Angola is a metropolis or, for that matter, much different from many other lake towns, but whatever each of them has, collectively, Angola appears to have them all.

For starters, there's its charming downtown square. Set off on the southeast corner is the Steuben County Courthouse. It was patterned after Boston's historic Faneuil Hall. The two-story brick structure was constructed in 1867–68.

In the middle of the square is the Soldiers and Sailors Monument, dedicated in 1917 to the 1,278 county residents who fought in the Civil War—more per capita than any other county in the state. The seventy-foot-high granite monument, topped by Columbia, has on its four sides figures representing the infantry, cavalry, artillery, and navy.

The square had been the place where farmers brought their wagons to town to sell their products, first to bands of Potawatomi and then to other white settlers. The railroad didn't arrive here until 1871.

Nestled around the square and adjacent side streets are shops and restaurants to accommodate the larger summer crowds that considerably swell the county's thirty-two thousand population. Old U.S. 27 runs north and south through the center of the town, but most people arrive by Interstate 69—also present-day U.S. 27—and drive the three miles on U.S. 20 to the east into Angola. U.S. 20 runs through town, east and west.

Trine University (formerly known as Tri-State University) is located near downtown Angola on a tree-lined four hundred-acre campus. Best known for its engineering school, it has twenty-five buildings, mostly brick. Of more recent note is its eighteen-hole Zollner Golf Course that has been the site of three national golf championship tournaments.

Summer activities in the community are considerable. Steuben is known as the county with 101 lakes. The lakes are left over from the last glacier to cover much of Indiana and began

HISTORIC COURTHOUSE. The Steuben County Courthouse, rather than sitting in the town square as usually is the case, is located on the southeast corner of the square. Its two stories are topped by a belfry and widow's walk.

IF YOU GO

GETTING THERE: From Interstate 69 take U.S. 20 east three miles to the Angola business district.

INFORMATION: The Steuben County Tourism Bureau telephone number is (260) 665–5386 or toll-free at (800) 525–3101. E-mail is lakes101@locl.net/ and the Web site is http://www.lakes101.org/.

FEES: Various venues have different fees. Call for information.

melting about fifteen thousand years ago. As blocks of ice broke away, they created today's kettle-hole lakes.

Around Angola are nine nature preserves, not including the Lonidaw preserve on the grounds of Pokagon State Park. Most are open to the public and have hiking trails. The best known is Wing Haven, north of Angola. It includes the Seven Sisters Lakes, scenic trails, slopes, valleys, a log cabin, and outbuildings. An art studio and visitor center is open the first Sunday of the month from 1 to 5 p.m.

The year is filled with festivals, including the July 4 celebration and September's Fall Fest with crafts, sidewalk sales, and entertainment around the square in Angola.

If all else fails, there's always shopping. Indiana's first outlet mall—the Horizon Outlet Center, now with fifty stores and called The Outlet Shoppes at Fremont—was built on Interstate 69 at its intersection with the Indiana Toll Road only a few miles north of town.

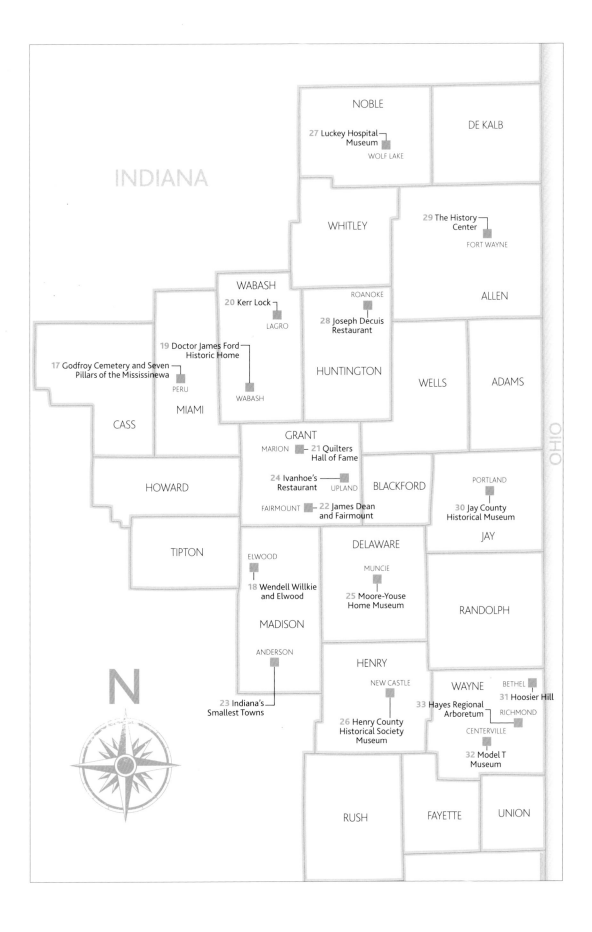

INDIANA

NOBLE

DE KALB

27 Luckey Hospital Museum

WOLF LAKE

WHITLEY

29 The History Center

FORT WAYNE

WABASH

20 Kerr Lock

LAGRO

ROANOKE

ALLEN

28 Joseph Decuis Restaurant

19 Doctor James Ford Historic Home

17 Godfroy Cemetery and Seven Pillars of the Mississinewa

PERU

HUNTINGTON

WELLS

ADAMS

WABASH

MIAMI

CASS

GRANT

MARION

21 Quilters Hall of Fame

HOWARD

24 Ivanhoe's Restaurant

UPLAND

BLACKFORD

PORTLAND

FAIRMOUNT

22 James Dean and Fairmount

30 Jay County Historical Museum

JAY

TIPTON

ELWOOD

DELAWARE

MUNCIE

18 Wendell Willkie and Elwood

25 Moore-Youse Home Museum

RANDOLPH

MADISON

ANDERSON

HENRY

WAYNE

BETHEL

NEW CASTLE

31 Hoosier Hill

23 Indiana's Smallest Towns

33 Hayes Regional Arboretum

RICHMOND

CENTERVILLE

26 Henry County Historical Society Museum

32 Model T Museum

RUSH

FAYETTE

UNION

OHIO

N

MANY YEARS AGO. These caves were carved over the centuries into the limestone cliffs of the Mississinewa River and were considered special grounds by the Miami for use in rituals and celebrations.

MIAMI CEMETERY. Francis Godfroy's tombstone in the Godfroy Cemetery. The Miami war chief died May 1, 1840. The last burial in the cemetery occurred in 1995.

ON THE HILLSIDE. The Godfroy Cemetery includes the burial plots of persons of Native American ancestry and their families. It stands on a hillside along winding Indiana 124 in eastern Miami County.

Godfroy Cemetery and Seven Pillars of the Mississinewa, Peru

PERU—If one of these days, you find yourself driving around in north-central Indiana with just a little time to spare, you might want to consider two stops east of Peru off Indiana 124. Both remind visitors of a time some two hundred years ago when Native Americans in significant numbers inhabited the area.

One is the Godfroy Cemetery, named in honor of the most prominent individual buried there, Francis Godfroy, the last of the Miami Nation war chiefs. Burial in this cemetery, at the top of a gently rising hillside next to the highway, is restricted to persons of Native American ancestry and their families.

For a time in the early 1800s, Francis Godfroy (1788–1840) was reputed to be one of the wealthiest merchants and largest landowners in what was to become north-central Indiana. That was because of his fur-trading expertise and land treaties signed with the U.S. government. According to *Indiana: A New Historical Guide*, Godfroy made most of his money from selling furs to East Coast companies out of two trading posts, each where one of his two wives resided.

The cemetery is across the highway from where one of his trading posts, known as Mount Pleasant, existed.

Words on Godfroy's weather-worn tombstone in the cemetery note that, at his death, he enjoyed "the confidence of his tribe" and was "beloved by his American neighbors." They conclude that "he died as he lived without fear or reproach."

A few miles to the west of the cemetery is a place where the waters of the Mississinewa River over time kept grinding against the limestone walls of the high bluffs as year followed year, then for hundreds of years and finally for hundreds of hundreds of years. Ultimately, low-lying caves were worn into the walls, in a geological formation known today as the Seven Pillars of the Mississinewa. They are best viewed from the opposite side of the river.

Historians believe the Mississinewa caves held a fascination for the Miami and were incorporated into a number of its tribal rituals, including the education of young braves and perhaps as well the torture of enemies.

SEVEN PILLARS. Caves of the Seven Pillars of the Mississinewa are carved into the limestone walls of the sixty-foot bluffs of the Mississinewa River east of Peru.

IF YOU GO

The *Historical Guide* also reports a legend that "'Little Indians,' fairy-like creatures who guided lost Indian boys home," resided in the caves. The legend goes that the "Little Indians" could only be seen by old women. It's also possible that the first trading posts in the area established by the French were located in the caves.

The Seven Pillars and the surrounding Mississinewa countryside also were favorite sites for Indiana painters, including T. C. Steele of the Hoosier Group and Homer Davisson, who painted at the Pillars several times.

You also can take the Frances Slocum Trail off Indiana 124 just before the bridge in Miami County and be on the Pillars' side of the Mississinewa. However, unless you are spry and prepared to do some perhaps risky climbing, you can't really see the Pillars—which are below you—from that side.

Neither of these spots—the cemetery or the Pillars—is a big tourist attraction, of course. Nor should they be. But if you have a historical interest and are of a reflective bent, you'll be interested.

GETTING THERE: Entering Miami County from the east, go west on Indiana 124. The Godfroy Cemetery is on the left shortly after entering Miami County where the road becomes winding. To see the Seven Pillars of the Mississinewa, continue west to 300 E and turn south. (This takes you by the Chief Richardville home constructed by the United States for another wealthy Miami leader.) At Mississinewa Road, turn left and follow it along the river. It becomes a gravel road before turning onto 400 E. The Pillars are at that junction, across the river.

INFORMATION: The Miami County Historical Society has published a driving-tour brochure with information about and a map of historic sites in the county. Call (765) 473–9183 or go to http://www.miami countymuseum.com/.

FEES: None.

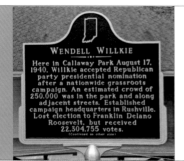

Wendell L. Willkie and Elwood

WHERE HE ACCEPTED. This historical marker in Elwood's Callaway Park tells of Willkie accepting the GOP nomination there with a crowd estimated at 250,000 in attendance.

SITE OF BIRTH. Wendell L. Willkie was born while his family lived in this house at 1900 S. A Street in Elwood. Actually, he was named Lewis Wendell Willkie, but the military reversed his first two names during World War I. Since he liked it that way, he never changed it back.

ALL THAT REMAIN. This arch near the library is one of two that remain of the high school that the Republican candidate for president attended while he lived in Elwood.

ELWOOD—Quick now, how many candidates for president of the major political parties were born in Indiana?

William Henry Harrison, elected as the Whig candidate in 1840? No, although he gained his major fame—the Battle of Tippecanoe—while he lived in what was to become Indiana. However, he was born in Virginia and elected from Ohio.

Abraham Lincoln, elected as the Republican candidate in 1860? Lincoln was born in Kentucky and elected from Illinois despite having lived his formative years in Indiana.

Benjamin Harrison, elected as the Republican candidate in 1888? Another no. Although he was elected while living in Indiana, the grandson of William Henry Harrison was born on his grandfather's farm in Ohio.

The only major party nominee born in Indiana was Elwood's Wendell L. Willkie, Republican candidate in 1940. (See the end of this article for a historical footnote.) Even though he lost to President Franklin D. Roosevelt, Willkie gained the most votes of any Republican candidate in history until the election of Dwight D. Eisenhower in 1952.

In April 1940 Willkie Clubs began springing up around the country, an honest-to-goodness grassroots effort to spur the candidacy of the little-known Hoosier, then a New York utility executive. First, there were only a few and then 20, 30, 40 a day until more than 750 existed by June with 50,000 Willkie volunteers working across the country. Then in Philadelphia, with a deadlocked convention and the galleries shouting "We want Willkie! We want Willkie!" the Indiana-born lawyer was nominated on the sixth ballot.

It was the final convention in the nation's history where a delegation was sent later to the nominee's home to notify him. As if he didn't know! Tens of thousands of people—estimates were as many as 250,000—poured into Elwood August 17 for Willkie's acceptance speech and parade on a blistering 100-plus-degree day.

Amazingly, most of the places involved in this once-in-history Hoosier event still stand in Elwood:

Willkie's birth home at 1900 S. A Street, now privately owned.

WILLKIE'S CARAVAN. The candidate's motorcade slowly makes its way through Elwood on August 17, 1940. A crowd estimated at more than 250,000 came to see the candidate and hear his acceptance speech.

IF YOU GO

The nearby home where the Willkie family moved as Wendell grew up at 1836 N. A Street, also privately owned.

In Callaway Park on N. Nineteenth Street, where Willkie accepted the nomination, a two-sided plaque marks the location.

Of course, Main Street, down which the Willkie caravan proceeded during the big parade with thousands of people packing the sidewalks and streets.

Two arches remain from old high school buildings, one next door to the Elwood Public Library at Main and Sixteenth streets and the second at the entrance of present-day Elwood Middle School on N. Nineteenth Street where he briefly appeared before making his acceptance speech.

And the library, a depository for numerous Willkie materials.

Historical footnote: Eugene V. Debs of Terre Haute ran five times for president on the Socialist ticket (1900, 1904, 1908, 1912, and 1920), once even while in federal prison! Indiana's other party candidate was James Hanley, who ran in 1916 for the Prohibitionists.

GETTING THERE: Indiana 28 runs through downtown Elwood and the Willkie sites.

INFORMATION: Staff members at the Elwood Public Library, including Nancy Sumner, Adult Services, are most helpful. Located at 1600 Main Street, telephone (765) 552–5001. Hours are Monday through Thursday 9 a.m. to 8 p.m., Friday 9 a.m. to 6 p.m., and Saturday 9 a.m. to 4 p.m.

FEES: None.

AUTHENTIC 1880 STOVE. This stove is an important part of the kitchen at the Doctor James Ford Historic Home in Wabash. The house appears as it might have looked around that time.

GRUESOME SIGHT. It isn't real but it might have been a situation Doctor James Ford dealt with while he was a Wabash physician. It's an exhibit at the restored Doctor James Ford Historic Home.

Doctor James Ford Historic Home, Wabash

WABASH—I'll take his word for it.

According to an article published by Historic Landmarks Foundation of Indiana, its retired president Reid Williamson said of the Doctor James Ford Historic Home restoration in Wabash, "foot by foot, inch by inch, it's one of the highest quality museums in the state." Williamson ought to know. He has been one of the nation's experts in saving historic landmarks.

I went to the Doctor James Ford Historic Home during a beautiful Saturday autumn afternoon—a great time to be out anywhere in Indiana.

Of course, the home has quite a history.

Around 1838, Ford and his wife, America Holton Ford, purchased three lots at the corner of Hill and Cass streets on the top of a hill north of downtown Wabash. They started their home in 1841, building a one-room brick house and moving into it with their small daughter. It is said to have been one of the first brick buildings in Wabash. The Fords added four additions built during four decades.

Doctor Ford apparently was one of those enterprising men of the recently settled frontier who could turn his considerable talents to any number of fields. In addition to serving as a medical doctor, including time in the army as a Civil War surgeon, he also was a writer, agronomist, surveyor, inventor, and architect.

As frequently happens, after the Fords' deaths and over time, the house passed out of the hands of the family and "languished under indifferent ownership."

That changed when Doctor Ford's great-grandson, Richard Ford, returned to Wabash later in the twentieth century. He set as one of his goals the purchase and restoration of the house to how it likely appeared around 1875. He wanted it to tell the story of his great-grandfather's family as well as of Wabash of that time. The restoration began in 2002 and was completed when it opened to the public in 2005. Volunteers staff the home during its open hours.

As was generally done at the time, Doctor Ford carried out his medical practice in the home, with surgery being

DOCTOR JAMES FORD HISTORIC HOME. Located in Wabash, the house is a few blocks north of downtown. The Victorian garden is to the left in the photo.

performed in the building next door where a parking lot now is located. When you turn to the right upon entering the home, you soon find yourself in a room typifying the building next door where the good doctor may have found a scene such as greets you—a man obviously in bad shape lying on a surgical bed with blood everywhere.

One of the pleasures of this restoration is that you can do your tour however you like. You can meander through the house, stopping here and there according to your fancy, or you can do it in a more organized way by moving from room to room, pausing to listen to recorded messages that provide additional information. (I probably missed a lot, but, being the meandering type, I chose to pick up detail through my own observation. In retrospect, probably not a good idea.)

Another pleasure of a visit is to stroll through the Victorian garden next to the house. A Queen Anne house formerly was there but was moved down the street. In the back of the property is a stone barn where the doctor kept his horse, Barney.

IF YOU GO

GETTING THERE: On Indiana 15 in Wabash, turn west on the north side of the courthouse on Hill Street. The Ford house is on the south side in the second block, 177 W. Hill Street.

INFORMATION: Open Wednesday, Thursday, Friday, Saturday, 10 a.m. to 5 p.m.; Sunday, noon to 5 p.m. For more information call (260) 563–8686. The Web site is http://www.jamesfordmuseum.org/.

FEES: Admission charged.

CANAL MARKER. On the site of the Kerr Lock at Lagro, this sign indicates the gift made by Charles Nottingham to mark the historic canal's passage through the Wabash County town.

MOVED TO CANAL SITE. This log cabin has been moved to the site of the Kerr Lock in Lagro.

Kerr Lock, Lagro

LAGRO—You find a little bit of everything in Indiana. Believe it or not, you even find an Irish war. It was a part of one of the great Hoosier stories—the building of the Wabash and Erie Canal. Here's the way the historians tell what happened.

As canal construction worked its way toward the Wabash County town of Lagro in mid-July 1835, an influx of Irish workers had been hired to do the hard work of digging and preparing the canal's bed, viaducts, culverts, locks, towpaths, and turnabout basins. Many of them previously had worked on other canals in the eastern United States.

Already two groups of the Irish workers had engaged in several fights along the way in Indiana. Canal historian Thomas Castaldi says they may have fought because of how many jiggers of whiskey they received in addition to their dollar a day, because of Catholic-Protestant differences, or maybe because the "Corkers" and the "Way Downers" just didn't like each other.

In any case, they apparently decided to settle their dispute on July 12, 1835, the anniversary of the Battle of Boyne, fought by the Irish against the British near Dublin, Ireland. Hundreds of the canal workers faced each other in a battle that may have been fought—or not fought—with working materials, rocks, and clubs.

Actually, historians aren't clear on how much of a battle it was. One reports "a pitched battle," another says it amounted "to a few fisticuffs," while yet another says "it did not take place" because state troops arrived, detained perhaps one hundred men, and arrested the ringleaders, said to number fourteen. They were tried in an Indianapolis court and at least some of them served brief jail terms.

Thus, the so-called Irish war in Indiana was over. Everybody went back to work, and the canal through Wabash County was completed within the next year and a half.

Such disturbances were not to be taken lightly, however. Several murders occurred, families often fled to caves and other shelters for their safety, and rumors of wars were frequent occurrences. A saying at the time was that the canal cost a life for every six feet of length.

KERR LOCK CANAL. The lock remains still are quite visible at Lagro. The lock was part of the Wabash and Erie Canal constructed across Indiana in the early part of the nineteenth century to provide transportation for goods, crops, and travelers.

Remnants of the canal still can be found throughout the state, including the Kerr Lock in Lagro. It's just off Washington Street as the centerpiece of a small park. Visitors are welcome to walk down to what remains of the lock to inspect it. The large stones that formed the sides of the lock are in place, and the bed of the waterway is evident.

Also on the site is a log cabin, given to Lagro by the Indiana Department of Transportation in 1992. Previously, it stood at the intersection of U.S. 24 and Indiana 524 for a number of years. It was a private residence and an antique shop at various times. Dismantled, it was moved to the canal site by the Lagro Lions Club.

"A member of our street department keeps an eye on it," says Maxine Baker, town clerk, "although we don't make any special use of it right now."

Many other reminders of the Wabash and Erie Canal still can be found throughout Indiana. One probably is near you if you live on a line that roughly runs across the state from the northeast to the southwest.

IF YOU GO

GETTING THERE: In Wabash County follow U.S. 24 to Indiana 524 and turn south into Lagro. Go east on Washington Street three blocks to the Kerr Lock.

INFORMATION: Call the Wabash County Convention and Visitors Bureau at (800) 563–1169, go to http://www.wabashcountycvb.com/, or call the Lagro clerk at (260) 782–2451.

FEES: None.

BUILT OF RECYCLED WOOD. This sign on S. Washington Street in Marion identifies the house where the Quilters Hall of Fame is located. The house was built of recycled wood from the former York Inn of Marion.

MARIE'S DESK. Marie Webster worked at this desk in 1915 in her Marion home when she published her first quilt book, *Quilts: Their Story and How to Make Them.*

Quilters Hall of Fame, Marion

MARION—What a small world it is! Hardly a new thought, but this truth was evident again when I visited the Quilters Hall of Fame in the old Marie Webster house on Marion's South Washington Street.

Turns out the house is located but four blocks from where I grew up. I now realize I must have gone by it a thousand or more times on my way to and from downtown Marion—we walked in those days—and to and from my first newspaper job as a sportswriter at the old *Marion Chronicle*.

Then, after visiting the Quilters Hall of Fame, I attended a semiannual reunion of Marion High School graduates. As fate would have it, I sat across from my grade school first love. When I mentioned the quilter's house, she said—which I apparently had forgotten—that her family once lived in that very house, not many years after Marie Webster left Marion.

Indeed, it is a small world.

I'm told thirty million people quilt. As for this house, its staff says it is the only quilters hall of fame in America located in the former home of a world-renowned quilter and the only National Historic Landmark devoted to a quilter.

In other essays about outdoor activities, I have acknowledged I really am not an outdoorsman. Neither am I a quilter, but I certainly do admire their work. I still have a quilt made by my paternal grandmother. (Wonder how many others have a similar one?) Along with them, I find myself fascinated by the designs, use of color, and just plain beauty of quilts.

Marie Webster without question was a master of the art. Born in Wabash in 1859, she was taught needlework by her mother. She traveled widely with her husband, George Webster, and became, according to her biography, "one of the most knowledgeable women of the day on the subject."

The Websters moved into their 926 S. Washington Street house in 1902—a house, by the way, which is said to have been built largely from recycled wood from Marion's old York Inn.

Webster wrote the first quilt history book in 1915 and published her quilt designs in the then-popular *Ladies Home Journal.* Because of the demand, she started a successful

QUILTER AND HISTORIAN. Marie Webster lived in this house at 926 S. Washington Street, now the home of the Quilters Hall of Fame.

mail-order pattern business that she ran out of her upstairs sitting room. That sitting room has been restored to look much as it might have in Webster's day.

She moved from Marion in 1942 and died in New Jersey in 1956. As the years passed, not surprisingly, the house was allowed to deteriorate. Two of Webster's grand-daughters aided its restoration over a twelve-year period, with the hall of fame opening in 2004.

The hall features changing exhibits, honorees of the Quilters Hall of Fame (I counted thirty-seven including four men), an extensive library, museum store with books, gifts, and handmade items by members of the Marie Webster Quilt Guild, and, outside, flower gardens tended for many years by the Grant County Evening Garden Club, now by Master Gardener Michelle Gerig and husband, Mark Gerig.

The house where I grew up? On this latest trip, I found it torn down and now simply a grassy lot. So it goes with writers, I guess. Along with Rodney Dangerfield, we don't get any respect.

GETTING THERE: At the court-house in downtown Marion, turn south on Washington Street to the Quilters Hall of Fame at 926 S. Washington Street. There is parking on the street and in the rear of the building.

INFORMATION: Open Tuesday through Saturday, 10 a.m. to 4 p.m., March through December. Closed Sunday, Monday, and most major holidays. Hours may change, so be certain to check. Telephone (765) 664–9333 or go to the Web site http://www.quiltershalloffame.net/.

FEES: Admission charged.

SCULPTED HEAD. This sculpture of James Dean sits atop his memorial monument in the small James Dean Memorial Park in downtown Fairmount.

FAIRMOUNT FRIENDS. The pastor of this small Friends Meeting in Fairmount presided at James Dean's funeral.

BOARDED UP SCHOOL. James Dean graduated from Fairmount High School. The old building since has deteriorated although plans surface from time to time to try to save it.

JAMES DEAN GRAVE. The headstone was stolen a few years ago but later found in western Indiana and returned.

James Dean and Fairmount

FAIRMOUNT—Indiana basketball is the stuff of which legends are made. As a sportswriter decades ago, my thoughts go back nearly sixty years to a weekend when a player almost fulfilled the dream of every Hoosier boy: Leading his small-town team to victory over the big city school in the annual "Hoosier Hysteria"—the Indiana single-bracket basketball tournament.

The player was Fairmount High School senior James Dean. The year was 1949. Six years later the actor was killed in a California automobile crash after he had made only three motion pictures.

At a time when the term "legend" is loosely used, he has become a true legend. *Newsweek* magazine at one time predicted eight of Tom Cruise's twenty-six movies will be watched fifty years from now, four of Russell Crowe's thirteen, four of twenty-eight for Julia Roberts, and one of twenty-three for Nicole Kidman. James Dean? Three of three.

But in 1949, Dean was simply a skinny 5 foot, 9 inch guard for Fairmount who wore glasses and scored a few points. After a so-so season, the Quakers faced Van Buren in the first game of the Marion sectionals. Van Buren had won both regular season games from Fairmount, but this time the Quakers won 42–39 with Dean scoring thirteen points. In the semifinals, against a much-favored Mississinewa team, the Quakers won an upset, 39–37, as Dean scored twelve more points.

The dream wasn't to become reality, however. That night, against the big city Marion Giants in the sectional finals, the Quakers finally fell, 40–34. Dean led all scorers with fifteen points, so he had scored 35 percent of all Fairmount's points in the three games.

His performance certainly caught the eye of local sportswriters. Dean was "largely responsible for Fairmount getting to the finals" and "had a spectacular long shot."

Dean also did his work as a defensive player. He was too small to play under the basket but usually took on the other team's best backcourt shooter. One opposition player said he "didn't have a lot of talent but was a sticky guard."

Today, Dean is remembered here with the annual James Dean Festival in late September, an exhibition at the Fair-

MEMORIAL PARK. Dedicated to motion picture legend James Dean in downtown Fairmount at Main and Second streets.

mount Historical Museum, his much-visited grave north of town, and, at a site often overlooked, the James Dean Memorial Park in downtown Fairmount.

It's only a small spot with some seating, landscaping, and a memorial bust. It's quiet, almost serene, contemplative.

The plaque on the memorial sculpture makes this point: "This is not a monument to a rebel. Those were only roles he played. James Dean was an American original who on a basis of high school honors and in a period of five years time rose to the very pinnacle of the theatrical profession and through the magic of motion pictures lives on in legend."

If the plaque has it right, the small park may be an appropriate way to remember an Indiana farm boy who nearly played out one dream on a Hoosier basketball court before he went on to play out yet another dream on a world stage.

IF YOU GO

GETTING THERE: In downtown Fairmount, the James Dean Memorial Park is on the east side of Main Street at Second Street.

INFORMATION: Fairmount Historical Museum, 203 E. Washington Street, (765) 948–4555, Web site http://jamesdeanartifacts.com/. Open daily, March through November, Monday through Saturday, 10 a.m. to 5 p.m., Sunday, noon to 5 p.m. Visitors also can be admitted December through February by calling the museum telephone number.

FEES: None.

WOODLAWN HEIGHTS. The tree-covered entrance into Woodlawn Heights, Indiana's seventh smallest town with seventy-three residents. Woodlawn Heights is located within the city limits of Anderson in Madison County.

Indiana's Smallest Towns

ANDERSON—A list and an Indiana map accompanying an article in the *Indianapolis Star* certainly caught my attention. "Indiana's Smallest Towns" was the headline over the list and map—part of a larger article about the twenty smallest towns in Indiana with populations of one hundred or less.

As I looked through the list and the map, I was struck by the fact that three of them appeared to be in eastern Madison County. Indeed, I found as I did a little more checking that all three lie within the city limits of the county seat of Anderson.

And that includes the smallest town in Indiana—River Forest, population twenty-eight.

I called my writer friend in Anderson, Holly Miller, who said, yes, she knew where River Forest is located and had some idea about the other two. So we decided to check them out. It turns out that River Forest consists of ten houses on a single, one-block street.

When we drove there, I talked with one River Forest resident who was standing in his driveway. Frank Phelps, retired and a River Forest resident for about fifteen years, said he thought the population actually might be a little less today than twenty-eight because "some of the kids have gone off to school."

The town is called River Forest because the street is called River Forest, he said. It was chartered in early 1953 by Doctor L. L. Nesbitt, who platted the "town," according to an article in the *Anderson Bulletin*, found in the archives of the Anderson Public Library. It's unlikely ever to grow because no vacant lots exist and the street is a dead end.

"We have our own town council; we're incorporated by the state as a town. We set our own taxes and have very few expenses," Phelps told me. Asked about the town's budget, he said it was around $6,000 a year— "mostly to maintain our road; fire protection and road maintenance—that's about it." He added, "It took us four years to get our streetlights because of our low budget." Fire and police protection are contracted with another nearby small town, Edgewood, located on the west side of Anderson.

The other two incorporated small towns—Woodlawn Heights, population seventy-three, and Country Club Heights,

RIVER FOREST. There's no outlet to the one-block long street of River Forest, where all ten houses of Indiana's smallest town of twenty-eight persons is located.

population ninety-one—actually are across Madison Street from each other on Anderson's near west side.

Woodlawn Heights extends from Madison Avenue west to Glendon Road, south to the White River and north to VanBuskirk Road. It has more than thirty homes—also no vacant lots. To the east, across Madison Avenue, is Country Club Heights. As its name suggests, it is closely associated with Anderson Country Club. You drive through the town to reach the club, which marked its one hundredth anniversary in 2002.

According to the latest population figures as published in the *Indianapolis Star* article, Woodlawn Heights is the seventh smallest town in the state and Country Club Heights the fourteenth.

None of them would necessarily be a destination point for Hoosier travelers. Indeed, I'm sure the residents aren't looking for visitors. But, if you're in the area, and you want to see for yourself, well—.

IF YOU GO

GETTING THERE: In Anderson, go west on Eighth Street until you cross Raible Avenue. A sign on the right marks River Forest just a short distance later. To go to Country Club Heights, turn north on Madison Avenue from West Eighth Street after going west through downtown. After crossing the White River, turn east (right) into the Anderson Country Club. Woodlawn Heights is west (left) off Madison also just north of the White River.

FEES: None.

Ivanhoe's Restaurant, Upland

ADDITION. The 1993 addition to the Upland landmark restaurant can be seen at the right. It doubled Ivanhoe's size.

MOMS COME BACK. Children of two former Taylor students enjoy their lunch at Ivanhoe's in Upland. Their moms—onetime college roommates from Indianapolis and Van Wert, Ohio—were at a nearby table. They were in Upland for the day and worked in a trip to the restaurant.

LINE UP. Customers line up at Ivanhoe's to place their food orders. Another line to the right down the hallway is devoted to ice cream.

UPLAND—When is the best time of the year to eat ice cream? Summer? Winter? Any time?

For people who stop at Ivanhoe's Restaurant, located just north of the Taylor University campus on South Main Street, probably the last answer is the correct one even though summer is when the Upland institution has its biggest days—sometimes one thousand or more customers.

While Ivanhoe's serves sandwiches and salads in addition to ice cream, it's difficult for most customers to resist a menu that includes one hundred different milk shakes and one hundred sundaes.

It wasn't always one hundred of each. When it first opened as Wiley's Drive-In in 1960, the restaurant's shake menu consisted of vanilla, chocolate, and strawberry. After Ivan and Carol Slain purchased the business, they would close it for about three months during the winter to go to Florida. En route, they started thinking up new milk shake ideas. "When they finally got to one hundred, they decided that was a good number to stop at," says Mark Souers, general manager. Today, each new menu printing brings changes within the one hundred. For example, Ivanhoe's recently added a Turkey Tracks milk shake.

Souers was one of five general managers when I visited the establishment (the others were Dennis Hunter, Jessica Buster, Shawn Rust, and Mark Slain—a second generation in the business). When the Slains started keeping the restaurant open year-round in the late 1970s, they found running the business was a full-time job—nearly seven days a week, open to close. So, they've welcomed son Mark to help share the load.

"Some of our regular customers come from as far as Kokomo," says Souers. "Others come because somebody talks to somebody else who has gone to Taylor and says, 'If you're going down on [Interstate] 69, you need to go to Ivanhoe's'" (three miles from the Upland exit onto Indiana 22).

The restaurant employs about fifty people, more than thirty-five of them high school students, working part time. "Most people think we would have college kids, but their

ONE OF ONE HUNDRED. Creamsicle shake is one of one hundred milk shake offerings at Ivanhoe's Restaurant in Upland, long a favorite of Taylor University students and customers from east-central Indiana—and farther.

college life is pretty busy, and they really don't have the time," says Souers.

The major building change occurred in 1993 when the restaurant's space was nearly doubled with the addition of a large dining room. The restaurant can seat about 120, but take-outs remain popular.

A restaurant highlight is the "100 Club," made up of those customers who have ordered all one hundred of the shakes or sundaes. The customer who reaches that point is awarded a T-shirt and has his or her name placed on a plaque. Jim Snellink was the first to have his name go up in 1976 with one hundred shakes. After a twenty-two-year dry spell, Justin Young in 1998 followed with another one hundred shakes. Thirty-one names have been added, however, since 2000—half of them for sundaes.

"I think it's because people have become more aware of it, and it takes a little while to order one hundred shakes or sundaes," says Souers.

Or maybe it's because today our ice cream appetite takes in every season.

IF YOU GO

GETTING THERE: Ivanhoe's is located at 979 South Main Street in Upland, just north of the Taylor University campus.

INFORMATION: Open Monday through Thursday 10 a.m. to 10 p.m.; Friday and Saturday 10 a.m. to 11 p.m.; and Sunday 2 to 10 p.m. Telephone (765) 998–7261, or go to the Web site at http://www.ivanhoes.info/.

IT HAD A CLOSET. This upstairs bedroom also had a small closet, out of view to the left, somewhat unusual in houses built early in the nineteenth century.

HAS TOURS. Furniture includes this small tea table in the Moore-Youse Home Museum, open for monthly tours by the Delaware County Historical Society.

Moore-Youse Home Museum, Muncie

MUNCIE—It's a somewhat familiar story: Newlyweds or their parents buy or build a house for the young couple, one or more of their children live there, followed by someone from the third generation, perhaps even the fourth, and finally no one is left who is interested in living in what is by now an old house.

In many cases, the probably one hundred-year-old property is sold and passes into history, or it is used for other purposes, or, more likely, it is razed. In a few situations, a relative sees the significance of the property or some history buffs come to the rescue and the house becomes part of the historical group.

Fortunately for the Delaware County Historical Society, the last possibilities are what happened to the Moore-Youse house, one of the oldest structures in the city. It was willed to the historical society at the death of Mary Youse Maxon.

Former Ball State historian Dwight Hoover outlined the three-generation story of the house's occupants in a pamphlet, "The Moore-Youse Home, a Three-Family Tale." It recounts how widower Charles Moore married Clara (Clarissa) Wilson in 1861. Her father, Samuel Porter Wilson, in 1864 bought them a Federal-style house of four rooms—two down and two up—at 122 E. Washington Street that had been built in 1849. The Moores' daughter, Mary (Mame) Moore, married Will Youse in 1893, following an eleven-year courtship, and the couple lived in the house, too, caring for her elderly parents. Finally, their daughter, Mary Youse, born in 1896, married Jack Maxon at age fifty in 1946 after a nineteen-year courtship. Since Mary wouldn't leave the house, the Maxons continued living there. Jack Maxon's death came in 1957 and Mary's in 1982, ending the three-family residential period that lasted nearly 120 years.

The original house was divided by a central hallway, and the two rooms upstairs possibly were reached by stairs outside the back of the house. The larger bedroom had a small closet, somewhat unusual for homes of the time. Later a dining room was added on the first floor and, still later, a larger two-story addition plus a garage.

HISTORIC HOME. The Moore-Youse Home Museum in downtown Muncie was the home of Moore, Youse, and Maxon families for nearly 120 years.

Much of the furniture now in the house was accumulated by the Moore and Youse families over the years. For example, in an 1896 photo of Clara Jane Moore, holding her infant granddaughter, Mary, her rocking chair, and a small table and a shelf, seen in the background of the photo, still are in the same second-floor bedroom.

Today, the Moore-Youse home is the centerpiece of the historical society and is open once a month and by appointment for tours. If docents aren't in an area for a tour, audiotapes are in place for details.

A second building on the grounds serves as the offices and library of the Delaware County Historical Society Inc.

While the Moore-Youse house dates back to 1849, it likely was not the first building on that site in downtown Muncie. A Ball State University intern at the house found what appeared to be another foundation for a smaller structure under the original Moore-Youse structure.

Henry County Historical Society Museum, New Castle

THIRTY-FIVE YEARS TO BUILD. This is the desk that architect Thaddeus Coffin built during a period of thirty-five years, consisting of 56,978 inlaid pieces—after he had lost all the fingers on his left hand. It's on display at the Henry County Historical Society Museum.

MUSEUM'S SITE. This former home of Civil War general William Grose and his daughter's home to the left house the Henry County Historical Society Museum. It is located at 606 S. Fourteenth Street in New Castle.

SUMMER KITCHEN. In what may have been the home's tack room, this summer kitchen has been created by the Henry County Historical Society. Few of the furnishings of the museum came from the original home, most coming from other Henry County homes and businesses.

NEW CASTLE—You've got to see it to believe it.

New Castle architect Thaddeus Coffin took thirty-five years (1870–1905) to build one desk, using 56,978 separate inlaid pieces of wood. One drawer alone includes 2,367 pieces and tells, in Morse code, the history of the Coffin family.

Ten years before starting on the desk, the then twenty-nine-year-old New Castle architect oversaw construction of this newly designed Italianate home, built for former Civil War general William Grose. The following year, Coffin lost all the fingers on his left hand while operating a woodworking machine. He waited another nine years before he began to build the desk, consisting of 324 varieties of wood from around the world.

This desk is but one of the objects found in the Henry County Historical Society Museum. The museum is made up of Grose's former home along with the adjacent home, built for the general's daughter. The general's home was purchased by the county to house the historical society in 1901. After the historical society obtained the daughter's home in the 1970s, the two houses were connected by a pavilion to form the present museum.

Coffin's desk is located in the large main-floor room of the general's home, in what was once three rooms but now is opened up to create a large display space. Another drawer of the desk has the music for "Taps." Coffin, a Civil War veteran, inlaid his military service medals in the desk's front center panel.

Although she's not certain, Marianne Hughes, the museum curator, believes one of the three rooms served as the general's office for his law practice when he returned to New Castle following the war. The other two rooms were the front parlor where guests were received and the family parlor. A large portrait of General Grose overlooks the present large room.

Most of the furnishings throughout the museum have come from other homes in the county and from business establishments. An additional room was added to the house in 1961 to accommodate furnishings from the New Castle home of

WHEN THE TORNADO HIT. This photograph is in a basement room of the Henry County Historical Society Museum. It shows a section of the city after a tornado went through on March 11, 1917.

William and Emma Bond. With no space available, the Bonds' daughter, Jean Bond Hough, paid to have the room added.

In all, the two homes contain twenty-seven rooms. Some of them are dedicated to special subjects. In the basement are found equipment used in an old barber shop, for health care, a clinic, and the Hoosier Kitchen Cabinet room. For decades, the popular cabinets were manufactured in New Castle.

On the second floor is clothing from the 1800s and the early 1900s along with displays of America's wars ranging from the Civil War through the Gulf War. Two other Henry County generals, Omar Bundy and Bruce Harris, are featured. The antislavery movement, natural history, Native American artifacts, and a Victorian bedroom are subjects of other displays.

In the daughter's home, the visitor can walk through the Pence museum of children's toys, political memorabilia and yearbooks, pictures, and other objects from Henry County schools. It also houses the museum's library and offices.

IF YOU GO

GETTING THERE: In New Castle, at the intersection of Indiana 3 and Indiana 38 (Broad Street) turn east [left] and go to Fourteenth Street. Turn right. The museum is on the left-hand side of the street at 606 S. Fourteenth Street.

INFORMATION: The museum is open Monday through Saturday 1 to 4:30 p.m. Large groups can be accommodated with prior arrangements. It is closed Sunday and holidays. The Web address is www.kiva.net/~hchisoc/museum and its telephone number is (765) 529–4028.

FEES: Admission charged.

FORMER NURSE SHIRLEY HILE.
Here she shows her 1960s miniskirt
nurse's uniform that is part of the
display of nurses' clothing at the
Luckey Hospital Museum at Wolf
Lake.

SURGERY ROOM. Luckey Hospital's surgery room now is located on
the first floor of the museum but at
some point will be moved to where
it was located on the third floor.

Luckey Hospital Museum, Wolf Lake

WOLF LAKE—As I followed Shirley Hile up to the second
floor of the Luckey Hospital Museum, she explained, "My
sister Mary [Goodrich] and I put 125 gallons of paint on this
building." That's just part of what the two great-nieces of
Doctor James E. Luckey have done to save this memorial to
small-town medical care as it existed in the 1930s.

Hile related the story as we toured the former hospital and
clinic, now mostly a museum with apartments on its second
floor. My brother-in-law, Doctor Robert Stone of Ligonier, told
me about the museum, suggesting it might make an interesting article.

It certainly does. In brief, here's what happened.

Doctor Luckey moved here in 1901 and built his house at
the intersection of U.S. 33 and where Indiana 109 ends. He
had a small office building, but mostly used his home for his
practice while also making house calls. With his two sons
joining him, he built the hospital/clinic in 1929–31, using his
old office as part of the building. Hospital patients entered the
south end, while clinic patients came into a waiting room at
the north.

The hospital/clinic consisted of a basement for food preparation, staff dining room, X-ray developing, laundry, pharmacy storage, and alcohol for instrument sterilization—"and
sometimes human consumption"—and was connected by a
tunnel to the house. The first floor had clinic facilities, emer-
gency room, doctors' offices, pharmacy, laboratory, business
office, X-ray room, and a two-bed room for patient overflow
or children with tonsillectomies. On the second floor were
sixteen patient beds including a four-bed maternity ward,
nursing station, and a four-bassinet nursery. A third floor had
a surgical room, labor and delivery room, sterilization and
pack room, and sleeping rooms for staff and visiting doctors.
After Luckey's death in 1938, his sons and other doctors operated the hospital until 1957 when the remaining two doctors
moved the clinic to a new building at Southeast Wolf Lake and
closed the hospital.

In succeeding years, the building was used as a nursing
home, Laundromat, beauty shop, video store, apartments,

LUCKEY HOSPITAL MUSEUM. The hospital/clinic at Wolf Lake in northern Indiana closed in 1957.

and as a private home, and when Hile and Goodrich purchased it in 2000 it was "in bad disrepair." A new roof, septic tank, well, water drainage system—and lots of paint—followed as well as tearing down a garage. The Luckey house long since had been demolished.

Hile and Goodrich, both former nurses, had been collecting medical artifacts for more than thirty years, so it naturally followed that they would open the hospital museum. On the first floor is a room of nurses' uniforms, caps, and equipment that includes some of Hile's uniforms. The surgical room presently is on the first floor rather than the third. The second floor, where patients were housed, is now mostly apartments.

Among the artifacts are instruments used in a bygone day for bloodletting. It was thought several centuries ago that "bad blood" needed to be removed from the body for healing. (Hile told me that red and white poles in barber shops denoted that they also practiced bloodletting.)

IF YOU GO

GETTING THERE: In Wolf Lake, the museum is on the west side where Indiana 109 intersects with U.S. 33.

INFORMATION: The museum is open Memorial Day through Labor Day Saturday and Sunday 1 to 4 p.m. and by appointment at other times. Call (260) 635–2419 or go to www.luckeyhospitalmuseum.org/.

FEES: Admission charged.

THE RESTAURANT. Entrance to the Joseph Decuis restaurant at Roanoke, which opened to the public in 2000.

THE CONSERVATORY. One of the five dining areas at the Joseph Decuis restaurant at up-and-coming Roanoke in Huntington County.

Joseph Decuis Restaurant, Roanoke

ROANOKE—Every newspaper has a reporter who is some kind of a food expert, perhaps even a gourmet. It's a shame Rose Meldrum couldn't have shared lunch at the Joseph Decuis—pronounced "day-queeze"—restaurant with one of them. Instead, Meldrum, executive director of the Huntington County Visitor and Convention Bureau, drew me as her luncheon partner. First off, let's get one thing clear. I paid the bill for my meal to get any journalism ethics questions out of the way.

Meldrum had talked earlier with me about this special restaurant in Roanoke. If I'd like to go sometime, she said, she would be happy to accompany me because she loves eating there.

Mind you, I'm not complaining—far from it. The gumbo soup, Joseph Decuis salad, and more-than-my-half of a chocolate dessert were as well presented and tasty as any food I've eaten.

The problem wasn't Joseph Decuis. The problem is me.

In terms of food, I'm just a plain ol' Hoosier meat-and-potatoes guy. I might wish I were different, but I'm not. That didn't take anything away from the experience. What the American Specialty people have done in Roanoke with this restaurant is amazing. Like many a small town, Roanoke was hurting badly before American Specialty chose it as its corporate headquarters in 1990. American Specialty offers consulting and high-risk insurance services for the sports and entertainment industries.

With representatives of high-priced people and events coming to town, American Specialty's Pete Eshelman wanted a fine corporate restaurant to serve them. So he founded Joseph Decuis in 1996, which he opened to the public in 2000. The name? Eshelman says he named it after an ancestor with that name who lived in Louisiana in the late 1700s. That "began our heritage of dining in the Creole tradition," he says.

Writing in his book, *Roanoke: The Renaissance of a Hoosier Village*, he says, "Many people thought a gourmet restaurant in Roanoke would never succeed," but "We had confidence that Joseph Decuis would become a destination restaurant: its

JOSEPH DECUIS. Pete Eshelman's ancestor appears with his wife, Celeste, in this painting by a Fort Wayne artist. It hangs in the Club Creole room at the Roanoke restaurant.

small-town location and New Orleans-style atmosphere would provide a completely different experience."

Did he succeed? *Indianapolis Monthly* in a review declared it to be "quite simply the best restaurant in the state."

The buildings once were, among other businesses, the First National Bank of Huntington—its vaults now housing a walk-in wine cellar and cigar humidor.

Joseph Decuis offers five settings today: Club Creole, the formal dining room and bar; Café Creole, which includes the open exhibition kitchen; the Conservatory, alfresco dining amidst ferns and gas lanterns (where Meldrum and I ate); the Gallery Board Room, for privacy or meetings; and the Courtyard, for seasonal outdoor dining surrounded by gardens. The restaurant raises its own beef as well as most of its own vegetables and free-range chicken eggs.

Nearby is the Inn at Joseph Decuis. Built in 1912, it's an early-twentieth-century décor, restored four-bedroom Victorian-style inn, available only to those who eat at the restaurant.

GETTING THERE: Turn off Interstate 69 at Exit 96 B onto Lafayette Center Road, south of Fort Wayne. Go west until it becomes Vine Street at Roanoke. At the traffic signal, turn right on Main Street for two blocks.

INFORMATION: Reservations are recommended by calling (260) 672–1715 or go to the Web site at www.josephdecuis.com/. (The menu, which changes, can be checked on the Web site.) Open Tuesday through Saturday with lunch 11:30 a.m. to 2 p.m. and dinner 5:30 to 10 p.m. Live jazz Friday and Saturday evenings.

FEES: Prices vary but tend to be on the high end, especially for dinner.

The History Center, Fort Wayne

"DRUNK TANK." In use until the early 1970s, this "drunk tank" in the old City Hall at Fort Wayne had wire screening inside its bars to thwart suicides. It's part of "the calaboose" in the basement historical display.

"MOST LAWLESS." According to a *Chicago Tribune* article in 1875, Fort Wayne was considered at the time "the most lawless town in Indiana." This law enforcement display includes the rope used in the last public hanging in the city.

FORT WAYNE—"When you look at those jail cells downstairs, you'll probably think they look primitive. They are, but Fort Wayne was still using them until 1971," says Jack Lee, a weekend employee at the History Center, operated by the Allen County–Fort Wayne Historical Society.

Lee has it right. The cells look as if Wyatt Earp might have thrown some of the bad guys in them more than one hundred years ago. It's a dark, oppressive basement area—a place to visit, perhaps, but certainly not one where you would want to stay. One cell, the "drunk tank," has a screen across the top of the bars to discourage suicides. According to a sign on the cell, oral history has it that at least two suicides occurred in the cell, nevertheless.

The museum is located on the first and second floors of the old City Hall building along with the basement display, called "the calaboose," an old slang term for a jail. In addition to the lockups, there's the rope that was used to hang Sam McDonald in Fort Wayne's last public hanging, local law enforcement artifacts, and a Harley Davidson police motorcycle.

The Fort Wayne and Allen County story is a somewhat happier one on the other two floors. The first floor centers on the city's history from its earliest days until the 1920s. You can see the camp bed that General Anthony Wayne is said to have used in the 1700s along with artifacts once owned by the Miami Indian chief, Little Turtle.

The city is named for Wayne, who selected the site for an American fort in 1794. Little Turtle lived near an earlier fort, built by the French.

Fort Wayne also is closely associated with Johnny Appleseed—John Chapman—who planted fruit trees throughout the Indiana-Ohio countryside. A flask used by Chapman, who died in Fort Wayne in 1845, is on display on the first floor.

Today, the second floor has an exhibition on women's clothing and Fort Wayne aviation. An introduction to Allen County history also is located on the second floor along with two audio/video kiosks that have brief historical vignettes—twenty at each one—about county history.

NOW A MUSEUM. The former Fort Wayne City Hall now contains the Allen County–Fort Wayne Historical Museum. The sandstone building was completed in 1893 and became the new home for the museum in 1980.

Part of that history is the story of Philo Farnsworth, called by some the "father of television"—at the very least, the inventor of the television camera—who lived in Fort Wayne and where once the Farnsworth-Capehart Company produced some of America's earliest television sets. A museum room dedicated to Farnsworth is part of the Dean V. Kruse museums just off Interstate 69 at Auburn.

Fort Wayne's old city courtroom, also used as the city council chambers, has been renamed the Freimann Room and is used for changing exhibits. Museum offices are on the second and third floors.

You may see some reference to the "Habsburg Horror" when you visit the museum. That's a reference to local residents' criticism of the cost of the then-City Hall in the 1890s—a "royal" figure of $69,000. The Habsburgs ruled Germany, and much of Fort Wayne's population had recently arrived from that European nation, so they were aware of royalty's spending habits.

IF YOU GO

GETTING THERE: In Fort Wayne on Jefferson Boulevard, take Barr Street north for 2 ½ blocks. The museum is on the right. Turn in the alley to the parking lot east of the building.

INFORMATION: Museum hours are 10 a.m. to 5 p.m. Monday through Friday, noon to 5 p.m. Saturday, and closed Sunday. For information call (260) 426–2882, fax (260) 424–4419, or go to www.fwhistory center.com/.

FEES: Admission charged.

"HONEST ABE." "The best photograph" of the new president, said his neighbors in Illinois following his election in 1860. But the Republican National Committee didn't believe he looked "dressed up enough," and few copies were made. This one was given to the Mississinewa chapter of a historical organization in 1919.

PORTLAND HOME. The Jay County Historical Museum is located on East Main Street.

Jay County Historical Museum, Portland

PORTLAND—An old newspaper adage holds that "names make the news." If that's true, then the Jay County Historical Museum located in near-downtown Portland contains lots of news. Many of the museum's walls are covered with photographs of graduating classes from the county's former eight high schools as well as a considerable amount of memorabilia from the schools.

Name follows name with those smiling high school seniors of yesteryear looking down on visitors strolling through the halls and rooms of the museum.

The museum contains much more of Jay County's history, of course.

Included are authentic Native American artifacts, Civil War relics, historical documents, a rare photograph of Abraham Lincoln—more about that later, mementos of the United States' wars, a horse-drawn mail wagon, antique farm machinery, blacksmith shop and old tools, a pioneer exhibition, business and industry displays, an early one-room schoolhouse, clothing from various periods of the county's history, antique toys, medical and dental equipment, and a reference library with numerous written and pictorial materials.

All in one county museum building?

Yes, indeed, and, if it's anything like other county museums, more is stored because of the lack of display space. Also, I noticed as I drove away from my visit, an yet-to-be restored clover huller housed in a shed behind the museum. That will be quite an attraction when restoration is completed.

The historical society that operates the museum works, as almost all do, with volunteers who staff the building five hours a day during the week, at special open houses, and by appointment.

It also has an ambitious nonmuseum schedule of tours, lectures, publications, memberships, newsletters, and, of course, fund-raising. Its store located in the museum offers more than forty Jay County books and pamphlets for sale.

The historical society also sponsors an annual two-day Fall Heritage Festival, usually the first weekend in October, with free admission. Ham and beans are the Saturday specialty

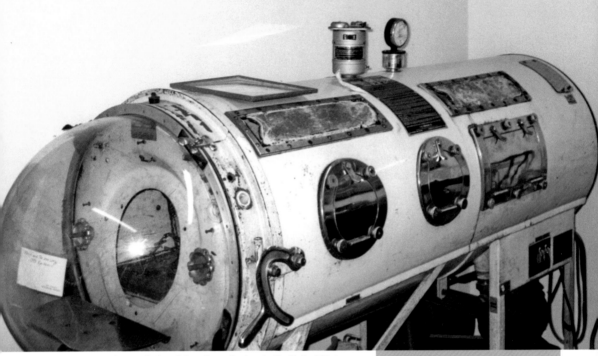

IRON LUNG. It's a reminder of the grim polio days in the United States. The iron lung is part of the Jay County Historical Museum in Portland.

IF YOU GO

with chili and hot dogs on Sunday.

Now, more about that Lincoln photograph.

I know, as a Lincoln buff, I haven't begun to see all the material our nation has saved about the man many consider our greatest president. But I've seen my share. Never have I, however, come across the photograph the Jay County Historical Museum has.

Apparently, New York portrait artist Charles Perry was sent to Illinois to take a photograph of the newly selected Republican candidate for president in 1860. His photo was rejected by party headquarters because they didn't feel he was "dressed up enough" in the picture. So very few copies were made.

Citizens back home, however, declared it to be "Honest Abe's best photograph." One of the few copies was donated to a local historical chapter in 1919 and since has come into the possession of the historical society.

Lincoln could not be considered a handsome man by any imagination, but in this photo with his tousled hair and distinctive features he has a most striking appearance. So, I tend to agree with his neighbors.

GETTING THERE: In Portland, turn from Meridian (U.S. 27) onto Main Street. Turn east (left) to the museum at the end of the street. Its address is 903 E. Main Street.

INFORMATION: Museum hours are Monday through Friday 10 a.m. to noon; 1 to 4 p.m. Go to history@jaycounty.info for e-mail. The museum's telephone number is (260) 726–7168.

FEES: Admission is free, but donations are appreciated.

MARKER. Indiana's highest elevation at 1,257 feet above sea level is cited on this marker at the eastern Indiana site. As the sign indicates, it has been named "Hoosier Hill."

LOGBOOK MAILBOX. Visitors can sign in at Indiana's highest point as well as leave notes if they wish.

Hoosier Hill, Bethel

BETHEL—Admittedly, by most states' standards, it isn't very high. Nor did it seem high as I approached it. I was driving across relatively flat Indiana farmland, went up a slight hill, and there it was: Hoosier Hill, Indiana's highest point.

Highest point? All of 1,257 feet above sea level, less than a quarter of a mile or about the length of four city blocks.

Rather puny, compared to Mount Whitney, highest in the continental United States and Hawaii, which rises 14,494 feet, or nearly three miles, into the sky in California's Sierra Nevada mountain range, or Mount McKinley in Alaska at 20,320 feet or nearly four miles, the highest in the United States' fifty states. Of course, that still only makes McKinley the 109th tallest mountain in the world! Most of the really big mountains, as you no doubt know, are in Asia.

So, we're not talking "highest high" here in Indiana. Still, Hoosier Hill holds the Indiana record. No place in the entire state, including some fairly high hills in southern Indiana, is higher above sea level. That's because Indiana, generally speaking, slopes down as it goes south, the result of glacier shifts and inland oceans that came and went over the eons.

For most of us, it probably makes little difference. I imagine the vast majority of people who live in east-central Indiana have never been to the spot and, in all likelihood, never will. Still it is a quiet, restful place, only a little off the road with a picnic table and a nearby bench. Also, it isn't difficult to find—just a short distance off Indiana 227, about fifteen miles north of Richmond.

To "states' highest points" enthusiasts, however, it's a big deal. At the site is a mailbox that contains a logbook, mostly filled in, it seemed, by persons who have set out to visit all of the fifty states' highest points.

On the day I stopped there, I noted that previous visitors included those from Arlington, Virginia; Plymouth, Michigan; Denver; East Kingston, New Hampshire; Portland, Oregon; Troy, Michigan; Boulder, Colorado; and Covington, Ohio, as well as various Indiana cities. Three persons there the day

INDIANA'S HIGHEST POINT. It's located at the top of this small hill in eastern Indiana, north of Richmond and near the community of Bethel.

IF YOU GO

before were a woman from the Houston, Texas, Volunteer Fire Department and two from Cyprus, Texas. One person who signed in declared it to be "one of prettier high point spots." Another from Fort Wayne wrote, "Started with one in my own back yard; 49 more to go." Quite a collection.

Some flyers placed in the mailbox indicated what might account for an extra number of "highest point" visitors nationally. They announced that "50 for Tibet highpoint team will climb the 50 U.S. state highpoints in one year between June 16, 2006, and June 15, 2007." The program was a fund-raiser to raise awareness of the occupation of Tibet by China and for the Roswell Fund for Tibet, established "to encourage and support the work of Tibetans in the language and visual arts who can make significant contributions to society." When I last checked the organization's Web site at www.50fortibet.org/, donations had exceeded $100,000.

GETTING THERE: From Indiana 227 in northern Wayne County, turn west at 1100 South, near the "Highest Point in Indiana" sign. Go a mile to Elliott Road and turn south; up a gradual hill at its highest point on your right is a sign, "Highest point." It's easy to miss the sign.

FEES: None.

CHARIOTS OF FIRE. This Model T Ford limo was seen in a motion picture. It was built in England rather than the United States.

DEVELOPING A RACE CAR. Racing cars naturally followed production of Henry Ford's famous automobile. This display at the Model T Museum is a 1926 dirt-track racer.

Model T Museum, Centerville

CENTERVILLE—You've probably heard this line from the early part of the twentieth century about Henry Ford and his Model T cars: Ford said a buyer could have any color he wanted so long as it was black. That may or may not be true but actually when Ford started producing his first cars, in fact they were painted different colors. When he developed his assembly line, however, so car buffs report, that's when he went to all-black models.

You can catch the spirit of the Model T Ford days—September 27, 1908, to May 1927—by visiting the Model T Museum, located at the Centerville exit just west of Richmond on Interstate 70. Actually, a museum visit can work for both men and women. Women may or may not be interested in Model Ts, but they probably will be interested in the next-door Warm Glow Candle Outlet. When I visited, I spent some time in the candle shop, too. It has a huge trade. The Model T Museum is housed in what was the former candle outlet store before the new one was constructed.

But back to the Model Ts, which have been called "the car of the century" and are usually referred to as the world's first affordable automobile. The world as we know it today is in part the creation of Ford. Assembly lines existed before his time, but nothing could equal what he organized and the speed with which the Model Ts were produced. Not only that, but to say that Ford "put the world on wheels" is not mere exaggeration.

The Model T Museum is the project of the Model T Ford Club of America. Jay and Barbara Klehfoth of Centerville, with the help of volunteers, spearheaded the museum. The Klehfoths are major players, too, in the Model T Ford Club of America; he is the chief executive officer and she is the secretary.

The club, founded in 1965, has members in all fifty states and in forty-one other nations with nearly 140 chapters in the United States and eight other countries. Believe it or not, the club even offers a repair manual for the Model T! The club's major publication, *The Vintage Ford*, also lists restoration

MODEL T MUSEUM. The new museum, located at exit 145 north of Centerville and just west of Richmond, houses the world-famous car of Henry Ford that put "the world on wheels."

IF YOU GO

manuals as well as videos—some thirty-five of them—and articles of club news and photos. (One recent article explained how to install modern valves in a Model T engine.)

The museum is the place to be indoctrinated into the story of the Model T. In those nearly twenty years between 1908 and 1927, Ford built 15 million Model Ts. What I didn't know until I visited the museum was that Ford also had Model T plants in other countries around the world.

For example, the 1923 right-hand drive Model T limo that appeared in the movie *Chariots of Fire*—remember it in the beginning of the film when the athletes arrived to start training for the Olympics—wasn't built here but was built in England. That car is part of the museum's displays.

The museum, which only recently opened, still is somewhat a work in progress, in that the Klehfoths and other members add to it from their own storehouse of Ford memorabilia and cars loaned for display. Some exhibitions are expected to rotate to accommodate the large number of vehicles that might be shown.

GETTING THERE: Take exit 145 off Interstate 70, just west of Richmond.

INFORMATION: Call (765) 855–2008 or go to www.mtfca.com/. Museum hours are 10 a.m. to 6 p.m. every day but closed on Mondays.

FEES: None, but donations are accepted.

FIRST RING. This tree's first ring came in 1540 when the sycamore was twelve years old. It was cut down in 1970 at Brookville as the area was flooded for a reservoir. Its base measured twenty-two feet, six inches in circumference. It is part of the nature center displays.

THEY'RE READY. Ready to go on a visit to the Hayes Arboretum, these youngsters head to the nature center before their tour.

ARBORETUM TRAIL. Wooded area off a bridge on the beech/maple trail at Richmond's Hayes Arboretum.

Hayes Regional Arboretum, Richmond

RICHMOND—The best time to visit Hayes Regional Arboretum? Pick your favorite season of the year—spring with trees and flowers budding, summer's glorious greenery, or fall's colorful foliage. Sorry about winter—the arboretum is closed between November and February.

The arboretum's slogan is "nature's gift in every season," and that hits the mark.

Actually, my most recent trip to this 466-acre arboretum and managed preserve came a few weeks ago somewhat between seasons. Summer was ending with just a hint of trees turning to their autumn colors. This particular Saturday was a busy one at the arboretum, located on the east side of Richmond and just north of the Old National Road, U.S. 40. Rain probably was coming but not yet.

A motorcade of cars and vans had delivered a host of youngsters who quickly spread out in all directions. Couples were walking hand-in-hand, exploring the trails. Some drivers in automobiles were starting the four-mile auto tour. In the annex, a wood-carving class was in session. Other visitors were looking at the two floors of displays in the nature center.

The center is the place to begin a visit. It's located in an 1833 remodeled dairy barn. Visitors can sit at a bird-watching window, look over the displays in the building, pick up a detailed map of the grounds, use the restrooms, or purchase tokens to enter the auto-tour gate.

You can walk for free, however, following one of the color-coded-trails, all a mile or less—blue through the beech and maple forest, yellow along the habitat trail up and down hills and over a spring, orange to the springhouse and fern garden, and red that passes by the Stanley W. Hayes estate home.

That's the Hayes who made the arboretum possible. In 1911 he moved a railway manufacturing business in Richmond. An inventor and holder of ninety-four patents, Hayes is said to have selected Richmond because of its central location, climate, native areas, and the people—"the best American character, friendly, hard working, and ambitious." He liked

GUESTHOUSE. The Stanley W. Hayes estate at the arboretum now serves as a guesthouse for visiting educators, consultants, and researchers as well as for staff and foundation directors.

country living and began purchasing forest and field lands and by the mid-1920s had acquired 285 acres, tying them together with gravel roads. Important to the arboretum, he began withdrawing the land from cultivation and use as a pasture, instead systematically planting trees, shrubs, and vines. With the exception of the beech and maple forest, almost all the woody plants were put in during a half century under Hayes's direction.

Before his death in 1963, he had created the Hayes Research Foundation, transferring land, equipment, and buildings to it and providing an endowment to keep the arboretum going. (What a blessing that was!)

The four-mile auto tour passes by almost all of the arboretum's features, including on its southern leg part of the former Richmond Race Track, once considered "the fastest one-mile dirt track in the world." That track had been designed by Robert Howard, who later turned his talents toward creating another track of some renown: the Indianapolis Motor Speedway.

IF YOU GO

GETTING THERE: From Interstate 70 east of Richmond, exit at the Old National Road and go west to Elks Road. Turn north (right) to the arboretum.

INFORMATION: Call (765) 962–3745 or go to http://www.hayes arboretum.org/. Address is 801 Elks Road. Hours are Tuesday through Saturday 9 a.m. to 5 p.m. Closed Sunday and Monday. Also closed November through February.

FEES: Admission charged for the auto tour. No charge for visitors hiking the trails.

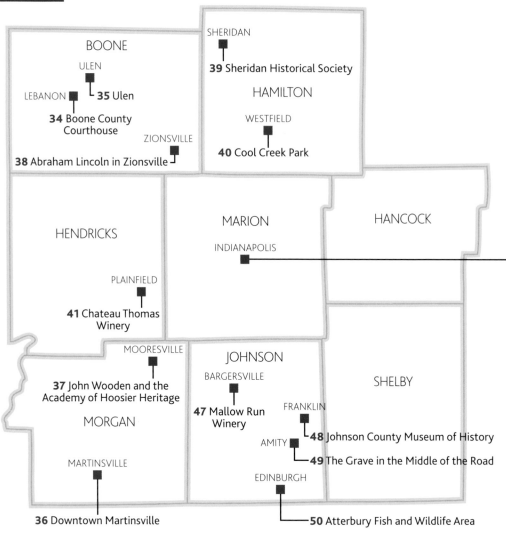

BOONE

ULEN

LEBANON

35 Ulen

34 Boone County
Courthouse

ZIONSVILLE

38 Abraham Lincoln in Zionsville

SHERIDAN

39 Sheridan Historical Society

HAMILTON

WESTFIELD

40 Cool Creek Park

HENDRICKS

MARION

INDIANAPOLIS

HANCOCK

PLAINFIELD

41 Chateau Thomas
Winery

MOORESVILLE

37 John Wooden and the
Academy of Hoosier Heritage

MORGAN

JOHNSON

BARGERSVILLE

47 Mallow Run
Winery

FRANKLIN

AMITY

SHELBY

48 Johnson County Museum of History

49 The Grave in the Middle of the Road

MARTINSVILLE

EDINBURGH

36 Downtown Martinsville

50 Atterbury Fish and Wildlife Area

N

COURTHOUSE. Boone County Courthouse as seen from the south-west corner.

THEY WORK! The clocks in the Boone County Courthouse dome actually work and record the correct time.

IN THE ROTUNDA. This quilt, produced by the Boone Bicentennial Sampler Committee for the July 4, 1976, two hundredth anniversary of the nation, hangs in the courthouse rotunda.

Boone County Courthouse, Lebanon

LEBANON—Over time and one by one, Indiana's grand old courthouses disappear, either because of weather damage, old age, or neglect. In other counties, however, it's a different story. In some cases preservationists have gone to work, and in other situations, practical-minded people apparently have seen that an investment in repairs and updating were more than worth the cost.

While I don't have county financial figures before me—and probably I wouldn't understand them if I did—that seems to be the case with the Boone County Courthouse, located on the downtown square in Lebanon.

It's a most attractive building from the outside. Inside, it is clean and obviously well maintained. It appears to the un-practiced eye to be as responsive to the county's needs in the twenty-first century as it was when constructed nearly one hundred years ago.

Part of what makes a courthouse work are the people in it, of course. During my unannounced visit, I found the police stationed there and other personnel to be cordial and helpful, even encouraging the taking of photos if I wished.

The courthouse account in Boone County is quite similar to that of other Indiana counties. As a matter of fact, nearby Jamestown actually was the first county seat, from 1830 to 1833. That's when it was changed to Lebanon. The first courthouse there, according to *Indiana: A New Historical Guide*, was a two-story log courthouse built in 1833. Then came a small brick building in 1840. What the guide calls "an impressive Gothic-style edifice" was the next courthouse, serving the county from 1856 until 1909.

That's when a Columbus architectural firm was employed to design a new courthouse. Built using Oolitic limestone, it was finished in 1911 and dedicated July 4, 1912.

The building has at least two outstanding features. Its dome measures eighty-four feet high and fifty-two feet wide, making it the second largest in Indiana. The clocks in that dome even keep the right time from my observation! Its thirty-five-feet high columns at the north and south entrances have been

GLASS DOME. Looking up at the glass dome in the rotunda of the Boone County Courthouse, constructed nearly one hundred years ago.

thought to be the largest single-piece pillars in the nation, according to the county's Web site.

Inside, as already noted, those public areas I saw were as clean as a whistle. The well-lighted central rotunda is in part made possible by the beautiful stained-glass dome, high overhead.

Equally magnificent is the quilt produced by the Boone Bicentennial Sampler Committee for the July 4, 1976, bicentennial of the nation. It hangs in the rotunda as well.

And, yes, you're right: Boone County was named for the well-known adventurer and frontiersman Daniel Boone. However, it was his brother Squire Boone who spent considerable time in southern Indiana and for whom one of the state's public caves near Maukport is named.

So the Boone boys had their impact on Indiana as well as Kentucky.

GETTING THERE: Approaching the northwest Indianapolis area, likely on Interstate 65, either take Indiana 39 or Indiana 32 into Lebanon. The courthouse is one block north of the intersection of Indiana 32 and Indiana 39.

INFORMATION: The courthouse is open Monday through Friday except for holidays 8 a.m. to 4 p.m. The Boone County Web site is http://www.boonecounty.in.gov/, and the Boone County Convention and Visitors Bureau is http://www.boonecvb.com/, and the telephone number is (765) 436–2909.

Ulen

ON THE GOLF COURSE. Two of the homes built for Ulen corporation executives.

LEBANON—Nestled about a half-mile north of the Boone County Courthouse in downtown Lebanon is the small town of Ulen—pronounced U-len. The 2000 census listed its population as 123. I'm not sure how many people in Lebanon, let alone Boone County, even know it is, indeed, a separate town.

Here's how it came to be, according to *Indiana: A New Historical Guide* and Internet sources. First came the Ulen Country Club golf course in 1924. It's an 18-hole, 6,363-yard, par-70 course, which on the Web site is termed a "great golf course for the money; old style with small greens; must drive the ball well to score well." Henry Charles (H. C.) Ulen designed the country club building and hired William H. Diddel to design the course.

Next door is the town of Ulen, obviously named for its founder. In the mid-1900s H. C. Ulen was corporate director of the Ulen Contracting Company, one of the world's largest international engineering and contracting firms. His own story is a nearly unbelievable rags-to-riches account. By his own admission, he was a tramp in his early years, constantly running away from his Lebanon home. Finally, he studied law, went into banking, and then very successfully into engineering and construction.

Consider this: In 1930 his firm was building three dams in Chile, doing a $23 million land-reclamation project in Greece, constructing Persia's (present-day Iran) only trunk-line railroad, and managing Brazil's public utilities. It was already well known for building the eighteen-mile tunnel through the Catskill Mountains and the dam that supplied all the water for Athens, Greece.

In 1929 Ulen moved his international offices from New York and Paris to Lebanon, Indiana! (Wouldn't that make quite a story in itself?) "Civic pride," *Time* magazine called it. About 75 percent of his employees took up his offer to move to Indiana—he paid all the expenses.

To accommodate his executives, Ulen designed and built all the town's homes within walking distance of the golf

FOUNDER'S HOUSE. H. C. Ulen's home in the town of Ulen, actually is inside the corporation limits of Lebanon, Indiana.

IF YOU GO

GETTING THERE: In Lebanon, Ulen is about one-half mile north of the courthouse. Turn east off N. Lebanon Street/Indiana 47 onto Ulen Drive.

INFORMATION: Go to http://www.ulencc.com or http://www.boone chamber.org or call the Boone County Chamber of Commerce at (765) 482–1320.

FEES: None.

course. They are on Ulen Drive, which makes a single loop through the town of Ulen. Ulen built his own home to overlook the ninth green. Its architecture is referred to as Mediterranean Revival. The brick house had a barrel-tile roof. Stately homes for other company officials quickly followed.

Today Ulen's census report shows 125 people living in 48 households, an average of 2.56 per household. As with many such small communities, residents pay the larger city, in this case Lebanon, for fire and police protection.

Ulen retired from his firm in the late 1940s, ending an international career that he began as a sixteen-year-old tramp. (One wonders if that would be possible today.) Ulen died at ninety-two in 1963. The corporation is also gone. What remains, however, is what the *Guide* calls "one of the most elegant residential areas in the India-napolis area."

MINERAL WATER CITY. This large downtown sign proclaims Martinsville as the "city of mineral water," known for its supposed medicinal cures.

VETERANS MEMORIAL. It, along with a neighboring Veterans Museum, are part of the current Martinsville downtown scene.

Downtown Martinsville

MARTINSVILLE—Let's have a show of hands. How many of you, while driving on Indiana 37 between Indianapolis and Bloomington have turned off the highway into downtown Martinsville? I suspect the number of hands will not be too many. I would not have been included until, on a recent southern Indiana swing, I deliberately left Indiana 37 to go into the downtown area. What I found was the somewhat typical Indiana square, surrounded by businesses and a few shuttered storefronts—what downtown doesn't have them these days?—along with the distinguished-looking Morgan County Courthouse.

First, some background about Martinsville.

Among its several claims to fame is that basketball legend Johnny Wooden of UCLA fame was born here. At one time it was the "gateway to beautiful southern Indiana" because the long ago Wisconsin glacier line more-or-less ends in the southern part of the county. The glacier left lots of rolling and rugged hills with a resultant southern Indiana beauty. Just south of Martinsville is the Morgan-Monroe State Forest, a destination of its own.

Another of Martinsville's claims is its history as the Artesian City, known for its mineral springs and health sanitariums. According to *Indiana: A New Historical Guide*, at one time in the early twentieth century Martinsville had a number—often averaging around seven—of different sanitariums, the last one closing as late as 1973. These were businesses where people could go to "take the cure" in the mineral springs that would supposedly cure about anything. In its heyday, it may have rivaled French Lick and West Baden as a place to go to be miraculously cured. Two of the sanitarium buildings remain, both on the National Register of Historic Places.

All of those days are gone now. Martinsville, however, sits in the enviable spot of being midway between Indianapolis and Bloomington—the big city and the big-time college town.

So what does the visitor find in downtown Martinsville today?

Surrounding the town square are assorted businesses including an icon candy store since 1919 known for its candy

HISTORIC BUILDING. Martinsville's historic county courthouse and bell tower dominate the public square in downtown Martinsville.

canes, the post office, lawyers' and other professionals' offices, banks, a Mexican restaurant, the courthouse annex, dance studios, and, as noted earlier, some empty storefronts. One especially interesting spot is the small veterans park and a not-too-often-open veterans museum.

The downtown has been greatly aided by a couple of recent rejuvenation projects that included putting up old-time streetlights as well as street resurfacing and new sidewalks, curbs, and storm sewers. The centerpiece, however, remains the 1857–59 county courthouse, a combination of Victorian and Italianate architecture with its dominating bell tower.

For those with long memories, the name of a Martinsville resident, Paul V. McNutt, will be recalled. He was a handsome, popular politician on his way up in the 1930s as the Democratic governor of Indiana. He probably had presidential aspirations but with Franklin D. Roosevelt firmly in place, that wasn't going to happen. He later became the administrator of the Philippines.

IF YOU GO

GETTING THERE: Turn off Indiana 37 into Martinsville by going west at the stoplight on Mahalasville Road, which becomes Ohio Street, south on Poston Road and then west again on Main Street after going around a cemetery to downtown Martinsville.

INFORMATION: Call the Greater Martinsville Chamber of Commerce at (765) 342–8110, or go to http://www.martinsvillechamber.com/.

FEES: None.

JOHN WOODEN. Some of his material at the Academy of Hoosier Heritage in Mooresville, usually shown during "March Madness" time along with other cases of basketball history.

ACADEMY BUILDING. This Mooresville structure was built by the Society of Friends in 1861 as a boarding school and now is the home of the Academy of Hoosier Heritage.

John Wooden and the Academy of Hoosier Heritage, Mooresville

MOORESVILLE—It is only a small display, but it is very much in keeping with the modesty of the man. Plus, it isn't even on display all of the time—temporary is the term—it is mostly just brought out around NCAA "March Madness" tournament time. He has a lot to be proud of—ten championships at UCLA.

The man, of course, is the legendary John Wooden, a Morgan County native, who coached UCLA to those ten championships. In doing so, he became an icon for winning the titles without blatant showmanship and, even today at an advanced age—he will be one hundred in 2010—is considered an expert on leadership.

The Wooden display case makes its annual appearance in the Academy of Hoosier Heritage, located in the historic 1861 Academy Building in Mooresville. The museum and Academy Building themselves are stories, but first some more about Wooden.

His teams won national championships in 1964 and 1965 and then seven—yes, seven—in a row from 1967 through 1973. His final one was two years later in 1975. In the years from 1967 to 1973 his UCLA teams won 201 games while losing 5! Two consecutive years they were 30–0. There's never been anything like it and, almost certainly, there never will be.

Wooden, as a youngster, played for the nearby Martinsville state championship high school team and then at Purdue. Later, he was the UCLA coach for twenty-seven years, from 1948 through 1975.

While Julie Lyle-Lee, museum manager, is happy to talk about Wooden, she is just as interested in telling visitors about the history of the Academy Building and the Academy of Hoosier Heritage.

The building was constructed by the Religious Society of Friends (Quakers) in 1861 to provide upper-grade education and was the first high school in central Indiana. The building was enlarged when a grade-school wing was added and given to the town by the Quakers in 1870. For more than 110 years through 1971, the building was used first for high school, then junior high and grade school classes (sometimes all three),

ONE-ROOM SCHOOL. Located at the Academy of Hoosier Heritage in Mooresville. Fourth-grade classes hold full-day field trips here, and other ages visit for special programs.

and the added wing was removed in 1936. Placed on the National Register of Historic Places in 1975, it underwent extensive renovation before its rededication in 2000 when the museum opened.

Now housed on the second floor is the Academy of Hoosier Heritage. It consists of two rooms. The first is entered from the front stairway and houses local and Indiana memorabilia, while the second is a replica of a one-room schoolhouse. The downstairs contains a public meeting room and offices of the Community Foundation of Morgan County Inc.

The Academy Building museum is the site of tours, pre-sentations, and special programs and events. A favorite is a full-day field trip for fourth-grade students studying pioneer and Indiana history with classes conducted by a "school marm" in the second-floor, one-room school.

Autographed copies of Wooden's latest books, includ-ing his autobiography, his book on leadership, and a children's book, *Inch and Miles: The Journey to Success*, are for sale at the museum.

GETTING THERE: In Mooresville, turn onto Indiana 267 (Monroe Street) to the Academy Building at 250 N. Monroe Street.

INFORMATION: Open Monday, Wednesday, and Friday 1 to 5 p.m. or other times by appointment. Call (317) 831–9001 or go to http://www.academymuseum.org/.

FEES: None, but donations are appreciated.

ERECTED IN 1936. Zionsville dedicated this plaque to Abraham Lincoln on June 14, 1936, seventy-five years after he stopped there to speak as he headed east by railroad to Washington, D.C.

Abraham Lincoln in Zionsville

ZIONSVILLE—In this day of instant communications and images by the thousands, even the millions, when the names and photographs of the well known are seen day-by-day by almost everyone in the nation on television, on the Internet news reports, in the newspapers and magazines—even on your telephone—it's perhaps difficult to imagine what it must have been like in the spring of 1861 when the newly elected president of the United States came to town.

Abraham Lincoln was the incoming president. Not that his name wasn't known, it was. However, with the exception of one key trip he had taken to the East Coast, Lincoln had never been seen by many of his countrymen east of Chicago.

The exception—and it was crucial to Lincoln's electio—had been his trip to New York City to deliver a speech at the Cooper Union Hall in Brooklyn. Some fifteen hundred people turned out, and the widely reported address became a sensation.

It also was on this trip that Lincoln had his photograph taken by Mathew Brady. Historian Doris Kearns Goodwin called it "the first arresting image many would see of Abraham Lincoln."

But other than some campaign materials, that was about it. So when Lincoln actually won the election and prepared to go to Washington the following winter for his inauguration, it was decided that his train would make a number of stops as it headed east during a twelve-day period in order for Americans to actually get a look at their new president.

One of those stops was at Zionsville, northwest of Indianapolis. The Zionsville railroad station, constructed in 1853, was in the downtown area where today a small city park, appropriately named Lincoln Park, is located. The presidential train stopped there on February 11, 1861, and Lincoln delivered remarks to the citizens who had gathered.

The presidential train went the short distance to Indianapolis where that evening Lincoln delivered his first major address of the trip to a crowd estimated at twenty thousand.

LINCOLN MEMORIAL PARK. Located in Zionsville, the park is at the site of the old railroad depot where Abraham Lincoln stopped to address citizens on his way to Washington, D.C., to be inaugurated as president.

His talk at Zionsville, of course, drew a much smaller group at the train station, no doubt mostly made up of local people. Like similar talks he made along the way in smaller communities, it was brief, of no great consequence, and filled with off-the-cuff remarks. Lincoln, well aware of the troubled situation facing the divided nation, was satisfied simply to let people see him. Also, he did not want to divulge his inaugural address material or further inflame the passions of the South.

Today, the small one-block area is a grassy and pleasant spot. No trace of the train station remains. At first it was called Depot Park, but the name later was changed to Lincoln Memorial Park to mark the president-elect's appearance there. A bronze plaque commemorates the occasion, placed on the site in 1936 by the Zionsville Lions Club.

Even if you're not into visiting historical places and reading plaques, remember that Zionsville's various attractions—antique stores, specialty shops, and dining are only one block away.

IF YOU GO

GETTING THERE: Lincoln Memorial Park is located between Oak and Cedar streets on First Street in downtown Zionsville.

INFORMATION: Call the Greater Zionsville Chamber of Commerce at (317) 873–3836, go to http://www.zionsvillechamber.org/, or, if in Zionsville, stop at its office at 135 S. Elm Street.

FEES: None.

ONE OF A KIND. Kenneth Biddle gave the museum one of its prized possessions, a 1908 Black automobile, made in Chicago. According to museum officials, no other Black is known to exist today.

HISTORICAL MARKER. Relates events from the life of George Boxley, who traveled to what was to become Hamilton County from Virginia.

Sheridan Historical Society, Sheridan

SHERIDAN—You certainly can't criticize the Sheridan Historical Society for not thinking big plans. The society isn't simply thinking them, however, it is starting to put some plans into action, although it realizes that the end result may be years away.

I was discussing these plans with Jim Pickett, the society's executive director, during a visit to see one of the plan's early projects: the rebuilt 1828 George Boxley log cabin located in Veteran's Park.

We were talking in the present Sheridan Historical Museum on Main Street in downtown Sheridan.

"We want to build a visitors center on [the] north side of [the] cabin and then build a new museum at the cabin site. What we would really like to do is to enclose the cabin inside the museum for its protection," he told me. A community building also is in the mix. "But we know all of this is going to take a lot of money," he added. "We are working on some grants and thinking about other fund-raising." A grant from the Destination: Hamilton County Community Development Fund is being used to study the feasibility of all these projects.

Pickett, a retired Sheridan Fire Department member—thirty-six years—has "been here at the museum for twenty-four, twenty-five years." The museum actually opened thirty-eight years ago when local industrialist Kenneth Biddle gave the building to the society. Biddle's firm manufactures precision parts and is directed now by a granddaughter.

Biddle also gave the museum one of its prized possessions, a 1908 Black automobile, made in Chicago. Pickett said the society has investigated and "as of today we don't know of any other one like it."

But back to the cabin and the plans.

Pickett says the historical society believes the cabin to be the oldest extant structure in Adams Township. It has been placed on the National Register of Historic Places and remains on its original site. Its renovation included dismantling the cabin entirely and restoring it.

Wood from the cabin was used along with new wood in rebuilding the sixteen-by-eighteen-foot cabin. The cellar was

BOXLEY CABIN. Meant to be the centerpiece of the hoped-for museum at Veteran's Park north of downtown.

also rebuilt, using new bricks. In the cabin are a working fireplace and new windows.

The cabin's original owner, the abolitionist Boxley, was the first settler in the township. Later, his son Caswell constructed a large house in front of the cabin, but it was destroyed by a fire in 1997.

Behind the cabin are what remains of a house and barn.

"We think it's where the house worker lived," Pickett said. The barn probably will have to be destroyed—or what's left of it. Archaeologists are to determine whether the house can be saved and it, too, restored.

Indiana University–Purdue University at Indianapolis archaeology students and their professor have been assisting the society with the current project. They conducted a field school in the area around the cabin to see what other evidence of its history they might find.

Oh, and when you visit, stop by the Twin Kiss Drive-in on the south side of Sheridan. It was Pickett's suggestion when I asked about a place to eat a quick meal. The tenderloin was great!

IF YOU GO

GETTING THERE: In Sheridan, where Indiana 38 turns to the west at the north edge of downtown go one more block north on Main Street to Veteran's Park. Take the gravel road to your left to the cabin.

INFORMATION: The Sheridan Historical Society is located at 308 S. Main Street. It is open Tuesday and Friday 1 to 4 p.m. The telephone number is (317) 758–5054, and the Web site is http://sheridanhistorical society.com/. The cabin is open by appointment or for special occasions.

FEES: None.

INTERACTIVE TREE. Can be entered at the side by children to learn more about nature. The "tree" is in the Cool Creek Park Nature Center.

WOODED TRAIL. Beech trail in Cool Creek Park at Westfield, operated by Hamilton County Parks and Recreation.

Cool Creek Park, Westfield

WESTFIELD—Mountain lion? Cougar? Panther? Or something else? When I visited Cook Creek Park Nature Center that was the question central to an interesting exhibit—now, over the seasons, replaced by others.

Newspaper articles over the years reported residents along the White River near here who claim to have heard—and in at least one case, seen—a large animal that was supposedly prowling around the river. A footprint—five inches across—was once found. Others said they had heard a cry—"the sound like a woman screaming"—most often on a summer evening. Locals started calling it "the beast of the White River."

That made it a good candidate, however, for the Strangers in the Night exhibition at the center, part of Cool Creek Park operated by Hamilton County Parks and Recreation. The exhibition was meant to help explain how different animals adapt to life at night. The exhibition, one of a series of seasonally changing displays, was only part of the varied activities at the center that offers a variety of nature programs throughout the year. In addition, the building also included wildlife viewing, a multipurpose auditorium, and library.

One of the interesting permanent exhibitions is the interactive Oliver the Oak Tree. It's delightful to watch youngsters as they walk directly into the tree to carry out their "investigations." They also can participate in a "critters and discoveries" scavenger hunt.

Another of the displays at the center is a collection of pennies used by visitors to guess the weight of Indiana birds—hummingbird (the lightest of the group), robin (the heaviest), nuthatch, goldfinch, bluebird, chickadee, and cardinal. The birds are rotated in and out by season. Since a penny weighs about two grams, the visitor picks up as many pennies as the bird might weigh. A scale shows how close the guess is.

The ninety-one-acre park offers three wooded trails, including the beech trail—1 mile, the tulip trail—1.5 miles, and the paw-paw trail—.5 mile, as well as a playground area and nearby shelter. Four other shelters are spread around the park and are available for picnics and rental.

STRANGERS IN THE NIGHT. This was an exhibition at the Cool Creek Park Nature Center at Westfield. They change seasonally.

While most walkers seem to follow the trails, other park visitors, if the weather is nice, stroll up and down the rolling countryside. I kept to the beech trail myself and, in the autumn when I was there, found it to be a delightful walk.

The park takes its name from the small Cool Creek that winds through the property. Apparently it dries up by late summer, and I really didn't observe it during my time there.

While it's out of season except during the summer, the Cool Creek Music Pavilion is home to concerts. A variety of jazz, blues, pop, and Western performers appear. Persons interested should note the telephone number—(317) 770–4400—to use in the spring for information about the schedule.

The park is one of the more recently opened in the Hoosier State—in this case, in 1990. Bird-watchers say it is one of central Indiana's better sites for viewing. Some 144 species have been sighted since the park opened, according to its Web site.

IF YOU GO

GETTING THERE: In downtown Westfield on U.S. 31, turn south to 151st Street and then east one-half mile to the park and nature center.

INFORMATION: The park is open year-round, dawn to dusk. Center Drive, through the park, is open April 1 to November 1. The nature center is open Tuesday through Saturday 10 a.m. to 5 p.m. and Sunday 1 to 5 p.m. The telephone number is (317) 848–0576, and the Web site is http://www.co.hamilton.in.us/.

PART OF STORAGE AREA. Barrels at Chateau Thomas Winery are marked for customers and other wineries that also store their wines at the large winery.

FIRST-FLOOR SHOW ROOM. Chateau Thomas Winery is one of Indiana's largest. Its banquet room is on the second floor.

Chateau Thomas Winery, Plainfield

PLAINFIELD—While writing about other wineries, I have noted that some of Indiana's wineries might be considered the state's last mom-and-pop stores—small operations and often run by a couple in a somewhat confined space with a relatively small customer base.

Not so Chateau Thomas Winery just west of Indianapolis in Plainfield.

Of the state's thirty-five wineries Chateau Thomas is one of the largest and best known. Its main headquarters is just off Interstate 70 west of Indianapolis International Airport. It has added a Nashville (Indiana) Tasting Room and Gift Shoppe in that Brown County tourist town as well.

According to the *Indianapolis Star*, California has more than two thousand wineries producing some 700 million gallons of wine a year, nearly 90 percent of all the wine produced in the United States. Indiana, however, is moving up. Not too many years ago the number of state wineries was around a dozen. Today's thirty-five produce about 800,000 gallons a year.

Chateau Thomas was founded by Doctor Charles Thomas in 1984. An Indianapolis ob-gyn, he became interested in wines as a hobby and made trips to California to study the industry.

He continues to experiment with wines. Recently, he unveiled his new no calorie, no carb red, white, and blush wines called Slender. He said it's sweetened with a natural sugar. (See http://www.slenderwine.com/.)

Chateau Thomas wines continue to win awards, now totaling more than 450, in recent years Best in the Nation, two of the best one hundred wines east of the Rockies, and four Governor's Trophies at the Indy International Wine Competition, the second largest international wine competition in the nation.

Its grapes come from vineyards in California, Oregon, and Washington. They are chilled to thirty-four degrees, shipped in refrigerated trucks to Plainfield where they are crushed and fermented. Aging takes nine months to three years.

In the production area, after the grapes are crushed and go into fermentation tanks, the majority go into barrels for a spe-

CHATEAU THOMAS WINERY. Near Plainfield, it's just off Interstate 70 west of Indianapolis.

cific number of months, then blended in tanks and finally bottled, often unfiltered.

If visitors happen to be in the production area, they will see family names on numerous barrels, representing their owners. This is the "Coopers Club": Buy a barrel of wine and receive a twelve-bottle case of that wine every year for three years; then you get the empty barrel, too. (Cooperage is the art of making the barrel.) Chateau Thomas also houses wine for different organizations in its fifty-five-degree warehouse.

The large display and gift shop in Plainfield has a 4,800-square-foot banquet room on the second floor. On the first floor is a one hundred-year-old grapevine, display of awards, and maps showing where its grapes are grown. In the gift shop is a sixty-foot tasting bar, open daily.

The programming at the winery certainly is one of the most extensive in the state, especially during the summer months. You will want to go to the winery's Web site for a full schedule—http://www.chateauthomas.com/.

GETTING THERE: West of Indianapolis on interstate 70, take exit 66. Follow the signs for one-fourth mile, making two right turns to the winery at a roundabout.

INFORMATION: Call toll-free, (800) 761–9463, or go to http://www.chateauthomas.com/. Hours are Monday through Thursday 10 a.m. to 9 p.m.; Friday and Saturday 10 a.m. to 10 p.m.; Sunday noon to 7 p.m. Nashville shop is (812) 988–8500. Its hours are Monday through Thursday 11 a.m. to 5 p.m.; Friday 11 a.m. to 8 p.m.; Saturday 10 a.m. to 8 p.m.; Sunday noon to 5 p.m.

FEES: None to visit, various for other activities.

CRISPUS ATTUCKS MUSEUM. The museum is located in part of the former high school on Indianapolis's near west side.

BUST. Crispus Attucks was killed in the 1770 Boston Massacre. The Indianapolis high school might have been named after Thomas Jefferson, but school officials in 1927 settled on using the name of the runaway slave, one of the first to die in what became the Revolutionary War.

TWO CRISPUS ATTUCKS GRADU-ATES. Major General Harry Brooks Jr. is pictured at the top and Brigadier General Norris Overton at the bottom.

Crispus Attucks Museum, Indianapolis

INDIANAPOLIS—There's a lot more to the Crispus Attucks Museum than basketball. That might surprise you, especially if you grew up outside of Indianapolis during the mid-1900s.

If so, you probably know at least the essentials of the Crispus Attucks basketball story: Losing in the semifinals in 1954 to a storied Milan team that went on to win the state title, but winning the state championship in 1955—the first all-black high school in the nation to win an open state sports championship, repeating as state champions in 1956, and winning a third title in 1959.

You need to go to the large hallway, called Gallery III, next to the main room of the museum to see this basketball account of photos, trophies, and information. The dominant figures are "The Big O"—star player Oscar Robertson—and coach Ray Crowe. Inside the main museum—formerly the girls' auxiliary basketball gym—is the rest of the Crispus Attucks story.

Who was Crispus Attucks? (Answer at the end of this essay.)

The museum, operated by Indianapolis Public Schools, is about the overall African American experience as well as about Crispus Attucks High School, and its place in the legend of Hoosier basketball. The museum's literature points out it "is not meant to be an inclusive review of history, but rather give a glimpse into a rich and valuable culture."

A large exhibition, Gallery II, deals with the forerunner of the African American story with artifacts and information about Africa and how the migration of blacks—more often than not, through slavery—influenced societies worldwide.

The first exhibition inside the museum's entrance tells the story of the high school, built in 1927 for one thousand students and meant to be a vehicle for segregation. Its first principal was Matthias Nolcox, who put together a faculty in which every teacher held at least a master's degree and many possessed doctorates.

Part of the museum's exhibitions detail how African Americans participated in America's wars. Special attention is given the "buffalo soldiers," who made up one out of every five U.S. cavalry troopers on the Western frontier in the 1800s,

HERE'S BASKETBALL. Lorna Brummer, assistant to the Crispus Attucks Museum curator, stands next to one of the school's trophy cases, this one highlighting the boys' state championships and girls' basketball victories.

and nearly one hundred years later the famed Tuskegee Airmen, black fighter pilots during World War II, several of them from Indianapolis, who overcame military prejudice to build outstanding aerial combat records.

Another display recounts the careers of two black American generals, Major General Harry Brooks Jr. and Brigadier General Norris Overton, both Attucks graduates.

The musical careers of African Americans is another dominant theme, again including a large number of Indianapolis natives who established themselves in this field. Of a wall of photographs of jazz leaders, nearly half are Attucks graduates.

The museum was created when Crispus Attucks was converted to a junior high school for grades 7-8-9 in 1986. It later became a middle school.

Who was Crispus Attucks? Attucks, a runaway slave, was killed by British soldiers in 1770 in what became known as the Boston Massacre, which contributed to the start of the Revolutionary War.

IF YOU GO

GETTING THERE: In Indianapolis, turn off Meridian Street west onto Eleventh Street. Cross Martin Luther King Jr. Boulevard where the Crispus Attucks Museum is on the northwest corner. Pull into the parking lot and go to the double doors at the far right of the lot. A guide will take you into the museum.

INFORMATION: Call (317) 226–2430, or go to http://www.crispusattucksmuseum.ips.K12.in.us/. The museum is open Monday through Friday 10 a.m. to 2 p.m.

FEES: None to tour the museum.

COMMEMORATIVE STAMP. This U.S. Post Office stamp was issued in 1998 to commemorate the life of the legendary African American entrepreneur and philanthropist Madam C. J. Walker, an early twentieth-century businesswoman who is recognized today in the *Guinness Book of World Records* as America's first self-made black woman millionaire.

INTERPRETER. Roberta James makes a point as she delivers her monologue, detailing the life and times of Madam C. J. Walker, who amassed a fortune in producing and selling hair products in the late nineteenth and early twentieth centuries.

Madame C. J. Walker Building, Indianapolis

INDIANAPOLIS—Remember that climactic scene from *Miracle on 34th Street*, when the judge is trying to decide whether Kris Kringle, played by actor Edmund Gwen, is crazy or really Santa Claus? Finally, bags of U.S. mail are dumped on the judge's desk—all addressed to Santa Claus—and apparently to be delivered to the defendant. The judge says, "If the United States Post Office declares this man to be Santa Claus," he won't disagree.

That same line of reasoning helps me decide that the name is spelled Madam C. J. Walker, not Madame. That's the way it is on the 1998 commemorative thirty-two-cent stamp issued by the post office to honor Madam Walker, who is the subject of an educational and entertaining half hour at the Walker Building.

Sarah Breedlove, who became Madam C. J. Walker, was born in Delta, Louisiana, in 1867. At age seven, after the death of her parents, she moved across the Mississippi River with her sister and worked as a maid and washerwoman. Sarah married at fourteen, and several years later had a daughter, Lelia. Her husband died, and she remarried, but the marriage soon ended. Later she married Charles Joseph Walker—that marriage lasted only four years.

In the meantime, she moved to Saint Louis and, after years of working as a laundress and in other domestic positions, began producing a line of hair products specifically for black women that were touted to cure baldness and beautify hair. As her business flourished she moved to Pittsburgh, and then she came to Indianapolis, looking for a location for a headquarters for the company, factory, and laboratory.

Success followed success. She became the first self-made black woman millionaire. She moved to New York City to be near the Mecca of black cultural life in Harlem, built a mansion by the Hudson River, increased business, made even more money, worked in politics and to get an antilynching bill passed, and, at the same time, lived a high society life.

Along the way, she added Madam to give her name "dignity and respect."

BUILT IN 1927. The historic Madame C. J. Walker Building on the near north side of downtown Indianapolis today hosts numerous cultural and musical events.

That's the way Roberta James, an Indianapolis Free-town Village interpreter, tells Madam Walker's story in a far more interesting fashion than I could ever attempt. Her presentation is part of a series of half-hour programs presented about Madam Walker in the Walker Building.

James closed her story, noting that Madam Walker "had a good heart and set a good example by giving away millions of dollars."

Built in 1927, the Walker Building has a theater on the first floor, numerous offices including those of Freetown Village, and a fourth-floor ballroom. It is home to a large number of activities throughout the year.

There is some dispute as to whether her name is spelled madam or madame. It is spelled both ways in her extensive literature. According to the dictionary, madam is a title of courtesy in addressing a woman or as a title before a rank of office. Madame is a French title of courtesy for a married woman. The Walker Building's Web site explains it this way: The building's name is Madame C. J. Walker Building, while Walker spelled her name "madam."

IF YOU GO

GETTING THERE: In downtown Indianapolis, go on Meridian Street to North Street—it's five blocks north of Monument Circle—and west four blocks to the intersection of West Street and Indiana Avenue.

INFORMATION: Call (317) 236–2099, or go to www.walkertheatre.com/. For Freetown Village call (317) 631–1870, or www.freetown.org/. For more about Walker, go to www.madamcjwalker.com/.

FEES: Free to visit the building and when presentations are made. There is a charge for guided tours.

Scottish Rite Cathedral, Indianapolis

SCOTTISH RITE CATHEDRAL. Completed in 1929, the Scottish Rite Cathedral in Indianapolis was built at a cost of $2.5 million. It is located on Meridian Street, just north of the city's Monument Circle.

ORIGINAL ORGAN. Now part of the cathedral's museum, this was the original Skinner organ console installed when the building was constructed.

YES, 186 BULBS. The Scottish Rite Cathedral's Ballroom chandelier has 186 bulbs. Tour guide Robert Holler said he thought he had counted 200 when the chandelier was lowered for cleaning, but the number was later confirmed as 186.

INDIANAPOLIS—It's one of those imposing downtown Indianapolis landmarks that you've probably driven by a hundred times.

The Scottish Rite Cathedral is worth a stop, especially during the times when members of the Tour Committee are available as escorts and sources of information.

Its four floors, mezzanine, and lower level fill a city block—330 feet long, 120 feet wide with a Gothic carillon tower rising 212 feet above sidewalk level. When the structure was finished in 1929, its cost was placed at $2.5 million. (Today it is insured for $95 million and its fine art is valued at $2.2 million.)

The carillon is one of the building's features. Consisting of fifty-four bells—the smallest at six inches and twelve pounds and the largest at seven feet and five and one-half tons—it was at one time the largest in the United States.

Equally a feature are the materials used in construction, including 15 train carloads of Carpathian white oak and Russian curly oak, 12 carloads of partition tile, 8 carloads of marble, 120 carloads of brick, and 4 carloads of glazed tile, according to the printed cathedral guide, a handy companion during a tour.

Robert Holler was the tour guide for several of us on a late fall morning. He explained he is one of about forty active guides for the tours—the number diminishing year by year as volunteers, as with other such organizations, become more difficult to find.

While the cathedral's main entrance faces Meridian Street on the building's east side, the west entrance, across from the parking lot, is the one used today. The building's exterior is Indiana limestone, quarried at Bloomington.

We began our tour with an elevator ride to the third floor where the ballroom balcony and museum are located. Among other artifacts and photos, the museum features the auditorium's original Skinner organ console, a grand square piano, and a small organ. Then we went to the mezzanine with its meeting rooms and Double Eagle Café.

Two of the cathedral's most impressive rooms are located on the second floor—the auditorium and ballroom.

SOCIAL ROOM. The cathedral's social room now mostly is used to host early arrivals for evening performances in the theater. In an earlier day, it was a prominent meeting place for businessmen.

The auditorium seats eleven hundred plus another two hundred chairs for stage plays. It is patterned after a Cologne, Germany, cathedral. The room's carvings were completed in Minneapolis and shipped to Indianapolis.

At the south end of the floor is the ballroom, surrounded by the balcony. Its special features are the parquet, laid over a system of springs and deadening felt paper; a hand-painted acoustic tile ceiling, and a gilded bronze 2,500-pound chandelier holding 186 lights.

On the first floor, our guide showed us lodge rooms and offices; the library, which features Indiana white oak; and the main lounge. The lower level mostly is taken up by the banquet hall, which can seat 2,850 guests—214 feet long, 82 feet wide, and 45 feet high.

George Frederick Henry Schreiber was the architect. Schreiber, a Mason, included many Masonic symbols in his design. No detail, it was said, was too insignificant for his attention: "Trifles make perfection, but perfection is no trifle."

IF YOU GO

GETTING THERE: On Meridian Street, the city's main north/south thoroughfare, the cathedral is located at 650 N. Meridian. Parking is available in the cathedral's lot to the west of the building.

INFORMATION: Tours start Monday through Friday and the third Saturday of each month 10 a.m. to 2 p.m. It's always a good idea to check before you go to make certain the schedule is to be followed. Telephone: (317) 262–3100 or (800) 489–3579. The cafeteria is open Monday through Friday 11 a.m. to 2 p.m. The Web site is www.aasr-indy.org/.

FEES: Tours are free. A tour guide book can be purchased.

ATHENAEUM. The building addition is to the right in the photo where the American Cabaret Theatre awning can be seen. To its left is the entrance to the Rathskeller Restaurant.

MEETING ROOM. Jim Gould, community events coordinator for the Athenaeum Foundation, stands in the restored meeting room. It was here that "German House" members could catch up on the latest news in papers, books, magazines, and documents.

TOP OF GRAND STAIRCASE. This stained-glass window on the Michigan Street side of the Athenaeum is viewed as visitors climb the grand staircase. Depicted in the window is a lyre, a classic symbol of the arts.

Athenaeum, Indianapolis

INDIANAPOLIS—"The great thing is that the building is still used for the purposes for which it was built—to develop strong bodies and strong minds and to get together to enjoy life," James (Jim) Gould, community events coordinator of the Athenaeum Foundation, said of the building's programming. The Athenaeum is the former "German House"—"Das Deutsch Haus," located at Michigan and New Jersey streets in downtown Indianapolis.

The name changed in World War I, when hostility toward anything German colored American life, despite the large German population in Indianapolis. At the turn of the century, close to a quarter of the city's one hundred thousand people could trace their roots to Germany, Gould says.

The Athenaeum's history goes back 150 years when German residents in Indianapolis founded the Turners society in 1851. After starts in different buildings, it finally constructed a new clubhouse between 1893 and 1898. The architectural firm was Vonnegut and Bohn.

"When they built the building, it was important that they put in a gymnasium. It represented the strong body part of the 'strong body, strong minds' concept. That was the main part of the clubhouse," Gould says.

"The building was meant to be a German clubhouse to celebrate fifty years of German life in Indianapolis. Many of them had come as part of the failed 1848 revolution in Germany, so they came here to enjoy the American freedoms. The idea was to get together and to enjoy life as well as developing their bodies and their minds," Gould continues.

It was the first section of the Athenaeum to be constructed, its architecture is representative of the German Romanesque style. The numerous German clubs of the city were invited to move their offices to the new building, bringing them together under one roof. Down the middle of the structure ran the "neutral" hallway. Clubs met in rooms on both sides, but the hallway was neutral territory.

The second floor was the dining room, serviced by a kitchen in the basement that today prepares food for the famed

"STRONG BODIES." Photograph shows youth using equipment in the old gymnasium at the Athenaeum. Even in the 1800s, youth classes were coeducational.

Rathskeller Restaurant, the city's oldest restaurant. The upper floor room is the yoga room for the YMCA branch located in the building.

Shortly after the east structure was opened, plans advanced for the west wing—"the strong minds" part of the equation. Built in the more refined German Renaissance Revival style, its main feature was the second-floor ballroom with a built-in stage. The entrance was through a lower level box office and then up the grand staircase to the second floor—still in use today. That's where theatrical performances took place as well as the social functions. It was until recently the home of the American Cabaret Theatre.

By the late 1970s the building was beset by financial problems. In 1991 the not-for-profit Athenaeum Foundation Inc. was formed and a campaign launched to renovate the building. With a $5 million grant from Lilly Foundation in 1998 much needed renovations were completed.

"But, like any old house, there is still much to be done," Gould says.

IF YOU GO

GETTING THERE: In downtown Indianapolis, turn east off Meridian Street on North Street five blocks to East Street. Go one block south and then right on Michigan—a one-way street west. Parking in the Athenaeum's lot on your left.

INFORMATION: For information about the Athenaeum building, call the foundation at (317) 655–2755, or go to the Web site at http://www.athenaeumfoundation.com/. For information about the Rathskeller Restaurant, call (317) 636–0396 or go to http://www.rathskeller.com/. Lunch, Monday through Friday 11 a.m. to 2 p.m. Dinner, Thursday 4 to 9 p.m.; Friday and Saturday 4 to 10 p.m. Reservations suggested.

FEES: None for a tour, but donations are welcomed. Charges vary for meals.

Robert F. Kennedy/Martin Luther King Jr. Sculpture, Indianapolis

CITY PARK. This park on Indianapolis's near north side is the place where Robert F. Kennedy addressed a large crowd following the assassination of Dr. Martin Luther King Jr.

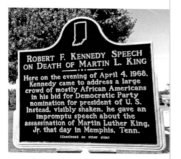

RECOUNTS EVENTS. This two-sided marker recounts the events of April 4, 1968, when Robert F. Kennedy spoke to an almost totally African American crowd in Indianapolis, telling them that Martin Luther King Jr. had been killed and asking them to return to their homes to pray for King's family and the country. The marker was dedicated in 2005 at the site of his talk.

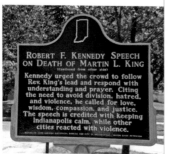

INDIANAPOLIS—Today, it's basically an open field city park on Indianapolis's near north side, settled in the midst of surrounding housing. The day I visited, not another person could be seen.

It wasn't always so. On April 4, 1968, fires blazed in 110 American cities as riots raged out of control leaving 39 dead, 2,500 injured, and some 75,000 National Guardsmen and federal troops in the streets across the country.

Not in Indianapolis.

In his book, *The Unfinished Odyssey of Robert Kennedy*, author David Halberstam recalls that April day in 1968 when Robert F. Kennedy's plane landed in Muncie for an afternoon speech at Ball State University. Kennedy had only a few days earlier entered the presidential primary campaign to challenge President Lyndon Johnson and Senator Eugene McCarthy for the Democratic nomination. Johnson, weary and perhaps sensing defeat, had dropped out of the race as the Vietnam War raged on.

Kennedy was greeted in the Ball State basketball gym by a full house—largely made up of students—as eager to see a celebrity of Kennedy's status as they were to hear what he had to say.

One of his last questions came from a young African American, wondering if Kennedy's faith in "white America" toward minorities could be trusted. Yes, Kennedy responded, adding "the vast majority of white people want to do the right thing."

Then, on his way back to the Muncie airport from the gym, Kennedy was told that Martin Luther King Jr. had been shot in Memphis, Tennessee. He landed in Indianapolis, where he was to address an evening audience expected to be almost all African Americans in a near-north-side depressed area. By then he knew King had died.

As Kennedy arrived, most of the crowd, not knowing of King's assassination, was in a festive mood. When Kennedy mounted a flatbed truck, "he was hunched in his black overcoat, his face gaunt and distressed and full of anguish," said historian Arthur M. Schlesinger Jr., in *Robert Kennedy and His Times*.

REACHING OUT. In Dan Edwards's sculpture, *A Landmark for Peace*, Robert F. Kennedy, left, and Martin Luther King Jr. reach outstretched toward each other in a demonstration of peace and understanding.

First, he told the crowd that King had been killed. "There was a terrible gasp from the crowd," Schlesinger writes.

Halberstam calls what followed "perhaps the best speech of the [1968] campaign, perhaps the best speech of his [Kennedy's] life."

In part, Kennedy said,

"For those of you who are black—considering the evidence there evidently is that they were white people who were responsible—you can be filled with bitterness, with hatred and with a desire for revenge. . . . Or, we can make an effort, as Martin Luther King did, to understand and to comprehend and to replace that violence, that strain of bloodshed that has spread across our land, with an effort to understand and to love. . . . So, I ask you tonight to return home to say a prayer for the family of Martin Luther King, that's true, but more important to say a prayer for our own country—a prayer for understanding and that compassion of which I spoke."

And the city didn't burn.

Two months later, Kennedy was assassinated in Los Angeles. A memorial and marker now stand in an Indianapolis field where Kennedy spoke.

IF YOU GO

GETTING THERE: From Fall Creek Parkway in Indianapolis, turn south on College to Seventeenth Street. Go one block west to Broadway and the city park.

INFORMATION: The site is identified as "Landmark for Peace in memory of Larry Conrad. Pacers Basketball Corporation Foundation, City of Indianapolis, and Citizens Neighborhood Coalition." The site design is by Don Colvin; Greg Perry, monument concept and design; and Dan Edwards, sculptor.

FEES: None.

PART OF THE VINEYARD. Chardonel and Leon Millot wines come from grapes grown on the property of the Mallow Run Winery.

INTERIOR. Tasting room of the Mallow Run Winery, located southwest of Bargersville in Johnson County.

Mallow Run Winery, Bargersville

BARGERSVILLE—A river doesn't run through it, but a creek does go across this Johnson County property—hence the name Mallow Run Winery.

"Mallow Run," says John Richardson, "was named for the Mallow family that settled here." He says his ancestor, George Mallow, came from Virginia in 1835 and built a barn along with the house where John's son, Bill, and his wife, Laura, now live. John lives "down the road" in another house on the property.

Mallow built the barn around 1880 that today is the showplace of the Mallow Run Winery.

More accurately, the barn still has the framework of the old building. For years, it had been used to store hay and keep farm animals. Since then, the siding and roofing have been removed as part of its total renovation.

Now, the old hayloft of the building is an attractive tasting and sales room for the winery with the timbers still showing. An outdoor deck with seating overlooks nearby Mallow Run. The large tasting room also offers Mallow Run wines, cheeses, jellies, sauces, gifts, and wine accessories.

Richardson is a retired New Albany English teacher who became intrigued with the wine business after reading an article stating that Indiana wineries were encouraging the growing of grapes. He and his son thought of their family farm near Bargersville as a likely spot for growing grapes, plus, Bill says, "It was a good chance to move back home."

The Richardsons started their vineyard in 2000. Rather quickly, they decided to open a winery, rather than selling their grapes. Their eight varieties of grapes include Leon Millot and Chardonel. In all, they have eight acres of grapes growing on their 600-acre farm. As with most other state wineries, it also imports additional grapes from neighboring states for some of its wines.

Things got off to a good start and then, following the actual "open for business" in early September, a grand opening attracted a turnout of more than 450 persons, according to John.

BUILT AROUND 1880. This barn has been reworked to house Mallow Run Winery.

Some of their wines are called "picnic"—blush, white, and red—named because of the property's history of a woods on the farm called Picnic Woods, where old settlers' picnics used to take place in the late nineteenth century, Richardson says.

Actually, Picnic Red made from Concord grapes has been the best seller so far, Richardson told me during my recent visit. Since then, they've also introduced a Winter White, a semisweet white blend, and expect to introduce blackberry and red raspberry wines.

According to the Indiana Wine Grape Council, the state now has thirty-five commercial wineries—in 1989 there were only nine—and more than three hundred acres of grapes. The council estimates more than eight hundred thousand people visit the state's wineries each year. Annual retail sales are approaching $9 million, according to the council, located at Purdue University.

Napa Valley? Hardly, but it's all part of the tourism/recreation/entertainment mix that is becoming a strong force in the state's economy, especially these days with gas prices restricting longer out-of-state trips.

IF YOU GO

GETTING THERE: From Indiana 37 south of Indianapolis, go east on Whiteland Road two miles to the winery.

INFORMATION: Go to http://www.mallowrun.com/, or call (317) 422–1556. Open with tasting hours daily from noon to 6 p.m.

FEES: Complimentary wine tasting daily.

Johnson County Museum of History, Franklin

NICK'S CANDY KITCHEN. The "place to go" on West Jefferson Street is a highlight of this exhibit. A popular spot in the 1950s and early 1960s, especially after games, Nick's sometimes had to lock the door when the store was filled to capacity.

A TIGHT FIT? Lewis and Sarah Hendricks lived in this log cabin from 1835 to 1838 with their seven children—later twelve—until a larger house was built. It was dismantled, altered, moved, and reassembled at the museum site.

FRANKLIN—Forgive me, first, this brief soliloquy. Many of us fail to appreciate the beauty and the treasures that surround our everyday lives. The truth is that my own backyard with its trees, grass, flowers, birds, and a porch swing on a quiet summer evening is more than enough to satisfy any longing I might have for the beauty of nature.

And what about the treasures offered in every Indiana community, not the least of which is its county museum?

To be sure some have better facilities than others. Some are extremely well maintained, others less. Some show the results of extensive accumulated work over the decades while others have struggled. But every one has its own fascinating—and sometimes unexpected—story to tell.

That occurred to me when I recently visited the Johnson County Museum of History, located just north of the courthouse in downtown Franklin.

Johnson County is fortunate in that its present museum brought together committed people with interests in history plus the capacity to raise considerable funds. The Johnson County Historical Society, in cooperation with county officials, bought the former Masonic Temple at 135 N. Main Street in 1988 and, after fund-raising efforts and renovation, the museum moved in during 1991.

More renovation followed before the third-story ceiling collapsed in 1997. A new $1.5 million renovation spanned 2002 to 2003 until the entire building reopened in October 2004.

The museum traces its history to 1923 when the county celebrated its centennial with numerous exhibits in store windows. Some were later stored in the recently built Masonic Temple. An actual museum came in 1931 when the Daughters of the American Revolution gained a room in the courthouse basement before moving to a house on West Madison Street in 1963.

As with a number of county museums, one feature of the current Johnson County museum is its extensive genealogy library. Another is the next-door 1830s log cabin. It has been moved twice, the last time dismantled, stored, and then reassembled. Antique farm machinery is housed at the Sawmill

FORMER MASONIC TEMPLE. Now the home of the Johnson County Museum of History since 1991. Over the years since then, numerous building improvements have been made.

Barn in Johnson County Park.

Yet another feature consists of three historical-marker driving tours for northern, central, and southern Johnson County. The central tour goes by the Theodore A. Pinkney home, supposedly an Underground Railroad station, although insufficient documentation exists for a marker to be placed there.

Also, similar to other county museums, it has permanent and changing exhibitions. Permanent ones include early inhabitants, pioneer settlers, Indiana infantry in the Civil War, Victorian life, war memorabilia, and the "fabulous '50s" with Nick's Candy Kitchen and the drive-in times of that era.

During my visit to the museum, I saw a temporary display about the Battle of the Bulge, the 12 Days of Christmas, during its last days—placed there by an outside group. It's been replaced by a quilt room with looms, used in teaching weaving classes at the museum.

It hasn't always been an easy road for the museum and its supporters. But today there it stands—an ongoing tribute to Johnson County history.

IF YOU GO

GETTING THERE: On Indiana 44 in Franklin, stay on Jefferson Street. Turn north off Jefferson one and one-half blocks on Main Street. The museum is on the right.

INFORMATION: Go to http://johnsoncountymuseum.org/, or call (317) 346–4500. Hours are Monday through Friday 9 a.m. to 4 p.m. and the second Saturday of each month 10 a.m. to 3 p.m.

FEES: Donations are recommended.

The Grave in the Middle of the Road, Amity

TELLS THE STORY. The marker describes the circumstances of the burial of Nancy Kerlin Barnett in 1831 and why her grave remains, dividing County Road 400 South near Amity.

AMITY—It has to be one of America's most unusual burial grounds: A grave that singularly divides a county road. At each end of the grave is a divided highway sign with a cross in the center, indicating a cemetery.

One can only wonder if there's another like it anywhere in the country.

Here's the story.

Nancy Kerlin was only fourteen—soon to be fifteen—when she married William Barnett in 1808. According to available records, her husband was the great-great-great grandson of Pocahontas and John Rolfe. Nancy and William lived near present-day Amity, a small community south of Franklin. Amity wasn't actually founded until a number of years later in 1855, however.

When she died in 1831, she was buried at what was apparently one of her favorite places—on a small hill overlooking Sugar Creek. In the following years, several others also were buried there, and a small cemetery was created.

Like many Indiana counties, Johnson County had innumerable small cemeteries. One researcher has identified 163 in the county with 54 of them lost and 9 removed. The biggest move of all came in the 1940s when a large number of graves were moved so Camp Atterbury could be constructed.

Over time a footpath developed through this small cemetery, and later a county road was planned through it. Other graves probably were moved, but one of Nancy's sons—she had eleven children—objected to moving her grave. Since it originally wasn't a problem, her grave was left behind.

The trouble developed in 1905 when the county wanted to widen the road to build a bridge over Sugar Creek. Now the county decided the grave would have to be moved in order for the widening to take place.

So the story goes, her grandson, Daniel Doty, went to the grave site with his shotgun and, in essence said, "over my dead body." How long he remained there and what was said by Doty and to whom isn't definitely known.

The upshot, however, was that the county agreed not to move the grave. Instead, they built the road around it. A

DIVIDES THE ROAD. Nancy Kerlin Barnett's grave site divides County Road 400 South in Johnson County near the village of Amity.

IF YOU GO

GETTING THERE: From U.S. 31 south of Franklin go east on County Road 400 South one and one-third miles to the grave.

FEES: None.

concrete slab was placed over the grave to protect it, and on August 8, 1912, a historical marker was placed at the site as well.

That's how things still stand today.

In almost any writing about unusual places in Indiana, you will see the grave site of Nancy Kerlin Barnett included. Also, it is easily seen by traveling a short distance north off U.S. 31 in southern Johnson County. (See "If You Go" box for more information.)

Incidentally, the grandson who protected his grandmother's grave was the son of one of Nancy's daughters, also named Nancy, the eighth of her eleven children. She was twenty years old, if records are correct, when she married John Doty in Johnson County in 1843. Daniel was the second of her nine children.

The first Nancy's husband, William, died by drowning in the Ohio River thirteen years after her death when a steamboat exploded during a return trip from New Orleans.

POW ROCK. This rock helps mark the entrance to Atterbury Fish and Wildlife Area to the north and Camp Atterbury Joint Maneuver Training Center to the south. Dated 1942, it was created by prisoners of war held at the camp.

PISGAH LAKE. Boats can be put in Pisgah Lake at this ramp inside Atterbury Fish and Wildlife Area. The man-made lake is sixty-two acres.

Atterbury Fish and Wildlife Area, Edinburgh

EDINBURGH—You get some idea of how big Camp Atterbury was at one time as you drive around the Atterbury FWA in the southeast corner of Johnson County. Meandering around its 6,026 acres is put in perspective when you realize that the original Camp Atterbury sprawled south down into Bartholomew County and covered more than 40,000 acres.

Established in 1942, it was first used as a training site for American troops during World War II. Later, part of Atterbury became a prisoner-of-war camp for Italians and Germans captured during the war. Deactivated in 1948, it was reopened for the Korean War and finally was closed again in 1954.

There it sat until 1965 when the area north of Hospital Road was purchased by the State of Indiana for a fish and wildlife area. The federal Job Corps program also is located there.

The area south of Hospital Road now houses the Camp Atterbury Joint Maneuver Training Center, utilized by the National Guard and Army Reserves. It is marked "U.S. Army, No Trespassing," but hunting is authorized on the military base when it doesn't conflict with training operations.

Atterbury FWA itself has changed from its former military days. Old barracks have been knocked down, although some remains still are apparent. Of the ten man-made impoundments, the largest are sixty-two acre Pisgah in the north center of the area and twenty-five-acre Stone Arch to the west. In addition, the recently opened Atterbury FWA Public Shooting Range features four combination trap/skeet fields and sixty-six rifle/pistol positions.

Wildlife management has developed marshlands and other habitats for game and birds. The Atterbury bird checklist includes more than 250 varieties of birds that have been identified on the property—some very rarely seen such as the lark sparrow, but others abundantly such as the Canada goose.

Hunting and fishing remain popular activities. Licenses are required, and daily hunt permit cards are also necessary. Hunting on the military base now is unlikely since the base has been mobilized.

ATTERBURY CHAPEL. Italian prisoners of war built this small "chapel in the meadow" on the grounds of Camp Atterbury in Johnson County where they were held during World War II.

IF YOU GO

In addition, nearby Driftwood State Fishing Area to the south, according to property literature, is said to be "ideal for bass, bluegill, catfish, crappie, and tiger muskellunge."

My visit wasn't for hunting or fishing, but rather to "check out" the area. When I went in the office for a map, I told the man at the desk I was "just looking a round." "Oh, thought you were looking for mushrooms; that's what most people are doing," he replied. He said the best places were in the woods and often in the open fields.

My other stop was at a small chapel that I had heard about over the years. Located on the western side of the property, across from Stone Arch Lake, it was built by Italian prisoners of war.

The small, three-sided chapel was constructed in 1943 and featured Christian artwork by the prisoners on its interior walls. Over the years, the chapel deteriorated considerably until it was restored in 1988 by the Military Department of Indiana. A glass front and door now protect the chapel.

GETTING THERE: From Interstate 65 south of Franklin at Indiana 252 (Flat Rock exit) turn west across U.S. 31 and on into Atterbury on Hospital Road. To reach the chapel, continue on Hospital Road to a gravel road turning right across a small stone bridge (not easily seen).

INFORMATION: Call (812) 526–2051, or the shooting range at (812) 526–6552.

FEES: None to enter property. Mandatory check-in for hunting fees for shooting range.

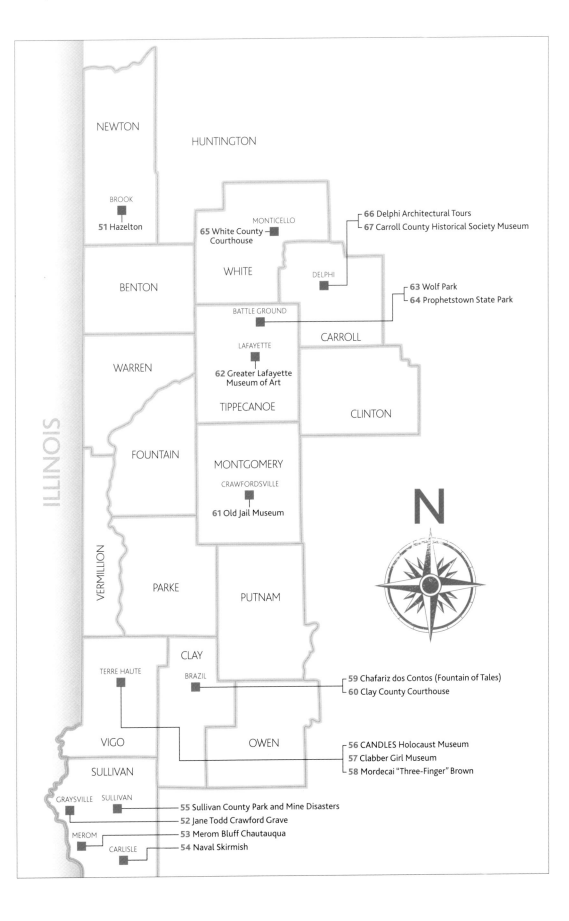

NEWTON

HUNTINGTON

BROOK
51 Hazelton

MONTICELLO
65 White County
Courthouse

66 Delphi Architectural Tours
67 Carroll County Historical Society Museum

WHITE

DELPHI

63 Wolf Park
64 Prophetstown State Park

BENTON

BATTLE GROUND

CARROLL

WARREN

LAFAYETTE
62 Greater Lafayette
Museum of Art

TIPPECANOE

CLINTON

FOUNTAIN

MONTGOMERY

CRAWFORDSVILLE
61 Old Jail Museum

N

VERMILLION

PARKE

PUTNAM

CLAY

TERRE HAUTE

BRAZIL

59 Chafariz dos Contos (Fountain of Tales)
60 Clay County Courthouse

VIGO

OWEN

56 CANDLES Holocaust Museum
57 Clabber Girl Museum
58 Mordecai "Three-Finger" Brown

SULLIVAN

GRAYSVILLE   SULLIVAN

55 Sullivan County Park and Mine Disasters

52 Jane Todd Crawford Grave

MEROM

53 Merom Bluff Chautauqua

CARLISLE

54 Naval Skirmish

ILLINOIS

ROADSIDE SIGN. It marks the Brook home of Hoosier author George Ade.

DESK IN ADE HOME. This desk is in a ground-level room of the George Ade home near Brook. Ade's work was written both while he lived in Chicago and later in this northwestern Indiana community.

Hazelton, Brook

BROOK—Historians call it "the Golden Age" of Indiana literature and well they might. Just look at the list of writers, most of whom were active around or in the early part of the twentieth century: Meredith Nicholson, Theodore Dreiser, Elmer Davis, George Jean Nathan, Booth Tarkington, James Whitcomb Riley, Charles and Mary Beard, Lew Wallace, Kin Hubbard, Claude Bowers, Charles Major, George Barr Mc-Cutcheon, Gene Stratton Porter, Lloyd C. Douglas, Emily Kimbrough, Edward and George Eggleston, and, last but certainly not least, George Ade.

Ade told the story, according to historian Howard Peckham, that when a Chautauqua lecturer came to Fort Wayne, he first told his audience he had heard of Indiana's literary reputation and, if an author was present, would that person please stand. Everyone stood except for one man. The speaker was a bit taken back but inquired about the one who didn't stand and was told, "Oh, no, he writes, too. He just deef and didn't hear your question"!

Because of our geographical and population settlement, the term "Hoosier" first supposedly was used in derision but later was embraced by natives. Ade, in referring to the state's literary heritage, described a Hoosier as "a puzzling combination of shy provincial, unfettered democrat and Fourth of July orator. He was a student by choice, a poet by sneaking inclination, and a story teller by reason of his nativity."

So, what's the connection between these writers, especially Ade, and a book on sites to visit in Indiana?

It happens that on a northern Indiana reporting swing, I drove into Brook in Newton County, close to the Illinois border and not far from Rensselaer. In doing so, I drove by Ade's former home. I almost missed it, as it is set back from the road, next to the George Ade Memorial Health Care Center about two miles east of Brook.

First, I went in the center but didn't quickly see anyone. I walked over to the house and tried the door. It was open, so I walked in. I spent a brief time just looking around. After all, this is the house where Ade hosted William Howard Taft dur-

GEORGE ADE'S HOME. Ade's home near Brook, where he entertained celebrities of the day, can be visited.

IF YOU GO

GETTING THERE: In northwest Indiana, turn west off Interstate 65 onto Indiana 16. The house is about two miles east of Brook.

INFORMATION: Call association member Rick Gerts at (219) 275–6161 at Gerts Funeral Home to make arrangements to see the house.

FEES: None, but donations are accepted.

ing the 1908 presidential campaign, Theodore Roosevelt in 1912, and, in between, literary figures of the day. On the wall is the famous photograph of Ade along with Tarkington, Riley, and Nicholson, four literary lions of the time.

I later found out that I was fortunate in finding the door open, as the caretaker probably was working somewhere in the house. It is now owned by the George Ade Home Association, which renovated it following twenty years of nonuse.

Ade is referred to as an American writer, journalist, and playwright. Essentially he was a humorist who made a fortune writing about America's "little man," especially the midwesterner and his efforts to cope with the new world as it shifted from an agrarian economy to one of industry.

Ade first worked on Chicago newspapers, and material from columns he wrote there was published in 1899 as *Fables in Slang*, his best-known work. His literary career stretched from 1887 to 1940. Born in 1866 in nearby Kentland, Ade died in Brook in 1944.

Jane Todd Crawford Grave, Graysville

ORIGINAL HEADSTONE. Jane Todd Crawford's grave in Sullivan County. The full ledger, which covers the grave, was placed there by the Women's Auxiliary to the Southern Medical Association.

HISTORICAL SIGN. The sign, posted along Indiana 63 at the Johnson-Hopewell Cemetery just north of Graysville in western Indiana, marks the grave of Jane Todd Crawford.

GRAYSVILLE—Frankly, until I wandered into western Indiana, I had never heard of Jane Todd Crawford or of her amazing experience early in the nineteenth century. But a visit to the Johnson-Hopewell Cemetery just north of here soon acquainted me with her heroic story. Her grave here is noted on a historic marker at the entrance to the cemetery, on a granite monument of the American Hospital Association dedicated in 1940 near her grave site, and at her actual 1842 tombstone, barely legible but next to the full ledger covering her grave, placed there in 1871 by the Women's Auxiliary to the Southern Medical Association.

Here's her remarkable story.

Jane Todd, born in Virginia in 1763, married Thomas Crawford in 1794. In 1805 they moved to Green County in Kentucky. It was here four years later that her place in history began. Jane, so the story goes, was told by doctors that her large stomach growth was likely twins. She was in considerable pain. Efforts were made to induce labor but brought no results. Finally, the diagnosis was that she had a huge ovarian tumor.

Somehow, and the story isn't clear about this, she heard of Doctor Ephraim McDowell in Danville, Kentucky, and determined to go to him for help. Apparently, she realized her only hope was for an experimental abdominal operation. But it was the dead of winter, and Danville was sixty miles away. So, in mid-December, she started out on horseback, eventually riding those sixty miles over the difficult trails of the time and by now in great pain.

Once she reached McDowell's home office, he confided that an ovariectomy, to his knowledge, had never before been performed. He would try, he said, but it would be dangerous and very painful. And there would be no anesthesia, since it had not yet been created.

Go ahead, Jane said. McDowell made a nine-inch incision and, in a twenty-five-minute surgery, removed what was said to be a twenty-two-pound cystic ovarian tumor. The story

GRANITE MONUMENT. The monument was placed by the American Hospital Association and dedicated in 1940 near the grave site of Jane Todd Crawford. She is depicted on horseback during her sixty-mile journey, headed toward the world's first successful abdominal surgery.

IF YOU GO

GETTING THERE: Take Indiana 154 to Graysville. The cemetery is about a mile north of Graysville on Indiana 63.

INFORMATION: Call the Sullivan County Historical Society at (812) 268–6253.

FEES: None.

continues that during the surgery on Christmas Day, she sang hymns. Not only that, but so the story also goes, McDowell found her five days later up and about, making her bed.

She returned to Green County, again by horseback. Some years later she moved to Graysville in western Indiana to live with her son, Thomas Crawford, a Presbyterian minister. Here she died, at age seventy-eight, in 1842, some thirty-two years following her historic surgery.

And historic it was. She was the first patient known to have a successful abdominal operation. McDowell's surgery made him world famous. His two-story home in Danville, a National Historic Landmark, was restored and has been open as a museum since 1939.

That sixty-mile path from Green County to Danville now is known as the Jane Todd Crawford Trail. It certainly should be.

COMMEMORATIVE PLAQUE.
A plaque tells about the historic Merom Bluff Chautauqua, held at this bluff overlooking the Wabash River in western Indiana from 1905 to 1936. Today, it is the site of a summer festival.

STRICTLY DECORATIVE. A cannon, mounted high on Merom Bluff overlooking the Wabash River in western Indiana, might have had a colorful Revolutionary War or War of 1812 history. In fact, however, it simply was placed at the Chautauqua site for decorative purposes.

Merom Bluff Chautauqua, Merom

MEROM—Picture the United States twenty-five years before motion pictures could be seen let alone be heard, thirty-five years before radio, and sixty-five years before television. It was the 1870s. Americans interested in entertainment or culture depended on printed material, mainly books, on the stage, traveling performers, and lecturers.

For teachers in rural America, the problem was especially acute. Frequently little older than some of their students, with only bare-bones work during one or two years of college, they struggled to improve their teaching with continuing education almost unknown.

Then, in upper New York State, someone had an idea. In the summer, along the shores of a nearby lake, better versed teachers, mostly drawn from religious education, gathered to lecture about the issues of the day, usually about moral topics. The idea caught on and spread. Ever-better prepared lecturers came, until eventually they included the intellectual giants of the day. The content widened to music, drama, dance, and other forms of cultural enrichment beyond religious instruction.

Since the movement started near this lake, it took its name—Chautauqua.

For forty-five years, chautauquas were a summer highlight across the United States. Traveling troupes crisscrossed the country, often staying in a community for several weeks as people would gather from far and wide to enjoy the lectures and performances. They reached an estimated thirty-five million people when the nation's population was only around one hundred million. Teddy Roosevelt supposedly called them "the most American thing about America."

Eventually, the Chautauqua concept reached the Midwest. Perhaps the most famous of the Hoosier chautauquas took place at the western Indiana town of Merom on a bluff overlooking the Wabash River, Illinois off in the distance. Today a Chautauqua festival takes place here each summer, although it bears slight resemblance to those events of a century ago.

More than fifty thousand people would come to Merom Bluff over a three-week summer period, according to *Indiana:*

ACROSS THE RIVER. Illinois, across the Wabash River from Merom Bluff, appears to be largely flat in contrast to the bluff that rises 150 feet above the river on the Indiana side.

A New Historical Guide. Some of the speakers were the best-known individuals of their day—William Howard Taft, Billy Sunday, William Jennings Bryan, Robert LaFollette, Jeanette Rankin, Warren G. Harding, Carrie Nation, and Indiana's own Eugene V. Debs.

Those days, which lasted from 1905 to 1936, are long gone. The famous Merom House, for example, built in 1822 and where many of these famous guests stayed, was torn down in 1940. However, the Chautauqua House still exists, located on a bluff adjacent to the Chautauqua grounds.

Today's Chautauqua festival at Merom Bluff Park follows a format of numerous present-day Indiana county events. It includes food, musical stage performances, vendors, tractor pull, bike show, Little Miss Pageant, Sunday church service, etc.

Still, it's possible to stand on the bluff 150 feet above the Wabash River, look out over the grounds, and in your mind's eye see the crowds gathering after a long winter for the great event—the Merom Bluff Chautauqua.

IF YOU GO

GETTING THERE: On U.S. 41 in southwestern Indiana at Sullivan, turn west on Indiana 154 and then south on Indiana 63 into Merom.

INFORMATION: Call (812) 356–4010.

FEES: Admission for summer festival, but none to visit otherwise.

Naval Skirmish, Carlisle

COMMEMORATES BATTLE. This plaque in Carlisle in western Indiana commemorates the only Hoosier "naval engagement" of the Revolutionary War when a British convoy was captured by an American force without a shot fired.

CARLISLE—The folks in western Indiana are proud of the plaque in downtown Carlisle that marks the "naval engagement" along the Wabash River in 1779 that is cited in what some history books call Indiana's only naval skirmish of the American Revolutionary War.

According to many accounts and the best historical evidence available, here's what happened.

As the Revolutionary War progressed, George Rogers Clark and his American force moved from Fort Kaskaskia on the Mississippi River in present-day Illinois toward Vincennes and Fort Sackville in present-day southwestern Indiana, which had recently been recaptured by the British. Their route in late January and early February 1779 took them along the Mississippi, Ohio, and Wabash rivers and flooded river bottoms, inundated by warmer weather melting snow and ice.

The British, thinking no army would attack during the winter months, were caught by surprise when the Americans were outside the fort, the town already under their control.

In a series of maneuvers, Clark then captured Fort Sackville. The British commander, Henry Hamilton, had wanted a three-day truce—not granted—and Clark quickly found out why: A British force from Detroit sent to supply the fort was proceeding down the Wabash River toward Fort Sackville.

With the fort captured, Clark sent Captain Leonard Helm up the Wabash River in three armed boats carrying about forty men—or was it fifty? Histories differ—to intercept the British flotilla of soldiers and supplies.

The full text of the plaque placed upon a large rock where a courthouse was once expected to be built in downtown Carlisle reads:

At Point Coupee west of here on the Wabash River, a decisive naval engagement took place one night about March 1, 1779, shortly after Ft. Sackville was recaptured from the British. General George Rogers Clark sent Captain Leonard Helm, Major Bosseron, Major Legras and 50 volunteers in three armed boats to intercept a British convoy bound for Vincennes. They captured 40 of the enemy, seven boats and supplies worth fifty thousand dollars.

AT A BEND IN THE WABASH RIVER. Possibly it was this bend where a small American force sneaked up on and captured British troops and supplies, sent to the aid of the British garrison at Vincennes during the Revolutionary War.

IF YOU GO

GETTING THERE: After following U.S. 41 into Carlisle, stop at the town square. The plaque stands at the southwest corner.

INFORMATION: Call the Sullivan County Historical Society at (812) 268–6253, or go to http://www .sullivancountyin.com/.

FEES: None.

Yes, it's true that the Americans surprised the British force and captured it and its supplies. Yes, it's true the Americans captured the seven boats the British were using. Yes, the stores included six cannon along with a supply of gold and provisions that the troops were escorting. Yes, it's true that when the British goods were distributed among the American force, including French militiamen, that everyone had about $1,000 each.

But "naval"? Yes, it's true that both the British and the Americans arrived at the spot of the capture by boats. The Americans landed on the banks of the Wabash where the British were encamped for the night, crept up on the convoy members—most probably already asleep—and simply took command.

"Engagement"? Not a shot was fired. So ended what *Indiana: A New Historical Guide* calls "what is considered the westernmost naval engagement of the American Revolution."

Engagement or not, it's a pleasure to stand at the riverside and watch the Wabash flow. How many generations have done just that?

Sullivan County Park and Lake and Mine Disasters, Sullivan

TWENTY MINERS KILLED. The Baker Mine of the Nora Coal Company explosion in 1937 killed twenty miners down more than two hundred feet. That mine was closed in 1951.

NEARLY ONE HUNDRED KILLED. This three-sided monument commemorates the three mine disasters that occurred in Sullivan County during the 1900s, taking the lives of nearly one hundred men.

SULLIVAN—What a contrast! It's a beautiful county park—certainly among the finest I have visited. A 461-acre lake offers the opportunity for motor boats and jet skis and lots of fishing. It also has a campground, nine-hole golf course, camp store, playground, picnic areas and grills, camping, and cabins. The visitor can easily picture people spending enjoyable, lazy summer days and nights there.

"There" is the Sullivan County Park and Lake, constructed in 1968 for flood control and conservation, located just east of the town of Sullivan in western Indiana.

Yet, when a visitor drives into the park and turns left toward the park office, to the right are reminders of some of the darkest days in the history of Sullivan County. Close to the road is a small coal car and a three-sided monument along with an unrelated grain millstone—also part of the county's history. This is coal mining country.

Hoosier coal mining has been centered in fifteen southwestern Indiana counties. One report, "Our Hoosier State Beneath Us," claims about nine hundred million tons of coal have been produced in the state since the beginning of mining in the early 1830s.

As recently as the turn of the century, some three thousand Hoosiers were engaged in mining, according to an Indiana University School of Business report. The number of miners in Sullivan and Greene counties combined makes up more than 5 percent of their total workforce.

However, underground coal mining always is a dangerous business. The United States Bureau of Mines Web site reports on hundreds of coal mine disasters over the years, especially before surface mining became more popular in the last century.

The three-sided monument tells of three county mine disasters that, together, claimed ninety-nine lives.

First, and the worst, was the City Mining Company underground explosion near Sullivan on February 20, 1925. It occurred at 10:30 a.m. and killed fifty-one miners. The coal was down 275 feet, a distance of about a city block. The mine, which produced nearly 600,000 tons of coal, was abandoned in 1929.

INSPECTING THE CAR. Indiana writer Alan Garinger, with whom I made my trip into western Indiana, inspects the coal car that is part of the monument to the coal industry and to the miners who died in Sullivan County explosions. It is located in the Sullivan County Park and Lake.

The second Sullivan County mine explosion was at the Little Betty Mining Company at Dugger on January 28, 1931, at 3 p.m. Twenty-eight died there, about 233 feet below the earth's surface. This mine was abandoned in 1938 after a total production of nearly three million tons of coal.

In the 1925 and 1931 disasters, rescuers were threatened and some made ill by so-called afterdamp—a combination of nitrogen and carbon dioxide left in a mine following an explosion or fire.

The third was the Baker Mine of the Nora Coal Company near Sullivan, which happened July 15, 1937, at 7:30 a.m. Twenty miners died in the mine where coal was reached at 212 feet. It closed in 1951 after it had produced nearly eight million tons. In this rescue attempt, gas masks and other safety devices were employed against afterdamp and any possible fires.

Today, it's estimated that only 2 percent of Indiana coal comes from underground mines, the rest from surface mining. So, it's unlikely those three Sullivan County plaques will be joined by a fourth.

IF YOU GO

GETTING THERE: Take U.S. 41 to Sullivan. Turn east at the stoplight and follow Washington Street through town to Foley and then north on to Picnic Drive. Signs also mark the route to the park and lake.

INFORMATION: For information about the park and lake or to make reservations, telephone (812) 268–5537.

FEES: None.

ONLY SURVIVORS. Russian liberators took this photo of prisoners freed from the Nazi death camp, Auschwitz 2, at the end of World War II. Eva and Miriam Mozes are seen in front. Eva Mozes Kor and Miriam Mozes Zeiger were the only survivors of their family.

LIBRARY AND RESEARCH CENTER. The library and research center is part of the CANDLES Holocaust Museum in Terre Haute, operated by death camp survivor Eva Mozes Kor.

CANDLES Holocaust Museum, Terre Haute

TERRE HAUTE—"To heal and be free, forgive your enemies," reads the large sign outside the CANDLES Holocaust Museum and Education Center, south of downtown Terre Haute.

For most of us, that would take some doing. Consider:

The quote's author, Eva Mozes Kor, entered Auschwitz 2, also called Birkenau, one of the Nazi death camps, with her twin sister and members of her family in the darkest days for Jews during World War II. When her family stepped off the cattle cars that carried them to the death camp, Eva was quickly separated from her mother, never to see her again. Eva and her twin sister, Miriam, along with other twins, were subjected to "experiments" by the infamous Doctor Josef Mengele, their bodies injected with germs and chemicals as part of his genetic tests. All of the other members of her family—mother, father, two older sisters—simply disappeared, apparently killed in the gas chambers of the concentration camp.

It's believed that between April 1942 and November 1944, more than a million Jews were gassed at Auschwitz 2 along with hundreds of thousands of non-Jews as the camp killed and cremated as many as nine thousand a day. Their corpses were reduced to ashes in crematoria.

Years later in 1995, with the war long over and now living in Terre Haute, Eva opened the CANDLES Museum—Children of Auschwitz Nazi Deadly Lab Experiments Survivors—in an effort to teach about the Nazi atrocities and the results of hate. In late 2003 an arsonist with a firebomb destroyed the museum.

But Eva had already moved on. Standing in the remains of the German concentration camp on January 27, 1995, she issued her "Declaration of Amnesty" . . . "to all Nazis who participated directly or indirectly in the murder of my family and millions of others. . . . I, Eva Mozes Kor, in my name only, give this amnesty because it is time to go on; it is time to heal our souls, it is time to forgive, but never forget; it is time to open up all the classified and personal files, not only for the sake of history, but to alleviate human suffering. . . . Here in

CANDLES. The Holocaust Museum in Terre Haute was destroyed by an arsonist in 2003. This is the new museum that reopened in 2005.

Auschwitz, I hope in some small way to send the world a message of forgiveness, a message of peace, a message of hope, a message of healing."

From the ashes of the burned Terre Haute museum has risen an even finer museum, which reopened in 2005. A large room is surrounded with photos from the Holocaust and is where groups meet, often to hear Eva discuss those days. A library and research center and smaller rooms complete the building.

One corner of the museum has a few burned remnants from the fire bombing to illustrate what happened.

In addition to the steady stream of adults who visit, are schoolchildren for whom World War II and the Holocaust must seem like ancient history. Shortly before my visit Hutsonville, Illinois, fifth grade; Eastern Greene County Elementary; Topics in History class, Bloomfield High School, signed the guest book.

A realtor, Eva helps support the museum by contributing 20 percent of her commissions to fund its operation.

IF YOU GO

GETTING THERE: From Interstate 70 at Terre Haute, take U.S. 41 north toward downtown. The museum is on the right about two miles after leaving Interstate 70.

INFORMATION: The museum is open Tuesday through Saturday 1 to 4 p.m., or by appointment. Call (812) 234–7881, or go to http://www .candlesholocaustmuseum.org/.

FEES: None if you look around yourself, but there is a charge for presentation by a docent. Contributions are appreciated.

Clabber Girl Museum, Terre Haute

MORE THAN BAKING POWDER. Some of the products produced by Hulman over the years are displayed in this case at the Clabber Girl museum.

"BASEMENT BESSIE." This race car was built in a northern Indiana basement. Powered by a 270-cubic-inch Offenhauser engine, the car finished ninth in 1950 and later won several one hundred-mile dirt track races. The car was still competing in 1965.

TERRE HAUTE—It's one of those successful immigration stories from the early years of America: A family comes to the New World from Europe in the mid-1800s, works hard, hits upon something people want, and makes its fortune.

Francis Hulman was the first to arrive, joined by brothers Diedrich and Herman in 1854. The extended family worked in the grocery business. After the death of Francis and his family in a ship fire in 1858, Herman expanded the grocery business by adding general merchandise. Herman died in 1913 at the age of eighty-two. True to his nature for hard work, he still was on the job until the day before his death.

Adding general merchandise helped the Hulmans have the funds to buy a distillery, reported to be one of the world's largest. Herman's big venture was to manufacture baking powder, spices, and coffee.

That's when the Hulmans' real success came.

Clabber Baking Powder in the late 1870s became a favorite leavening used by housewives, rather than following the time-honored tradition of mixing clabbered (sour) milk, baking soda, and refined ashes from wood-burning stoves.

With the introduction of its new baking powder in 1879, sales needed a boost. Housewives were unsure what the product was replacing. Its name changed to Clabber Brand Baking Powder, but in 1923 with a law requiring ingredients to be listed—and since no clabber was included—the final change to Clabber Girl Baking Powder came. The label now showed a girl holding a plate of biscuits rather than churning butter.

It still is just one of the products coming from the Hulman and Company building at Ninth Street and Wabash Avenue in downtown Terre Haute. For example, while I was there, I tried a cup of Rex decaffeinated coffee. Most coffees seem much the same to me, but this was different. It had an especially good taste, I thought, so I bought a pound of the beans.

What will draw the visitor, in addition to the products, is the museum. It has been greatly expanded since I last visited. The museum, general store, and café now occupy the first floor of the building. It includes a Hall of Memories, Victorian Parlor,

ONE HUNDRED YEARS AGO. One of the old-time delivery wagons from around 1905, now in the museum. It was used to deliver Hulman company products. The company owned wagons and stables for use in its deliveries.

Pig & Whistle Saloon, a communications display, and stories about the Hulman families and products.

The building itself is worth seeing. In 1892 the Hulmans dedicated the building at Ninth and Wabash. According to *Indiana: A New Historical Guide,* Samuel Hannaford designed the building and used red bricks with limestone and granite accents. It is Romanesque Revival and remains much the same more than one hundred years later.

The Hulmans are tied to the Indianapolis 500-mile race track, too, so expect to see a race car in the museum. When I last visited, it was "Basement Bessie," an Offenhauser built in a northern Indiana basement by mechanic Ray Nichels and Paul Russo, who drove it to a ninth place finish in the 1950 race.

Herman Hulman's great-great grandson, Tony Hulman George, now owns and operates the Indianapolis Motor Speedway, purchased by his grandfather in 1945. The most famous race in the world still remains the greatest spectator attraction in Indiana.

IF YOU GO

GETTING THERE: From Interstate 70 at Terre Haute, take U.S. 41 north into downtown and Wabash Avenue and turn right to Ninth Street.

INFORMATION: Call (812) 478–7119 (tours), (812) 478–7223 (store), (812) 478–7189 (bake shop), or go to http://clabbergirl.com/. Guided tours must be scheduled in advance. Museum hours are Monday through Friday 10 a.m. to 6 p.m. and Saturday 10 a.m. to 3 p.m.

FEES: None. Tour fees available upon request.

HEADSTONE. Where Chicago Cubs ace pitcher Mordecai "Three Finger" Brown and his wife, Sarah, are buried. She died ten years after the famed Hoosier baseball player.

Mordecai "Three Finger" Brown, Terre Haute

TERRE HAUTE—Enough visitors stop by Roselawn Memorial Park Cemetery to see one special grave site so by now the woman at the desk in the office simply pulls out a cemetery map and gives it to a visitor with its place identified—No. 218.

That's where Mordecai Brown was laid to rest in 1948.

Who, you ask, was Mordecai Brown? If I add his nickname—"Three Finger"—maybe you know. Then if I add the Chicago Cubs and the Cubs' last World Series win in 1908, you are still more likely to know.

If not, let's look at a little history.

So, the connection with Mordecai "Three Finger" Brown? The Hoosier-born pitcher was the Cubs' pitching ace back in that 1908 series, winning two games and allowing no runs in eleven innings pitched.

He began playing ball with a company team while working as a coal miner. He played with Terre Haute in the old Three-I minor league (Indiana, Illinois, and Iowa) in 1901 and two years later joined the Saint Louis Cardinals, reaching the big leagues when he was twenty-six years old. He was traded to the Cubs in 1904.

Then began some great years for the pitcher who had lost his index finger and part of another on his right hand—his pitching hand—in a corn shredder accident when he was seven years old. It's baseball lore, at least, that his thumb was paralyzed and stopped growing and his pinkie finger was impaired too. It's said that these factors gave Brown the ability to snap off a wicked curve ball that fooled many a big-league hitter.

He won twenty-nine games in 1908 and became the first pitcher in big-league history to win four consecutive shutouts. He won more than twenty games six years in a row. He was the star pitcher as the Cubs won the World Series in 1907 and 1908 as well as pennants in 1906 and 1910.

Like many other pitchers of his day, he went out to the mound every third or fourth day and usually pitched the entire game. He pitched 250 or more innings every year from 1906 through 1911. After an injury in 1912, he continued playing with the Cubs until 1916 and then became a player-manager

CUBS PITCHER. Mordecai "Three Finger" Brown is buried in the south end of Section J near Terre Haute's Roselawn Memorial Park cemetery office.

with other teams before giving up the game in 1920. In all, he won 239 major league games while losing 130, had a 2.06 earned run average—the third lowest in baseball history—and struck out 1,375 batters. Not only that, but he had a lifetime batting average of .248, remarkable for a pitcher.

That record was more than enough to cause Brown's induction into the Cooperstown, New York, Baseball Hall of Fame in 1949, the year following his death, and to make him the first Indiana-born inductee into the hall.

Grave site No. 218 is located in Section J of Roselawn, only a short distance from the cemetery office. Buried with him is his wife, Sarah Brown, who died in 1958.

Brown's birthplace is to the north in Parke County at Nyesville. A historical marker has been placed at the site of Brown's boyhood home where he was born in another eventful year—1876—one hundred years after the American War of Independence.

Who knows? Maybe "next year" will be the Cubs' year, too. Or, when you read this piece, they may already have done it.

GETTING THERE: Take Indiana 41 north through downtown Terre Haute and follow Business Route 41 north of town. The cemetery's address is 7500 N. Clinton Street and is north of Sky King Airport.

INFORMATION: Call the cemetery at (812) 466–5221 or visit the Web site at http://www.rlmp.net/index.html. Another source is the Terre Haute Convention and Visitors Bureau at (800) 366–3043 or http://www.terrehaute.com/.

FEES: None.

Chafariz dos Contos (Fountain of Tales), Brazil

HISTORY RELATED. This plaque recited the history of Chafariz dos Contos (Fountain of Tales) in Brazil. The monument stands along Indiana 59, approaching Brazil from the south.

BRAZIL—With the coming of spring the water was to have been turned on at any time at the Chafariz dos Contos (Fountain of Tales) monument in Forest Park, according to then-Brazil Mayor Tom Arthur. At the time of my visit in 2006, the city was preparing a ceremony to mark the fiftieth anniversary of the fountain's dedication in 1956.

The granite fountain, located at the edge of the park facing Forest Avenue, also Indiana 59, is visible to drivers approaching the city from Interstate 70.

The connections among the fountain, the country of Brazil, and this Indiana town—some five thousand miles apart—got its start as a happenstance.

(Two well-known twentieth-century figures were born in Brazil early in the 1900s. Their names are at the end of this essay.)

The town got its name shortly after it was platted in 1844, according to *Indiana: A New Historical Guide*, when a local resident was reading about the South American country, so he suggested the name of Brazil for his community.

The fountain story is a little more involved.

The Brazilian ambassador visited Brazil at the request of Brazilian President Eurice Gaspar Dutra. On his visit, the ambassador made an offer of a fountain. An act of the Brazilian Congress created a committee to study the subject, and sculptor Tito Bernucci was commissioned to copy one of Brazil's historical and artistic monuments.

On May 17, 1950, Indiana's Brazil had a "Brazil Day" during which it entertained the ambassador and his party. Part of the day's ceremonies included dedicating the site for the "friendship fountain." The monument was shipped to the United States in late 1953 and arrived by railroad.

The Baroque-style fountain of Portugal-sculpted granite is mounted in a heavy brick wall. The sculpture, weighing sixty-two tons in its mounted form, is twenty-six feet high and forty feet long. The last bolt was placed on May 19, 1956.

It was dedicated a week later, May 26, 1956. Due to a downpour, a parade was canceled and the dedication held in the park auditorium. Among the dignitaries attending the

CHAFARIZ DOS CONTOS. The English translation is "Fountain of Tales." The monument was a gift from the South American country of Brazil.

IF YOU GO

GETTING THERE: In western Indiana on Interstate 70, take Indiana 59 north into Brazil.

INFORMATION: Contact the Clay County Chamber of Commerce at (812) 448–8457 or the mayor's office at (812) 443–2221.

FEES: None.

ceremony were three of Indiana's political leaders at the time, Senator Homer Capehart, Governor George Craig, and Congressman Bill Bray.

Restoration took place in 1996–97. A plaque on the fountain reads, "From the Republic of Brazil, a token of friendship to her namesake, the City of Brazil 1954." Another in front of the fountain reads, "A gift from the Republic of Brazil to Brazil, Indiana, proffered to the City of Brazil, 1950, erected in 1955–56. This fountain is an exact replica of the fountain in Ouro Preto, Brazil, started in 1745, dedicated in 1760."

Oh yes, those two twentieth-century figures who were born in Brazil.

One was James (Jimmy) Hoffa, former head of the Teamsters union who mysteriously disappeared late in the last century. He is believed to have been murdered and his body disposed of. Hoffa was the son of a coal-mining father and was born in Brazil in 1913. The family lived in Brazil until 1922.

The other was George Craig, former national commander of the American Legion and later governor of Indiana.

LOG CABIN. The cabin was moved from Brazil to Bowling Green. It sits not far from the site of the old courthouse square in Bowling Green.

Clay County Courthouse, Bowling Green and Brazil

BOWLING GREEN—"They stole our courthouse!" That may have been what locals in Bowling Green shouted when they awoke on January 26, 1877.

According to *Indiana: A New Historical Guide*, here's what happened.

Bowling Green was the earliest settlement in Clay County in the present-day western part of central Indiana. The first white settler came into the area in 1812, only four years before Indiana statehood, and a few years later had a trading post going, serving travelers making the journey between Spencer and Terre Haute.

In 1827 the town was established to be the county seat of the new Clay County. It was named Bowling Green after Bowling Green, Virginia, in honor of the home town of one of the Hoosier community's early citizens. It was a bustling small town—"the center of business and civilization in Clay County," as the historical guide calls it.

Then an all-too-familiar story followed. First the National Road—to become U.S. 40—crossed the state, but several miles to the north. Next, the railroads bypassed the town. In short order, the inevitable happened: Bowling Green failed to grow while, to the north, the neighboring city of Brazil prospered as the major town in the county, in part because of the national highway and the railroads and also because of coal mining and the clay factories. Next the inevitable step occurred: A petition to change the county seat from Bowling Green to Brazil was successful.

A group of men from Brazil, realizing that anything could happen before the transfer of government took place, sneaked into the Bowling Green courthouse under the cover of night on January 25, 1877. They gathered up the county records from the courthouse and carefully crept away, depositing them without incident in the newly constructed Brazil courthouse.

Today, Brazil itself has been bypassed to its south by Interstate 70. Busy U.S. 40 still runs through the heart of the town, however, and Brazil remains an important place although the heyday of its coal and clay-making industries has passed.

COURTHOUSE. The Clay County Courthouse is located in Brazil. The site of the courthouse was removed from Bowling Green in the late 1800s in a disputed decision.

For example, the Hoffa family resided here in the early 1900s with James Hoffa, the son of a coal-mining family later becoming a powerful union leader as president of the International Brotherhood of Teamsters. Remember him? He disappeared one day and has never been found. It's believed enemies kidnapped and murdered him, depositing his body in some forlorn spot.

Brazil now has a twentieth-century courthouse for the center of Clay County official activities. It sits on U.S. 40 just east of the downtown business district.

Meanwhile, in Bowling Green where the courthouse once was, is an open square. The 1853 courthouse building was destroyed by lightning in 1910 after serving as a public meeting place.

Although Bowling Green lost its courthouse, it did gain one "victory" over Brazil a hundred years later. In 1973 an old log cabin, now owned by the Bowling Green Historical Society, was moved here from where it had been built in 1836 at Brazil!

In Brazil be sure to stop at the Clay County Museum a few blocks west of the courthouse. Ask about the safe robbery.

IF YOU GO

GETTING THERE: Take Indiana 59 into Brazil. At U.S. 40 (National Road) turn east to the courthouse. To reach Bowling Green, continue south on Indiana 59 from Interstate 70 to Indiana 46 and back east to Bowling Green.

INFORMATION: Call the Brazil/Clay County Chamber of Commerce at (812) 448–8457.

FEES: None.

Old Jail Museum, Crawfordsville

JAIL MUSEUM. This eight-room house is where the Montgomery County sheriff and family lived. The rotary jail is attached behind it.

IN AND OUT OF CELL. This corridor opened to each of the cells as it was revolved in the Crawfordsville rotary jail. The turning mechanism is at the right.

DOWN BELOW. In the jail basement is the underside of the rotary jail turntable mechanism. At first, steam heat was distributed through this pipe. It also carried waste from the toilets in the cell block to the city sewer system.

CRAWFORDSVILLE—They had federal patent No. 244,358, issued in July 1881. With their patent in hand, two Indianapolis men—William H. Brown and Benjamin F. Haugh—set about completing the design for the first of their rotary jails to be built in Crawfordsville in neighboring Montgomery County.

Their idea was ingenious even if it seemed like something out of the Middle Ages: One jailer would turn a hand-operated crank that would revolve a tiered, metal turntable. On each tier would be jail cells, built much like slices in a pie. The jailer would crank the turntable until the cell he wanted was next to a single opening—the only exit from each tier of the jail. When the door to the steel cage that surrounded the turntable cells would be opened, a prisoner could be taken out or put in.

Between the steel cage and the outside brick wall with its barred windows was a narrow area—the jail's bullpen or recreational area. The second floor held women's cells and solitary confinement. Up on the third floor were three cells for ill prisoners.

The purpose of this unusual structure was to enable a single jailer to handle the comings and goings of all of the prisoners—as many as thirty-two, two to a cell, plus nine more on the third floor—without having contact with any of them.

The jail opened in 1882, and for ninety-one years it housed the prison population for Montgomery County. It closed in 1973.

Similar to many of the jails built at the time, the quarters for the sheriff and family were attached to the jail.

According to the records here, only seven rotary jails were constructed. By 1930, this one was under serious attack. Unsafe, poor natural lighting and ventilation, dark, and "insanitary" were the charges brought in 1930 by a state board.

Those weren't the only criticisms. A central pipe ran up the middle of the rotary jail to carry steam from a basement boiler to heat the cells along with steam radiators. However, it wouldn't radiate properly. Finally the radiators were moved and repaired to try to solve the problem.

As the 1930s passed, the jail was condemned despite efforts to make improvements. In 1939 the turntable was immobi-

HELD TWO PRISONERS. One of the pie-shaped cells in the rotary jail. A narrow "bullpen" circled the cells inside the walls of the jail. A second overhead bunk has been removed from the cell.

lized, and in 1967 a county grand jury ordered the structure closed. It was not used after 1973.

Two years later, the Montgomery County Cultural Foundation came to the structure's rescue, and the Old Jail Museum opened. In 1975 the foundation received what it calls "a generous bequest" from one of its founders, Max Tannenbaum. Until then, it depended on small gifts. Extensive renovation of both the sheriff's living quarters and the jail followed.

The tour guide said that this jail is the only operable one, out of three, that survives. The others are in Iowa and Tennessee.

The sheriff's residence is used by the community for receptions, programs, and workshops. It also houses historic displays and exhibits, often of quilts. The displays include costumes, local business and industry artifacts, natural history specimens, materials from Crawfordsville's pioneer period, and items from the jail.

IF YOU GO

GETTING THERE: In traveling west through Crawfordsville where Indiana 32 turns left in the city, turn right one block. The Jail Museum is on your left at 225 N. Washington Street.

INFORMATION: The telephone number for the Old Jail Museum is (765) 362–5222. It is open March through December, Wednesday through Saturday 10 a.m. to 5 p.m., and Sunday 1 p.m. to 5 p.m. The toll-free telephone number of the Montgomery County Visitors and Convention Bureau is (800) 866–3973, the Web site is http://crawfordsville.org/.

FEES: Admission charged, twelve and under are free.

Greater Lafayette Museum of Art, Lafayette

THE SUN WAS SETTING. It was deep into a late winter Saturday afternoon when I arrived at the Greater Lafayette Museum of Art. Actually, the door had just been locked for the day. Did I get in? Read the essay to find out.

LAFAYETTE—It was 4:05 p.m. on a Sunday afternoon when I pulled my car into the parking lot of the Greater Lafayette Museum of Art. The museum's Mary Maxine had just set her stuff down outside the door as she prepared to lock up the building.

I gave her my song-and-dance about writing a travel column and told her—truthfully—I thought the museum closed at 5 p.m. "I really have to be somewhere soon," the Purdue English doctoral student said, but she volunteered to let me have "a quick look." One thing led to another and, ultimately, she insisted I take the full hour.

Was it the power of the press? More about that later.

In any case, the museum is an impressive operation that goes beyond what one normally assumes to be a museum of art. For example, deep in the bowels of the building and despite the fact that it was closed, artists were at work in the pottery studio. Other classroom facilities include a general studio and a darkroom.

Art classes offered throughout the week at the time of my visit ranged from "Junior Drawing and Painting" and "Youth Papermaking" through "Photography" and "Figure/Portrait Painting" for teens and adults. Classes change with the seasons. The museum also collaborates with other community not-for-profit organizations for children's programs.

Another example would be museum field trips—for instance, an all-day trip to the Art Institute in Chicago to see the Hopper/Homer Exhibit was a recent spring trip.

Other museum programming at that time of my visit included "Art a la Carte," a lunch-and-learn presentation by a local female artist and high school art teacher, plus a "Salon des Artistes" program that looked at an exhibit, Matter Mind Spirit—the work of twelve contemporary female artists in painting, sculpture, photography, and fiber—along with dancing and readings.

In another art form, the museum was accepting Tippecanoe County photographs taken during the past year from which one hundred were to be selected for display. The winning photographs will become part of the permanent collection

MATTER MIND SPIRIT. This exhibition of twelve Indiana female artists was on display in the East and McDonald galleries of the Greater Lafayette Museum of Art when I visited.

of the Tippecanoe County Historical Association. Every other year, the museum has an exhibit of Indiana photography. One of the museum's most popular annual shows is "New Artists," a juried show highlighting the work of talented regional high school artists.

Similar to other art museums, it has both permanent and changing galleries as well as art and art objects that can be purchased including jewelry, drawings, photographs, paintings, pottery, art glass, and textiles. The museum shop is filled with the works of more than forty local artists.

The museum focuses on nineteenth- and twentieth-century American art, especially on Indiana art.

Among works in its permanent gallery of paintings are those by F. Luis Mora—its first acquisition in 1911, Henry Ossawa Tanner, George Winter, Lyla Marshall Hareoff, T. C. Steele, Will Vawter, and E. K. Williams.

We finished our tour. Why had she unlocked the building and been so helpful? Well maybe it wasn't the power of the press; more likely it is because Mary Maxine is kind and helpful.

IF YOU GO

GETTING THERE: In Lafayette, Indiana 26 becomes Columbia Street near downtown Lafayette, a one-way street going west. Turn left at Tenth Street, cross South Street with the Tippecanoe County Historical Museum on your right and next door is the Greater Lafayette Museum of Art parking lot.

INFORMATION: The museum's main entrance is on Tenth Street. There is also handicap access on Ninth Street if you ring the bell. The Web site is http://www.glmart.org; the e-mail is glma@glmart.org; the telephone number is (765) 742–1128; and the fax is (765) 742–1120. Its hours are Tuesday through Saturday 11 a.m. to 4 p.m.

FEES: No charge for admission, but donations are accepted.

RELAXING TIME. A wolf takes it easy before evening activities begin at Wolf Park near Battle Ground.

TAKE CARE OF THEMSELVES. These bison will later mix with wolves during the early part of a Sunday "hunt" at Wolf Park, as the wolves seek possible bison weaknesses. The bison, all healthy and weighing up to one ton, can more than protect themselves.

Wolf Park, Battle Ground

BATTLE GROUND—Wolves. There is research and education about wolves and then there is the version of wolves portrayed in horror movies.

If you want to find out about wolf research and education, the best place to go is Wolf Park, a sprawling complex ten miles north of Lafayette and less than two miles from historic Battle Ground. The facility offers a wide array of programs, seminars, and internships for up close learning about socialized wolf behavior.

Wolf Park wolves interact with humans—they are socialized—beginning at two weeks of age when they are taken from their mothers and hand-reared at the park. For the rest of their lives they have a lot of human contact—an average of three thousand hours with humans before they are put back with other wolves, explained a young intern who showed me around Wolf Park on a Sunday afternoon.

The result is that researchers, including those who intern, and visitors to Wolf Park have the opportunity to observe wolves behaving in a relaxed manner in their seminatural enclosures, an opportunity that is rarely available anywhere else. The intern also explained a bit about wolf status in the pack, how body language helps identify the alpha—lead—male and female.

The park, started in 1972 by a retired Purdue professor, Doctor Erich Klinghammer, whose expertise is the study of animal behavior, has as its mission giving "the public an accurate picture of one of the most misunderstood animals of all time" and improving "the lot of wolves both in captivity and in the world."

Two popular program highlights are Howl Night and wolf-bison demonstrations.

Howl Nights are at 7:30 p.m. Saturday evenings year-round and Fridays from May through November, weather permitting. In early evening, when the wolves are most active, park visitors hear a lecture about wolf behavior and life in a pack, and then it's howl time. Members of the audience—perhaps two hundred people the evening I was there—are encouraged to howl, and the wolves quickly join in.

LET'S ALL HOWL. Wolf Park founder Doctor Erich Klinghammer's Chihuahua—held in his arms—begins to howl along with the wolves when the founder encourages it by his own howling. It was all part of Howl Night at the park. That's Klinghammer's wife, Peggy, at his side.

The intern told me a large number of park visitors come for the day—1 to 5 p.m., leave to eat, and then return for Howl Night.

On Sundays at 1 p.m., also from May through November, park visitors see "the first stage" of the hunt when wolves are put with a healthy herd of bison—meaning none of the bison has a physical problem that might cause it to be brought down by the wolves. Instead, the wolves test the bison—trying to find any weaknesses in the herd.

In addition, Wolf Park schedules kids' seminars and day camps run for two days, 9 a.m. to 5 p.m. The kids' seminar is 1 p.m. Saturday to 4 p.m. Sunday. Photography seminars usually are on Monday, while the three- and five-day seminars deal with topics such as wolf behavior, wolves for artists—using wolves as their subjects, the natural history of dogs, and a wolf intensive weekend.

Then there are the horror movies. The night I was at Wolf Park, Lon Chaney Jr.'s *The Wolf Man* produced around 1940 was to be shown on an outside screen following Howl Night. It's to remind people of how different wolves are depicted from wolves seen at Wolf Park.

IF YOU GO

GETTING THERE: In western Indiana on Interstate 65, take exit 178. Go north on Indiana 43 to Indiana 225. Turn east (right) two miles to Battle Ground. Cross the railroad tracks and angle left. After one block, turn left on Jefferson Street and follow it for a mile and a half. Signs direct you into Wolf Park.

INFORMATION: Call (765) 567–2265, or go to http://www.wolfpark .org/. Current seminar signups are at www.wolfparkstore.com/. Not open on Monday.

FEES: Admission charged.

FARM HORSES. Horses get a workout at this "working farm" at Prophetstown, near Battle Ground, where the famous 1811 Battle of Tippecanoe took place.

PLAYGROUND. This play and sports area at Prophetstown State Park near Battle Ground in western Indiana officially opened in the fall of 2004.

MODERN CAMPSITE. These campsites at Prophetstown State Park have graveled areas, water, electrical hookups, and waste connections. Its 110 sites have 45 full hookups and 45 electric places.

Prophetstown State Park, Battle Ground

BATTLE GROUND—When our New York City granddaughter arrived for a summer visit, I asked her as we approached Muncie, driving through the fields south of the city, "Well, Rebecca, what do you think of Indiana?"

"Lots of corn," she answered.

Asked about Prophetstown State park, a visitor might answer, "Lots of prairie grass."

One of Indiana's newer state parks, Prophetstown isn't intended to be the usual Hoosier park—hills, trees, hunting, fishing, boating, and maybe a lodge, although most of these eventually will come, too. Rather, its goal is to emphasize the history of this part of western Indiana, where the Tippecanoe and the Wabash rivers meet. It lies to the east of Interstate 65, close to the small town of Battle Ground.

We're told that when the first white frontiersmen arrived in what is now western Indiana around present-day Lafayette, they were greeted by "a vast sea of tall grass stretching as far as your eyes could see," according to the park brochure. The state park is located on the edge of what was this grassy prairie, caused in part by long-ago glaciers and the rich soil that later formed over the glacier deposits.

Critical to the area's history was the famed nearby 1811 Battle of Tippecanoe, where a confederation of Native Americans under the leadership of the Prophet, brother of Tecumseh, struck an American force commanded by William Henry Harrison.

Harrison won the battle and immediately burned the nearby Native American village, called Prophetstown, lying along the Wabash River. (A visit to the park certainly should also include a trip to Battle Ground and the battlefield memorial.)

The park, presently made up of 2,200 acres, offers a campground with shelters and playground, in addition to picnic areas just north of the Wabash River. Hiking and bicycle trails and bird-watching are other park activities, too, and the park has seasonal interpretive services.

It's the natural beauty of the park that probably will most attract visitors. Restoring the prairie is a vital and on-going process with more and more grass and wildflowers planted

CENTERPIECE. The Gibson farmhouse is the central feature of Historic Prophetstown's depiction of Tippecanoe County farm life during the 1920s.

annually—a few more acres each time. The wetlands attract seasonal birds and waterfowl.

The goal is to have two-thirds of the park resemble the land as it might have been seen by those first pioneers and the Native Americans who inhabited the region.

Across Indiana 225, lies Historic Prophetstown, part of the state park and a 300-acre complex featuring two accounts of Indiana's bygone days.

One is a Woodland Native American Village re-creation with a council house, wigwams, cooking shelter, chief's house, and a medicine lodge. Historic Prophetstown has year-round programming, and guided tours of the grounds also are available for groups.

A second is the 1920s Wabash Valley living history farm that re-creates Tippecanoe County farm life of the period. The Gibson farmhouse also can be rented for parties, receptions, meetings, and retreats. Year-round horse-drawn carriage rides as well as seasonal sleigh rides also are available.

For a look at Indiana's past, Prophetstown State Park is well worth the trip.

IF YOU GO

GETTING THERE: Take exit 178 off Interstate 65. Turn left (south) on Indiana 43 and take the first road to the left, Burnett's Road, following it to Ninth Street. Turn right (south) and take the first left, Swisher Road, to the park entrance.

INFORMATION: For information about the park, call (765) 567–4919. For campground reservations, go to http://www.camp.IN.gov/, or call (866) 622–6746. For information about Historic Prophetstown, call (765) 567–4700, or go to www .prophetstown.org/. Prophetstown is open daily from 10 a.m. to 5 p.m.

FEES: Admission charged.

White County Courthouse, Monticello

MODERN BUILDING. White County's newest courthouse, built in the mid-1970s following the devastating tornado that swept through Monticello in 1974, destroying the old limestone courthouse.

MONTICELLO—If you're trying to build an economy focused heavily on tourism—and almost everyone is these days—then you're probably not too interested in publicizing your community's more somber news from the past.

That's fair enough, so it's understandable why advertising about White County has little to say of the April 3, 1974, day when a tornado swept through northwestern Indiana, taking a number of lives and causing an estimated $100 million in damages—in 1974 dollars.

It was particularly devastating when it struck the county seat of Monticello, located on a bluff overlooking the Tippecanoe River. The town sits on the county's eastern border with Carroll County. Included in the losses that day was the historic White County Courthouse in Monticello.

The three-story courthouse was typical of those found in a number of Indiana counties. Built in 1895 of limestone, it featured a clock tower and was a community landmark. As with most other Indiana county seats, the courthouse was the latest in a series of structures, the first a log cabin built in the early 1800s.

That limestone building was no competition, however, on this particular April afternoon for the killer winds that raced through Monticello, destroying much of the downtown district. Gone in moments were homes, businesses, schools—anything that stood in the tornado's path, including the courthouse.

Monticello literature does cite the tornado under the heading "Community Pride," by noting that the county's residents quickly came together in response to the disaster. Within two years, a $2.5 million brick and concrete, three-story courthouse had been designed, built, and dedicated.

More than thirty years later, White County residents certainly can take pride in the building. In appearance, it looks to have been constructed "yesterday." It doesn't have that "Indiana courthouse look" about it, but it's an attractive structure, both inside and out. While I didn't talk with any of its workers the day I visited there, county business seemed to be quietly and, hopefully, efficiently conducted.

COURTHOUSE FEATURE. Chandelier suspended in the foyer of the current White County Courthouse in White County, northwestern Indiana.

IF YOU GO

Adding to the building's interior attractiveness is a handsome chandelier, suspended three floors above in the courthouse's center foyer.

Right now, though, White County—not unlike almost every other county in Indiana—likes to focus on economic development and what it can offer the tourist.

High on this county's list, of course, is Indiana's largest amusement park, Indiana Beach, with its more than 150 acres of vacation attractions that, along with man-made lakes Shafer and Freeman, annually draws more than 850,000 visitors.

While Van Buren in Grant County proclaims itself the "popcorn capital of the world," White County declares itself to be "the largest producer of popcorn in the world." Perhaps both are true, but White County also boasts that it's headquarters for the popular Orville Redenbacher popcorn and for the Whirley Popcorn Popper.

And, yes, Monticello is named after Thomas Jefferson's home in Virginia.

GETTING THERE: U.S. 24 goes through Monticello in northwestern Indiana. The highway turns south where the courthouse is located on Main Street. (It jogs on Railroad Street to Washington Street.)

INFORMATION: Call the Greater Monticello Chamber of Commerce and Visitors Bureau at (574) 583–7220, or go to http://www.monticelloin.com/.

FEES: None.

LINCOLN WAS HERE. Abraham Lincoln is said to have stayed in this Delphi home, prior to his becoming president. The house was built in 1858 by Enoch Rinehart, an early Carroll County sheriff.

DOWNTOWN BUSINESSES. The New York Store and Clifford Grocery were housed at 101–105 W. Franklin Street in Delphi. The buildings are part of the town's two architectural tours.

FDR STOPOVER. Franklin D. Roosevelt stopped here in Delphi in 1920 during his campaign to become vice president of the United States. He was the guest of Mindwell Crampton Wilson, publisher of the Democratic *Delphi Citizen*.

Delphi Architectural Tours, Delphi

DELPHI—The four houses are within seven blocks of each other in this Carroll County town. They are part of two architectural tours in a town once proclaimed to be the typical midwestern city. Their owners' stories tell much about an America of the last two centuries, particularly its political mixture.

The 1857 house on East Monroe Street is referred to locally as "the Brick," since it is a brick house and was built by William Barnett, who was in partnership with John Archer, a brick mason. Listed on the National Register of Historic Homes, it later was owned by Mindwell Crampton Wilson, publisher of the *Delphi Citizen* and a strong Democrat. Among Wilson's guests over the years was Franklin D. Roosevelt while he was campaigning to be vice president on the Democratic ticket in 1920.

One block to the south on East Franklin is the 1895 house where Margaret Afflis lived. It's of the so-called Free Classic architecture. Afflis was prominent in Democratic politics from the 1930s to the 1960s and also was the mother of "Dick the Bruiser," a well-known professional wrestler.

Two blocks to the south and two to the west is an Italianate house at West Front Street, constructed in 1858 by Enoch Rinehart, whose paper mill at one time stood behind his home. It's said that Abraham Lincoln stopped at the Rineharts before he became president.

Two blocks west is another Italianate structure at West Front Street. Constructed in 1860, it was once the home of Mabel Fraser, a dominant figure in Indiana Republican politics. Perhaps the highlight of her decades' long political activity came in 1948 when she was appointed an Indiana delegate to the Republican National Convention that nominated Thomas Dewey as president.

These are four of the buildings identified in the handsome booklet, *Delphi, Indiana, an Architectural Tour*, which details two tours—one the downtown loop of a mile and the second the city loop that swings away from the downtown area, covering a mile and a half.

Delphi was an important canal town in the mid-1850s after

1896 HOME. Numerous architectural styles are found in this Delphi home at 201 E. Franklin Street. Built by a city jeweler, it cost $3,000 to construct in 1896.

the Wabash and Erie Canal reached the city in 1840. That heritage today is marked by the impressive Canal Interpretive Center. The canal, however, began to fade, in part when the Norfolk and Western Railroad came to Delphi in 1856. Nevertheless, the ever-expanding programming at the canal center has become an important tourism destination point for the city.

Two of the public buildings are the Carroll County Courthouse and the Carnegie Public Library. Both are part of the downtown loop tour.

The courthouse is Carroll County's third, built in 1917 at a cost of $250,000. The exterior is of Indiana sandstone. The Carnegie Library was constructed in 1905–6, beginning with a $10,000 grant from the Andrew Carnegie Foundation. Renovations were completed in 1990.

Other homes on the two tours were at one time occupied by U.S. Congressman Charles B. Landis, 421 W. Main; a well-to-do banker, 404 E. Main; a judge whose grandson captained a U.S. destroyer during World War II, 221 E. Franklin; the only home with a cupola, 304 W. Front; and others.

IF YOU GO

GETTING THERE: Delphi is in western Indiana at the intersection of Indiana 18, Indiana 25, and U.S. 421/Indiana 39.

INFORMATION: Tour brochures can be picked up at the Carroll County Museum in the courthouse building. The museum is open Tuesday, Thursday, and Friday 9 a.m. to 5 p.m. and by appointment. Closed for an hour at noon. Call (765) 564–3152. The Web site is http://www.carroll countymuseum.org/, and the e-mail is cchs@dcwi.com/.

FEES: None for the brochure, but donations are accepted.

REAL HORSEHIDE. William Davis had his horse's hide tanned and processed in 1920 and made into a coat and gloves. It cost him $10.50. His daughters donated them to the museum.

SANK IN THE RIVER. Resting in the rotunda of the Carroll County Courthouse, this bell graced the present courthouse's two predecessors. The bell sank in the Ohio River as it was being shipped when two steamboats collided in 1839.

SCANNING PHOTOS. Carol Oliver checks her most recent photo scanning, part of the Carroll County Historical Archives Project, as Phyllis Moore, museum curator, looks on.

Carroll County Historical Society Museum, Delphi

DELPHI—Carol Oliver sits at her desk in the Carroll County Historical Society Museum, scanning historical photographs onto her computer as part of the museum's Historical Archives Project.

While Oliver has only been scanning photos since 2000, the number she has processed has long since passed the 100,000 mark. Many are photographs that have suffered from old age even though today they are stored in acid-free folders in boxes. By scanning them onto the computer, they can be easily retrieved and the originals preserved. Some 1,300 glass plates also add to the collection.

So now, as a bow to modern technology, the present 116,500 photographs are on the museum's Web pages.

Only a few feet away from Oliver is a Conestoga wagon—a prairie schooner—used by the Peter Ruch family in its move in 1853 from Pennsylvania to Indiana. It was given to the museum by Ruch descendants in 1973.

In a way, Oliver's scanning of photographs and the Conestoga wagon represent the museum's efforts to marry the old to the new—gathering the county's history and using the technology of today to preserve it for the future.

In another bow to today and our difficult economic times, the county has ended its funding for the museum staff. Now volunteers carry on the work as best they can.

The county's historical museum traces its beginnings back to the early twentieth century. A room was dedicated to county history in the courthouse, while a call went out to bring in items about Carroll's history. They've been doing just that ever since.

There was a time, however, when the museum room was mostly closed until a local sorority cleaned it and had it open for some special occasions. Finally in 1967, the society petitioned for and received control of the museum. They have operated it since then. Space quickly became a problem. The "old assembly room" on the courthouse's first floor was repaired, and that still is where the museum is located today.

The museum can be accessed by a door on the south from the grounds of the courthouse. Or the visitor can climb the

COURTHOUSE. Carroll County Courthouse, location of the county museum in downtown Delphi.

IF YOU GO

steps to the courthouse, enter the rotunda, and go down to the museum.

The museum is packed with historical artifacts and data. While perhaps some object is somewhere in the museum that curator Phyllis Moore doesn't know about, it's unlikely. She's been the curator since the museum opened. On my visit, she immediately had an answer or went to the object in responding to every question.

The courthouse itself also is of interest. It's the county's third, built in 1917 of Indiana sandstone at a cost of $250,000. The first and second courthouses' bell is on display in the rotunda, along with an account of its perilous journey to Delphi. It seems that it sank in the Ohio River when two steamboats collided as it was being delivered from a Cincinnati foundry in 1839. The county's good citizens collected ninety-five dollars to raise it and two dollars to have it delivered.

Times aren't easy for any museums these days as already indicated. Fund-raisers to pay the costs include a history publication, *Carroll County Legacy, 1824–2005*.

GETTING THERE: The museum and courthouse sit on the downtown square in Delphi in western Indiana's Carroll County. The address of the courthouse is 101 W. Main Street.

INFORMATION: The museum is open Tuesday, Thursday, and Friday 9 a.m. to 5 p.m. and by appointment. Call (765) 564–3152. The Web site is http://www.carrollcountymuseum .org/.

FEES: None to visit the museum, but donations are accepted.

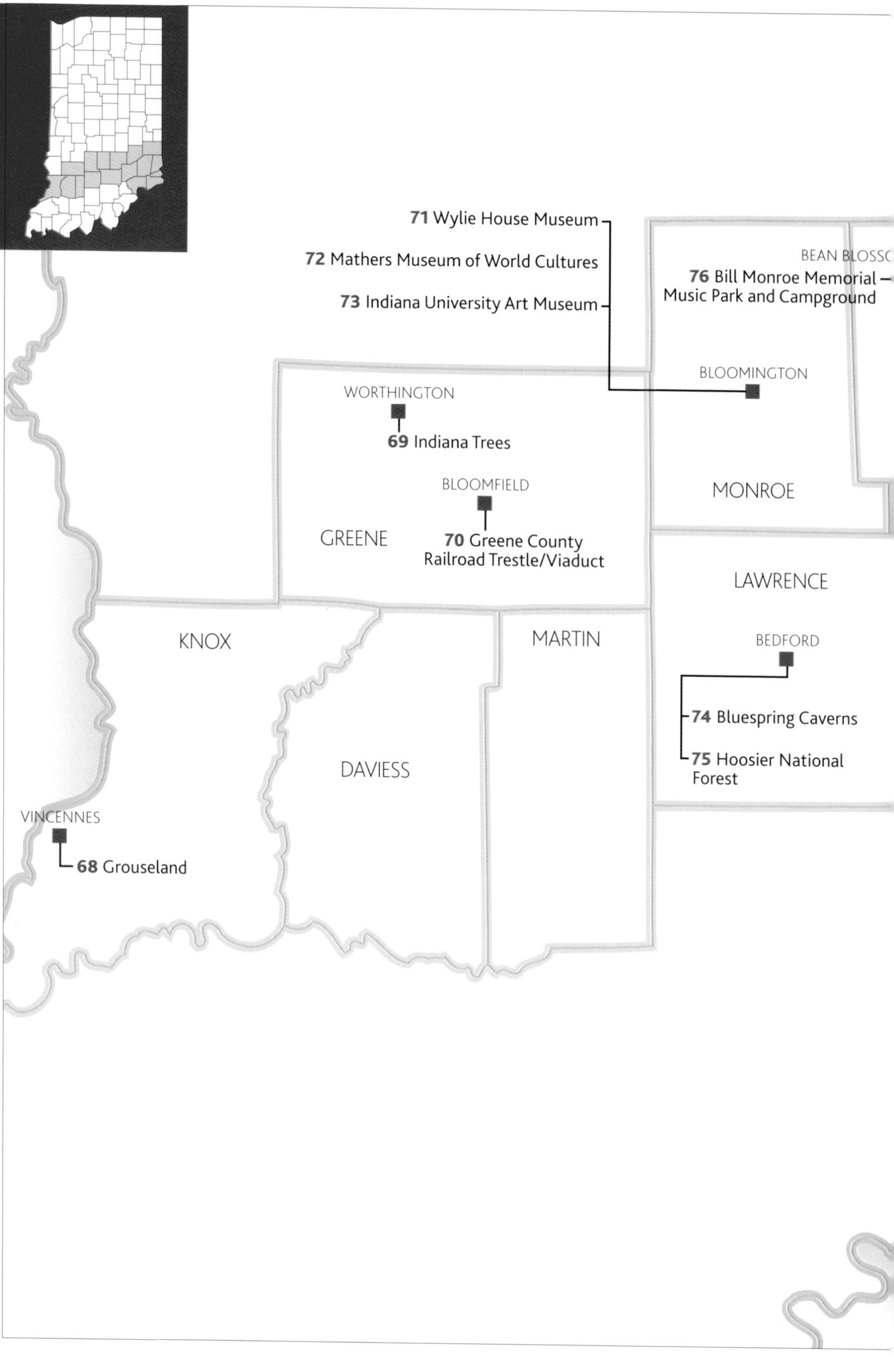

71 Wylie House Museum

72 Mathers Museum of World Cultures

73 Indiana University Art Museum

BEAN BLOSSO
76 Bill Monroe Memorial
Music Park and Campground

BLOOMINGTON

WORTHINGTON

69 Indiana Trees

BLOOMFIELD

MONROE

GREENE

70 Greene County
Railroad Trestle/Viaduct

LAWRENCE

KNOX

MARTIN

BEDFORD

74 Bluespring Caverns

75 Hoosier National
Forest

DAVIESS

VINCENNES

68 Grouseland

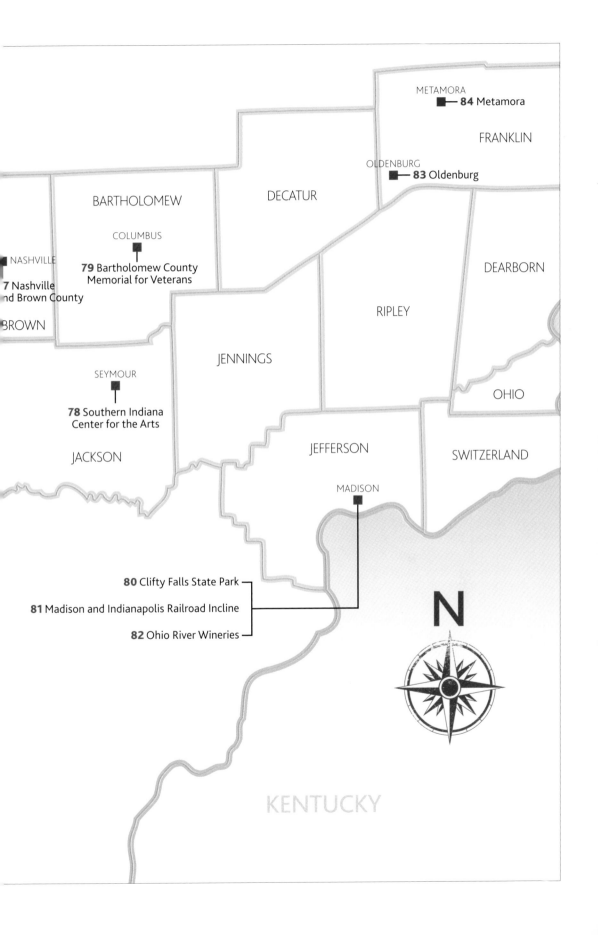

METAMORA
■— **84** Metamora

FRANKLIN

OLDENBURG
■— **83** Oldenburg

BARTHOLOMEW

DECATUR

DEARBORN

COLUMBUS
■
79 Bartholomew County
Memorial for Veterans

NASHVILLE
■
7 Nashville
nd Brown County

RIPLEY

BROWN

JENNINGS

OHIO

SEYMOUR
■
78 Southern Indiana
Center for the Arts

JACKSON

JEFFERSON

SWITZERLAND

MADISON
■

80 Clifty Falls State Park —

81 Madison and Indianapolis Railroad Incline —

82 Ohio River Wineries —

N

KENTUCKY

Grouseland, Vincennes

HARRISON. This William Henry Harrison portrait hangs in Grouseland's front hallway. The territory he governed from 1800 to 1812 included the present states of Indiana, Illinois, Michigan, Wisconsin, and Minnesota, east of the Mississippi River.

MORNING ROOM. This room, on the first floor of Grouseland's "dependency" structure, was where Anna Harrison spent part of her mornings when the Harrisons lived in Vincennes in the early 1800s.

FORMAL DINING ROOM. As the governor of the Indiana Territory, William Henry Harrison and his wife, Anna, entertained guests at their home. It was only a few decades after George Rogers Clark and his men had sloshed through wintry waters to capture the fort at Vincennes from the British in the Revolutionary War.

VINCENNES—There's that famous scene depicted in books, motion pictures, and television in which William Henry Harrison, governor of the Indiana Territory, talks to Tecumseh, chief of the Shawnee, at Harrison's home in Vincennes in one of their two historic meetings. The Shawnee had been slowly but definitely pushed west by the Americans in one treaty after another. A crisis is at hand.

Later, Tecumseh and his brother, the Prophet, formed a confederation to wage war with the Americans. Harrison's forces defeated the Prophet's warriors at the Battle of Tippecanoe in 1811—Tecumseh was not at the battle—and Tecumseh at the Battle of the Thames in 1813, where Tecumseh was killed.

But now, the two men are talking. Perhaps some peaceful solution can be found.

From the porch of Grouseland, Harrison's home at Vincennes, you see the place where the two men met. It's not that easy to visualize the meetings today. You're in the midst of the city of Vincennes.

Inside Grouseland, Harrison's home is filled with even more history.

After you ring the bell, a tour guide admits you. In my case, it was Alice Roberson, who said Harrison designed his home after an ancestral home in Virginia, the Berkeley plantation. Bricks for the outside and inside walls were fired not far away. Stone was brought up from the nearby Wabash River.

Grouseland actually was built as two structures—the front "great house" and the back "dependency" where servants stayed and Anna Harrison had her "morning room." The passageway in between was covered and eventually walled to form one building. The thirty-one year-old Harrison and his wife moved in during 1804 while he was governor of the Indiana Territory.

The home was built over a two-year period on three hundred acres of cleared land Harrison purchased. The family stayed here until 1812 when Judge Benjamin Parke moved in. A Harrison son came into possession in 1821 and Grouseland remained in the Harrison family until 1850.

GROUSELAND. When you stand on this porch, you can look out over the place in Vincennes where Governor William Henry Harrison and Tecumseh held their meeting. They were unable to settle differences between the Shawnee and the Americans. Ultimately, the Battle of Tippecanoe followed.

The home later was neglected, serving as a hotel, then a residence, and finally as storage. It was ready for the wrecker's ball in 1909.

That's when the Francis Vigo chapter of the Daughters of the American Revolution rescued it and began a restoration project, opening two rooms in 1911. Now all three floors have been restored and are open.

To the left of the entrance hall is the parlor or "council chamber" where a number of treaties were signed. To the right is the formal dining room.

If you get a little confused about the Harrisons, it's no wonder. There were five Benjamin Harrisons before 1770, including William Henry's father, a signer of the Declaration of Independence. William Henry also was the grandfather of the twenty-third president of the United States, another Benjamin Harrison, elected while he lived in Indianapolis. President Benjamin Harrison's father—John Scott Harrison was one of ten children born to William Henry and Anna Harrison.

William Henry Harrison was elected president, using the campaign slogan "Tippecanoe and Tyler too." He took office in March 1841 as the ninth president and died in office on April 4.

IF YOU GO

GETTING THERE: From U.S. 41 take the Hart Street exit (second exit) and drive to First Street. Turn right across the railroad and turn left on Scott Street.

INFORMATION: Open daily from 9 a.m. to 4 p.m. except Thanksgiving, Christmas, and New Year's Day. January and February hours are 11 a.m. to 4 p.m. For more information call (812) 882–2096 or go to http://www.grouselandfoundation.org/.

FEES: Admission charged.

Indiana Trees, Worthington

THE FAMOUS ELM. Indiana's most famous tree, or what is left of it, is sheltered under this sandstone canopy at Corydon. It is the Constitutional Elm, under whose branches delegates to the 1816 Constitutional Convention sought relief during the hot summer as they drafted the state's first constitution.

LARGEST AROUND IT. This massive sycamore trunk, measuring fifty-one feet in circumference, is all that remains of the tree that once grew along Wildcat Creek near Kokomo.

WORTHINGTON—No one in the early 1900s was really certain how old those two big sycamore trees were—more than several hundred years but probably not fifteen hundred years. About their size, however, there could be little argument. In fact, one of them may have been the world's largest.

Today's U.S. Forest Service Web site reports that sycamores frequently grow to a height of 120 feet with a circumference of about 9.5 feet.

Sycamore stumps can be found in various places around the state that have been hollowed out to form large containers, sometimes three feet or more in diameter. While they're impressive, the remains of these two Indiana sycamores are reminders of the massive trees found by settlers moving into the state in the 1800s.

In southern Indiana at Worthington, a limb from "the Big Sycamore" is all that's left of a huge tree that grew in the White River bottoms, about a 1.5 miles east of the city park where the limb was moved in 1925 and placed under a shelter.

Indiana: A New Historical Guide notes the tree was claimed to be "the nation's largest deciduous tree"—one that loses its leaves at the end of the growing season. A plaque in the park reports the tree stood 150 feet high and had a spread of 100 feet.

The trunk had a circumference of 45 feet, 3 inches measured 1 foot above ground and 42 feet, 3 inches at 5 feet above ground. Where it divided, one branch measured 27 feet, 8 inches, and the other 23 feet, 3 inches.

The tree became a tourist attraction when a postcard was published in 1911. Wind and lightning destroyed most of the tree over time. Finally, a 20-foot limb was brought to the park and mounted on a concrete base.

Farther north at Kokomo is another piece of a gigantic tree, "the Sycamore Stump." It was moved from its original site along the north edge of Wildcat Creek to Kokomo's Highland Park, in 1916. The estimate is it stood 100 feet—not as tall as the Worthington tree, but the 12-foot high stump measures a record-breaking 51 feet in circumference.

A LIMB FROM THE BIG SYCAMORE TREE THAT GREW
IN WHITE RIVER BOTTOMS ABOUT 1½ MI. EAST OF
WORTHINGTON AND WAS PLACED IN THE PARK IN 1925.
IN 1915 THE AGE OF THE TREE WAS ESTIMATED TO BE
500 YR., HEIGHT 150 FT. AND THE SPREAD 100 FT.
CIRCUMFERENCE 1 FT. ABOVE GROUND WAS 45 FT. 3 IN.
CIRCUMFERENCE 5 FT. ABOVE GROUND WAS 42 FT. 3 IN.
EAST BRANCH 27 FT. 8 IN. WEST BRANCH 23 FT. 3 IN.

ONLY A LIMB. The Worthington sycamore limb rests under this shelter at the city park in the southwestern Indiana town. Remember, this isn't the trunk but a limb of the tree.

So the folks at Kokomo claim to have the "world's largest sycamore stump."

The story goes that, when hollowed out and used as a phone booth, twenty-four people got in it. Over time, people started carving their initials into the tree trunk, so it was placed inside a protective cover at the park.

The Kokomo stump has a second historic companion at Highland Park. That's Old Ben, a stuffed steer measuring more than sixteen feet in length, more than six feet in height, and weighing in at more than two tons.

While Worthington's limb and Kokomo's stump represent the giant sycamores of a bygone day, neither is Indiana's most famous tree. That would be the "Constitutional Elm" at Corydon.

Again, most of this tree is gone. Unlike the sycamores, however, what remains hasn't been moved.

Tradition has it that delegates to the state's constitutional convention during the summer of 1816 met at least some of the time under the shade of the elm. Elm disease killed the tree in the 1920s. A sandstone covering was constructed in 1937 to protect the surviving trunk.

IF YOU GO

GETTING THERE: In Worthington, from Indiana 67 take Second Street and jog onto Worthington Street to the park. In Kokomo, from U.S. 31 turn west on Boulevard Street to the park. To Corydon, take Indiana 135, business route into the city.

INFORMATION: For Worthington, call the Linton/Stockton Chamber of Commerce (812) 847–4846 or go to its Web site at http://www.lintonchamber.org/. For Kokomo, call the Kokomo-Howard County Visitors Bureau at (800) 837–0971 or go to its Web site at http://www.kokomo-in.org/. For Corydon, call the Harrison County Convention and Visitors Bureau at (888) 738–2137.

Greene County Railroad Trestle/ Viaduct, Bloomfield

CROSSES THE VALLEY. Looking up at the pine lumber deck of the railroad track viaduct, known as X75–6, which goes for half a mile across a valley in southwestern Indiana.

STILL IN USE. A view of part of the half-mile viaduct in Greene County that still brings railroad freight trains across the Richland Creek valley.

BLOOMFIELD—Maybe I'm just not very good at understanding directions. All I can tell you is that it took four sets of directions and two and a half hours of driving—and later three telephone calls—for me to identify the route I took to what Greene County locals call the viaduct, a high railroad trestle that is supposedly one of the largest such steel structures in the world.

Even after I found it and tried to retrace my route, I wasn't certain exactly how I got there—hence, the follow-up telephone calls. The last was to Kerry Conway of the Greene County Foundation who suggested a better route than the one I tried. (See "If You Go" for directions that *might* work—plus hers.)

Here are the essentials of the trip:

Arriving in Bloomfield in Greene County, just west of Bloomington and Monroe County, I asked six persons for directions. The first two didn't have a clue. Four others each gave different sets of directions. One later telephone respondent simply stated, "When you turn on County Road 325 North, you just stay on the main paved road and it takes you right there."

The task is made more difficult because out in the county the roads change numbers as they twist and turn.

Even my trusty copy of *Indiana: A New Historical Guide* and its always precise directions failed me this time. In fairness, though, the *Guide* has this sentence: "Despite its size, the bridge is difficult to find without explicit directions."

Though several people told me there is no such intersection, I'm positive I finally at one point turned right at a T-intersection of CR 410N and CR 410E and, lo and behold, found CR 480E. The next moment, I was standing at the base of one of the viaduct's towers.

What about the trestle/viaduct?

It is only surpassed by about one hundred feet, so my information reports, by a similar railroad bridge in France. If the viaduct—officially Bridge X75–6, according to the Illinois Central Gulf Railroad—was placed on end, it would rise more than one thousand feet above the Eiffel Tower.

CEMENT BASES. The bases support the spiderlike girder spans of the Greene County viaduct, seen in the lower part of this photograph.

Its length, according to published reports, varies from 2,295 to 2,307 feet, or roughly one-half mile. (I suppose it depends on where you start measuring.) Everyone seems to agree on its height, standing 157 feet above the Richland Creek valley at its center span. It's supported by seventeen 75-foot deck plate girder spans, eighteen 40-foot girder towers, two 50-foot spans at the west end, and two 60-foot and two 45-foot spans at the east. Its weight is estimated at 2,895 tons.

The engineers' estimate back in 1905 to build the trestle/viaduct—not a bridge since it crosses only a small creek—was $200,000. The final cost was detailed by some writers to be closer to $1.5 million. One railroad official says its modern cost would be more than $20 million.

Hundreds of workers spread across "work camps" labored on the project. They mostly were blacks and Italian and Austrian immigrants. The viaduct was completed in about nineteen months.

The trestle/viaduct, which still has freight trains passing over it, was dedicated December 18, 1906.

IF YOU GO

GETTING THERE: Remember, now I was lost a number of times. But, here's how I think I got there. At Worthington, go south on Indiana 157. At 325N, before getting to Bloomfield, turn east (left). Drive through a railroad underpass and continue beyond the Beechwood Lake Christian Camp. Go under another railroad underpass and past a white frame Wesleyan church. Turn right to 480E at the T-intersection of 410N and 410E. The bridge should be in sight on your right.

Kerry Conway at the Greene County Foundation says the best way is to come in from Solsberry on the east. In Solsberry, go past Yoho's Store on 970E to 550N to 1000E. Stay to the left on 560N for several miles. At the fork, stay on 850E, crossing a bridge over Richland Creek. Turn left on 700N to Newark. Continue west out of Newark on CR 740/715/700N. Turn left on 450E. This takes you directly under the viaduct, she says.

FEES: None.

Wylie House Museum, Bloomington

TOUR GUIDE. Naomi Lawlis stands in the first-floor bedroom of the Wylie presidential home at Indiana University in Bloomington. For major occasions, the Wylies moved the furniture to the walls to augment their living room.

BLOOMINGTON—We can only imagine what life must have been like in the Wylie House in the middle of the 1800s. Fortunately, we have tour guides such as Naomi Lawlis to help us.

Andrew Wylie, the first president of Indiana University, and his wife, Margaret, built their two-story home on Second Street in 1835. Wiley presided over the new university and helped his wife supervise their ten children in their large-for-the-time house.

Actually, they had twelve children but only ten of them were with the family when they moved in. The Wylies also entertained, and, at times, they would push the pieces of furniture in their first-floor bedroom up against the wall and open the doors to have an enlarged space for their guests.

That's the way Lawlis explains it as she guides visitors around the home. During my visit, she seemed to know about everything anyone could ask concerning the Wylies and their historic home.

One example—probably well known to IU enthusiasts— would be that the present IU campus was not the site of the original campus when Wylie arrived. Rather, it was a couple of blocks down the hill to the west of the house at Second and Walnut streets. Later, it was moved to its present site, starting at Dunn Meadows.

Members of the Wylie family owned the house for nearly eighty years, first Andrew and his family and then his half-cousin, Theophilus Wylie, who was an IU librarian and science professor. The house had only one other owner before IU purchased it and restored it as the Wylie House Museum, part of the University Libraries. It is listed on the National Register of Historic Places.

According to *Indiana: A New Historical Guide,* the restorers used lumber from old houses, hand-forged iron works, and hand-tooled shutters to make the restoration as authentic as possible. Even today the house as a museum uses no electricity, although it has electricity for security systems and cleaning.

HISTORIC HOME. Built by Andrew and Margaret Wylie in 1835, this house of Indiana University's first president now is the Wylie House Museum on Second Street in Bloomington.

One of its exterior features is a double porch, one on each of its two floors. The roof also has a "captain's walk."

The grounds are worthy of note, too. The grapevines and rose bushes supposedly date back to the Civil War.

Some of the furnishings are from the Wylie family, some are carefully manufactured reproductions, and others are gifts used in other homes of the mid-1800s.

If you've toured similar houses, you will be struck by the size of the rooms, almost all of which are considerably larger than in other buildings of the period.

But, then, if you're sleeping ten children and their parents and entertaining guests, you had better have some space!

The latest project is the construction of a new education center behind the house. It will resemble a large nineteenth-century barn. Made possible by a bequest from a great-grandson of Theophilus and Rebecca Wylie, it will provide more display space, a large multipurpose room, small gift shop, and accessible restrooms.

A small back porch removed during the 1960s restoration will be replaced. The bequest also included a number of family heirlooms and family letters.

IF YOU GO

GETTING THERE: In Bloomington, take College Avenue or Walnut Street to Second Street and turn east to the Wylie House Museum at 307 E. Second Street. (The city visitors bureau is north of the city, is well marked, and is an excellent source of information.)

INFORMATION: Call (812) 855–6224 or go to http://www .indiana.edu/~libwylie/. Tours are March through November, Tuesday through Saturday 10 a.m. to 2 p.m. or by arrangement. For the Bloomington Convention and Visitors Bureau, go to http://www.visit bloomington.com/, call (800) 800–0037, or go to the office at 2855 N. Walnut Street. (In the city, it is College Avenue one-way going south and Walnut Street one-way going north.)

FEES: Tours are free.

IT'S ALL ABOUT CULTURES. The Mathers Museum of World Cultures commands East Eighth Street between Indiana and Fess avenues at Indiana University in Bloomington.

IT LOOKS LIKE OURS. If this looks like your kitchen, it might be in a museum! This is the kitchen, typical of a 1960s American home that is part of the Mathers Museum of World Cultures in Bloomington.

Mathers Museum of World Cultures, Bloomington

BLOOMINGTON—I admit, it's a pretty scary thought. Here I am, looking at a kitchen that appears to be much like the one in our last house and not that far removed from the one in our present house. And it's part of a museum display!

Well, it's not quite *that* bad.

The Mathers Museum is comparing what it was like to live in a ranch-style house in Bloomington in the United States in 1967 with living in Fanchan Tudu, Nigeria, in Africa. In other words, it's an attempt to explore these two cultures existing at the same time about forty years ago and, of course, their kitchens are part of that look.

The Mathers Museum of World Cultures is Indiana University's museum of anthropology and thought to be the only such specialized anthropology museum in Indiana. Its goals are to show the diversity of world cultures and, at the same time, illustrate the underlying unity of cultures as well as depicting universal life stages from birth to the afterlife.

As its Web site puts it, the museum gives the visitor the chance to take a trip around the world and "learn more about objects from Australia to Zimbabwe." Its primary purpose, however, is to be a teaching museum within a university setting.

Its collections include some 20,000 objects and 10,000 photographs. Obviously, as with almost all museums, not all can be on display at the same time.

When I visited for example, exhibits included Lost and Found: Art through Recycled Objects, Laughter on a Stick: Turkish Shadow Theater, Liberian Collections Project: Preserving the Past for Building the Future, To Have and To Hold: African Containers, Images of Native Americans: The Wanamaker Collection, and Thoughts, Things, and Theories . . . What Is Culture?

That's a lot to cover in less than 10,000 square feet of display space, plus making everything walk-in accessible to viewers.

The museum is made up of two buildings—according to *Indiana: A New Historical Guide,* a remodeled former fraternity house and a limestone structure constructed at a cost of a

FORMER FRATERNITY HOUSE. This building also is part of the Mathers Museum complex in Bloomington.

little more than $3 million. The museum opened in 1983.

Next door is the Glenn A. Black Laboratory of Archaeology, dedicated in 1971. Black was a self-educated archaeologist whose most prominent work was the excavation of Angel Mounds at Evansville.

Both institutions during the school year have students at work on various tasks along with staff members leading family programs, workshops, university classes, and research projects.

It has a small gift shop, featuring gift items from around the globe including jewelry, toys and games, masks, figurines, and pottery.

If you tie in a visit with some other IU activity, remember that parking on a major campus is almost always a problem. Metered parking is available a block away from the museum in the McCalla School parking lot at Indiana Avenue and Ninth Street. (See "If You Go" box for more information.)

If you park along the street in spaces reserved for residents, you run the risk of getting a ticket. I know.

I'm still having trouble seeing something resembling our kitchen in a museum!

IF YOU GO

GETTING THERE: In downtown Bloomington, at Seventh Street turn east onto Indiana Avenue. Turn north one block to the museum. Free Visitor and "A" IU permit parking available near the Indiana Avenue museum entrance. Metered and "C" and "E" IU parking available at the McCalla School parking lot. Free parking on streets during the weekends.

INFORMATION: The museum is open during school days Tuesday through Friday 9 a.m. to 4:30 p.m. and Saturday and Sunday 1 p.m. to 4:30 p.m. The entrance is at Fees Avenue and Eighth Street. The address is 416 N. Indiana Avenue. For more information or to schedule a tour, call (812) 855–6873, or go to http://www.indiana.edu/~mathers/.

FEES: None.

IMPRESSIVE ATRIUM. This photo looking up into the 110-foot atrium at the Indiana University Art Museum in Bloomington gives a view of one of the museum's most impressive features. The building was designed by the I. M. Pei and Partners architectural firm.

ANGULAR DIMENSIONS. The distinctive architectural design of the IU Art Museum on the Bloomington campus is displayed in this photo. The atrium is seen in the middle.

Indiana University Art Museum, Bloomington

BLOOMINGTON—Fortunate the art museum that is housed in a building, itself a work of art.

Naturally, art museums make do with what they have. In some communities—mostly because of the lack of funding—it's often a case of taking an older building and converting it into a museum, utilizing the space in the best way possible. More often than not, it somehow works.

If the museum actually is built as an art museum and if, in the best of all worlds, it is designed by one of the world's most renowned architects, then that community indeed is fortunate.

Such is the case at Indiana University where the firm of I. M. Pei and Partners in the mid-1970s was employed to design a new art museum. The university had established a small art gallery in 1941, mostly used as a teaching collection. Two locations later, Pei was named as architect for the new museum building. Ground was broken in 1978 with construction completed in 1982.

Today, the museum stands both as a work of art itself—essentially two triangular buildings joined by an open atrium area. It houses, according to the museum's Web site, more than 30,000 objects—paintings, prints, drawings, photographs, sculptures, ceramics, jewelry, and textiles, ranging from ancient gold jewelry and African masks to paintings by Monet and Picasso.

Its signature piece, however, may be the impressive red structure, *Indiana Arc*, made of aluminum, which graces the grounds at the museum's entrance. Created by Charles Perry, a Helena, Montana, native, it was given to the university in 1995 by anonymous benefactors in honor of former IU President and Mrs. Thomas Ehrlich.

Others easily could argue the most impressive part of the museum, located in the heart of the Bloomington campus, is its triangular atrium at the main entrance, reaching 110 feet. Serving as a backdrop for the atrium are angular stairs leading to the mezzanine and upper floors.

Inside the museum are three 10,000-plus-square-foot permanent exhibition galleries and a nearly 6,000-square-foot

INDIANA ARC. A painted aluminum sculpture by Charles Perry stands outside the main entrance to the IU Art Museum on the Bloomington campus.

IF YOU GO

special exhibitions gallery in addition to conservation and photography laboratories, a fine arts library, and, what every museum never has enough of, storage.

The permanent galleries feature art of the Western world, from Byzantine to modern times, on the first floor; Asian and ancient art on the second floor; and art from Africa, the Pacific and pre-Columbian America on the third floor. A gallery map is available and docent-led tours also are available with advance reservation.

Amenities include a coffee shop on the second floor and a gift shop on the mezzanine level.

The visitor's first concern, of course, when arriving at IU or any other major university, is parking. (See the "If You Go" box for information.) Once that's resolved, it's up to the visitor how much time to spend at the museum and, perhaps, at the nearby IU Memorial Union's art collection, too.

A monthly calendar of events is available both in electronic form and by U.S. mail upon request from the museum.

GETTING THERE: In Bloomington, from College Avenue turn onto Seventh Street toward the campus. Parking is available in the IU Memorial Union paid lot; at a few meters behind the museum; at Fee Lane and Tenth Street, north of the museum; and on Jordan Avenue, east of the museum. Bring an IMU parking ticket to the museum desk for a discount validation.

INFORMATION: Call (812) 855–5445 or (812) 855–1045 to schedule a tour. Hours are 10 a.m. to 5 p.m. Tuesday through Saturday, and noon to 5 p.m. Sunday. Gift shop hours are 11 a.m. to 4 p.m. Tuesday through Saturday. Closed on most national holidays. The Web site is http://www.artmuseum.iu.edu/.

FEES: Admission is free, but donations are encouraged.

"SHIPS PASSING IN THE NIGHT."
At least it seems that way in semidarkness as one boatload of Bluespring Caverns visitors passes another while exploring the underground Myst'ry River of the caverns.

CLOSE TO THE SIDES. Boat passengers touring Bluespring Caverns sometimes pass quite close to the sides of the caverns on their 1.25-mile trip.

Bluespring Caverns, Bedford

BEDFORD—One day the large pond was there and the next day it was gone.

It occurred during the early 1940s on the George Colglazier farm south of Bedford. Following a heavy rain, the pond simply disappeared into the earth. Not only that, but an entrance into the earth also was revealed. That entrance, still used today, allowed a look into what now is called Bluespring Caverns.

The caverns are part of a huge, pie-shaped area, beginning south of Indianapolis and spreading out across southern Indiana. Some cave experts believe more than 2,500 caves and caverns—a large cave or system of caves—exist in this part of the state, many of them still unexplored, even unknown.

The caves' histories go back thousands and thousands of years, including those times when glaciers made their way from the north, pushing rocks and soil south before them. As these glaciers later melted and receded, they left the debris they had deposited. Over more time, streams and rivers cut passageways through and around them, down into the earth to form underground streams and rivers.

Bluespring Caverns is what is considered a "young" cave—with a subterranean river, "Myst'ry River," still running through it. The underground river drains about twenty square miles and flows into the east fork of White River

Of the four public caves in southern Indiana, Bluespring is the only one in which visitors tour by boat—specially built shallow draft boats with ten seats on each side, back to back. Blind fish and crayfish live in the waters of the caverns in perpetual darkness. In addition to what tourists see, more than twenty additional miles of cave passages make Bluespring Indiana's longest public cave.

Tours are scheduled on arrival, sometimes every 15 minutes, others every 45 minutes or so—depending on the season, according to Jim Richards, who opened the caverns commercially in 1974. The tour lasts about an hour.

The tour starts at the hospitality center from where visitors walk downhill through the entrance discovered in the 1940s

TOUR ENDS. Coming back to the landing—in the middle of the photo—at Bluespring Caverns in southern Indiana. The trip through the caverns also includes a short walk to reach the boats that are one hundred feet below the surface.

and board custom-built boats for the trip of about a mile into and back out from the caverns. In some places, the boats pass within inches of the caverns' walls. Passengers are admonished not to touch the walls because residue from their hands, over time, could change the walls' physical texture.

A key moment in every cave tour comes when the guide turns off all the lights, leaving visitors in complete darkness. In Bluespring, boat passengers are asked to try to see "your hand in front of your face." Of course, they can't.

Darkness isn't the only cave constant. Another is temperature. It's always just a little above fifty degrees at Bluespring, so visitors are advised to wear at least a light jacket for warmth. Also, in times of heavy rains, tours are canceled because the underground river can be too high.

IF YOU GO

GETTING THERE: South of Bedford on Indiana 37, turn west on U.S. 50 and go one-half mile to Bluespring Caverns Road. Turn right and go one-half mile to the park entrance.

INFORMATION: Go to http://www .bluespringcaverns.com/ or call (812) 279–9471. Bluespring Caverns Park has a varied yearly schedule. The park and caverns are open in April and May, Saturday and Sunday only, 9 a.m. to 5 p.m.; Memorial Day through October 31, everyday, 9 a.m. to 5 p.m.; closed for season from November 1 through March 31, except for Overnight Adventure tours on Friday and Saturday nights for organized youth groups. Participants camp out and have breakfast one hundred feet underground as well as walking, crawling, and climbing through undeveloped parts of the caverns.

FEES: Admission charged for tours of the caverns.

FOREST OFFICE. This sign marks the Brownstown ranger district and national forest headquarters at Bedford. Most of the Hoosier National Forest lies to the south.

INSIDE THE FOREST. Many roads wind through the Hoosier National Forest in southern Indiana as do numerous hiking and horse trails, offering camping, hunting, and fishing opportunities.

Hoosier National Forest, Bedford

BEDFORD—It extends into nine Indiana counties, covering some 200,000 acres. Its rustic setting provides roads; hiking, mountain bike, and horse trails; campgrounds and picnic shelters; and hunting and fishing areas that offer scenic views of hills, valleys, and trees.

Yet, for whatever reason, many Hoosiers—especially those in northern and central Indiana—are only vaguely aware of this largest of all Indiana attractions.

It is the Hoosier National Forest.

Essentially, it is in two parts. One lies south of Brown County State Park and Yellowwood State Forest in parts of Brown, Jackson, Monroe, and Lawrence counties.

That's the smaller piece. The second, the much larger section, mostly stretches along Indiana 37 and Indiana 66 from Bedford south to the Ohio River and includes land in Lawrence, Martin, Orange, Crawford, Dubois, and Perry counties.

According to the U.S. Department of Agriculture Forest Service, the Hoosier National Forest is largely the result of poor timber cutting and farming practices and the Great Depression of the 1930s.

Southern Indiana was exploited for its virgin timber from the mid-1800s until shortly after the turn of the last century. A conservative estimate of 30 billion board feet was harvested. Families tried to farm the cut-over hills, but life was hard in this hilly land, especially with the coming of the Depression. Many farmers simply packed up what little they had and left. Population in what today is the Hoosier National Forest in 1930 was but 57 percent of that in 1890.

The national forest had its beginning in 1934 when Governor Paul V. McNutt and the Indiana legislature asked the U.S. Forest Service to begin buying land. Purchase of the first parcels followed in 1935.

Within the Hoosier National Forest boundary today is a hodgepodge of ownership: land owned by the State, the Corps of Engineers, the Defense Department, county and municipal governments, and privately owned.

The forest has twenty-eight trails, totaling 260 miles and ranging in length from one to 46.7 miles. Many are for mul-

TREES AND MORE TREES. A typical forest scene in the approximately 200,000 acres of the Hoosier National Forest, located in southern Indiana.

tiple use—hikers, mountain bikes, and horseback riders. Ten campgrounds and picnic areas are available, most of them open year-round with occupancy on a first-come basis unless reserved. (Forest information about each is available through publications, telephone, and the Web site. See "If You Go" box.)

Forest special features include the Charles Deam Wilderness of 13,000 acres; the Pioneer Mothers' Memorial Forest, an eighty-eight-acre virgin old-growth forest south of Paoli; Hemlock Cliffs, a valley of sandstone formations, waterfalls plants, and rock shelter, north of Interstate 64 between English and Birdseye; and Hickory Ridge Lookout Tower, the only remaining fire tower in the forest, offering a panoramic view of the Deam Wilderness.

If you're considering a trip into the Hoosier National Forest, the autumn months would be considered by most Hoosiers the best time to go. That's when the foliage is most colorful—one of the great things about Indiana with its four seasons, each offering its own beauty and appeal.

IF YOU GO

GETTING THERE: To go to the National Forest headquarters, turn left on the north edge of Bedford off Indiana 37 at the Forest Service sign and then left again to the office.

INFORMATION: The forest supervisor's office and Brownstown ranger district office are located at 811 Constitution Avenue, Bedford, telephone (812) 275–5987. The Web site is http://www.fs.fed.us/r9/hoosier/. A second office is located in Tell City at 248 Fifteenth Street, telephone (812) 547–7051.

FEES: None.

BLUEGRASS "FATHER." Bill Monroe, known as the father of bluegrass music, purchased land at Bean Blossom in 1951 to establish his festival and hall of fame museum.

GIFT SHOP. Oh, yes, there is a gift shop inside the Bill Monroe Hall of Fame and Country Star Museum at Bean Blossom. It is open year-round while the festival programming usually begins in mid-June.

Bill Monroe Memorial Music Park and Campground, Bean Blossom

BEAN BLOSSOM—I can only imagine what the Bill Monroe Memorial Music Park and Campground is like every June when the Bill Monroe Memorial Bean Blossom Bluegrass Festival takes place.

Scheduled for eight days, the festival is called the "oldest, continuously running bluegrass festival in the world" and the "Mecca of bluegrass music." In 2000 the International Bluegrass Music Association declared it to be the "event of the year." Photos of recent festivals show row after row of lawn chairs pulled up in the wooded amphitheater in front of its main stage.

In midwinter when I visited, the campgrounds where the stage also is located were empty—what else would you expect, of course?—but the phone was busy in the office of the Bill Monroe Bluegrass Hall of Fame and Country Star Museum with callers inquiring about summer campsites.

That was fine with me, because it was the hall of fame and museum I had traveled to Bean Blossom to see.

Incidentally, be prepared for a winding and hilly drive into Bean Blossom whether you come from the north or the south. The recommended route is into Nashville and then north on Indiana 135 five miles to Bean Blossom.

The museum consists of six rooms devoted mostly to bluegrass music. Many of the showcases hold photographs, clothing, instruments, and other memorabilia of bluegrass and country singing stars. Possibly the most eye catching is a red-sequined dress belonging to Dolly Parton, who, as everyone knows, is still a force in bluegrass and country music.

Naturally, Bill Monroe is featured, the so-called father of bluegrass who purchased the fifty-five-acre site in 1951. Included are memorabilia from his long career. Monroe moved his bluegrass museum from Tennessee to Bean Blossom in 1984. The Bean Blossom Hall of Fame and Country Star Museum was dedicated in 1986. A walkway of stars paves the museum's entrance.

Monroe first discovered Bean Blossom when he performed at the Brown County Jamboree in 1951 and, according to the museum's Web site, "fell in love with the area immediately."

CENTER OF BLUEGRASS. The Bill Monroe Bluegrass Hall of Fame and Country Star Museum is located on Indiana 135 in Bean Blossom, five miles north of Nashville in Brown County.

Monroe was considered a pillar of the Grand Ole Opry for fifty-seven years, mostly while singing his tenor vocals and playing his mandolin accompanied by his band. It's estimated nearly three hundred different musicians played as part of these bands during a sixty-six-year period.

Among his numerous citations and inductions was the National Medal of the Arts awarded him in 1995 by President Bill Clinton. Monroe died September 9, 1996, four days short of his eighty-fifth birthday.

The Bean Blossom campground opens in May and operates through November 1. Promotional materials report six hundred campsites are available, wooded and open, with electric and water hookups in addition to primitive tent sites as well as fully equipped and primitive log cabins.

Ten festivals and events were scheduled at the site the year I dropped by, beginning with the Monroe Memorial Bluegrass Festival in mid-June and concluding with the annual WM Bentley Wagon Train Jam in October. The Web site has the full list and dates.

IF YOU GO

GETTING THERE: From Nashville go north five miles on Indiana 135 to Bean Blossom.

INFORMATION: The museum is open Tuesday through Saturday 10 a.m. to 4 p.m. from November to March and daily, 9 a.m. to 5 p.m. April through October. Telephone is (800) 414–4677 and the Web site is http://www.beanblossom.com/. Reservations and general information are available at beanblossombg@ hotmail.com/.

FEES: Admission charged. Children twelve and younger, free.

DINING ROOM AND COUNTRY STORE. A longtime favorite of visitors to Nashville is the Nashville House with its dining room and country store of wares. It is on the main thoroughfare, Van Buren Street.

THE "NEW" PLAYHOUSE. For years, the Brown County Playhouse was a barn and tent structure. In 1977 the "new" playhouse was constructed. Its marquee is barely visible, nestled in between shops on Van Buren Street in downtown Nashville.

Nashville and Brown County

NASHVILLE—The autumn favorite for many a Hoosier is a drive to Brown County and especially Nashville. The trees are at their peak in color and the weather usually hasn't turned too cold. So, before autumn is gone, thousands of Hoosiers head for Nashville, generally on a weekend.

That's the problem, of course, it is bumper-to-bumper traffic. Restaurants and shops can be packed. It seems as if half the state has chosen the weekend you have for the trip.

One way to avoid the biggest crowds is to go during the week. Another tactic is to pick out some place other than the two best-known sites—Brown County State Park and downtown Nashville.

One possibility would be to drive into Nashville and then, instead of turning right into the downtown, hang a left and follow Indiana 46 to Yellowwood State Park. It doesn't have all the conveniences and special activities of Brown County State Park, but if it's trees you want to see, then Yellowwood with its 23,400 wooded acres certainly has them.

If you make it into downtown Nashville and you haven't already selected exactly what you want to do, it would be a good idea to go by the Brown County Visitors Center at the northwest corner of Main and Van Buren streets.

The center is well stocked with brochures about the county. Its personnel seem to have information at their fingertips. While I was there, a steady stream of people were in for help.

Visitors to Nashville and the county are drawn there for reasons beyond the fall colors. Brown County historically has been an arts and crafts and painting center for the state. T. C. Steele was perhaps the best known of the so-called Indiana Group of artists who flourished in the early 1900s.

That's another trip possibility—stay on Indiana 46 to Belmont, heading toward Bloomington, and then turn left. That will take you to Steele's home and painting studio, "the House of the Singing Winds." Today, a strong resident community of painters, mainly of landscapes, still exists, centered in Nashville.

BROWN COUNTY COURTHOUSE. This 125-year-old red-brick court-house still serves as the seat of government for Brown County. It is on the northeast corner of Main and Van Buren streets, across from the visitors center.

One not-to-miss spot is the Brown County Art Gallery and Museum, a not-for-profit started in 1926, making it one of the Midwest's older galleries.

Along with the artists in Nashville and around the county are art dealers as well as other specialty art shops—in all, more than 350 of them. Many visitors park their cars and then spend hours slowly moving up and down the streets, ambling into this shop and then that one. This is one trip you don't want to hurry through.

Nashville also is increasingly known as an entertainment center. Its two best-known venues are the Brown County Playhouse and the Little Nashville Opry.

The playhouse, Indiana's longest-running professional summer theater, presents programming through October. The Opry brings in top-flight stars from the other Nashville—and at realistic prices. Its presentations run from March through November.

Also, take a moment to go a block beyond the courthouse to the Pioneer Village and Museum. It alone can be worth the trip.

IF YOU GO

GETTING THERE: Indiana 46, accessible from Bloomington, Indiana 37 on the west, and Columbus and Interstate 65 on the east, all go to Nashville and Brown County.

INFORMATION: Go to the Brown County Visitors Center's Web site at http://www.browncounty.com/, call (800)753–3255, or stop at the office at the northwest corner of Main and Van Buren streets in Nashville.

FEES: Depends on the venue.

TEACHER AND STUDENT. Joan Olson instructs a young student in a second-floor studio at the Southern Indiana Center for the Arts.

THE CAGE. Former Center Executive Director Allen Dale Olson opens the metal cage used as a prop by John Mellencamp in his motion picture, *Falling from Grace*.

MISSY. This 1992 oil on canvas painting by John Mellencamp is one of his earlier works. It is part of his collection on display at the Southern Indiana Center for the Arts.

Southern Indiana Center for the Arts, Seymour

SEYMOUR—The Southern Indiana Center for the Arts can't complain about the rent—one dollar every two years. That's what John Mellencamp charges for the 1851 Greek revival, two-story-brick house and property located on the north side of Seymour.

Mellencamp bought the house in 1989 for use in a motion picture, *Falling from Grace*. It was filmed in the Seymour area and released in 1993. Later, he felt he wanted to do something for the arts in southern Indiana, so he made the local arts council a deal: Use the property for the arts and you can have it for one dollar every two years.

"John is a good landlord," Allen Dale Olson, the center's former executive director, told me when I visited there. "If the roof blows off, he repairs it. If we kick it off, we have to pay for it. He made sure it got rewired, the trim gets painted—all the things a landlord should do. He never attempts to manage, but he does come to visit."

The center has the only public venue of paintings by Mellencamp and also some by his mother, Marilyn Mellencamp.

"John started painting rather late in life," Olson said. "He is largely self-taught. When he was a kid, he thought he was not a very good painter. He watched his mother paint and thought, probably as part of his rebellion, 'I'm not going to paint.' At a time when he thought his music career was over, he went to museums in Paris with a friend and saw paintings there, and said, 'Hey, I can do that.' So, he came back here and, with a few lessons, took off painting," Olson revealed.

Olson has an average of one request a day to buy one or more of Mellencamp's paintings. "Theoretically, they're all for sale," Olson stated.

The center, in addition to its connection with the Mellecamps, offers a broad array of art instruction, programs, and exhibits, with more on the way. Funding comes from the Mellencamp Fan Club "and many other sources," said Olson. Recently, the Southern Indiana Center for the Arts has done more than in the past to sustain these programs, according to Dick Parman, the current director.

SOUTHERN CENTER. This 1851 brick home is the main building for the Southern Indiana Center for the Arts, located north of Seymour. It was built by a local merchant, John Kester, and is owned today by musician John Mellencamp.

During the summer, for example, the center hosts three weeks of summer art camp.

A permanent external gallery at the Seymour Memorial Hospital, juried art shows, arts education classes, lectures, workshops, a visiting Louisville potter, open house at the pottery shop in the barn every Saturday, exhibitions, arts library, and outdoor programs when weather permits are other center activities.

Also on the premises, and of considerable interest to Mellencamp fans, is the cage used by Mellencamp in his semibiographical motion picture. According to Mellencamp's character in the movie, "The daring thing for redneck, good old boys to do was to get in a cage while your friends drove a pickup truck as fast as they could down a gravel road. Then they would push you out and drag you a few miles while you tried to hold on to straps inside the cage. The sparks would fly."

The movie, still seen from time to time late at night, ends with Mellencamp recovering in a hospital.

IF YOU GO

GETTING THERE: From Interstate 65, take exit 55 and continue south on Indiana 11 toward Seymour for two and one-half miles. The center is on your right. Its address is 2001 N. Ewing Street.

INFORMATION: Call (812) 522–2278 or fax (812) 524–8406. Its e-mail address is sica@hsonline.net. The Web site is http://www.soinart.com/. The center is open to visitors Tuesday through Saturday noon to 5 p.m., or by appointment.

FEES: None for a tour. Donations, of course, are accepted.

26 November 1944
From Daddy to my sweet little darling Emmylou.
    I know your sweet mother and Grandma will show you a nice Xmas and the way the war news sounds, I am sure that your Daddy will be back next year sometime.
    So, you keep your Mother in good spirits.
    Love,
    Daddy

PFC Erven Meyer, U.S. Army, was killed in action in Belgium January 7, 1945.

MEMORIAL LETTER. Erven Meyer's letter to his daughter, written a little more than a month before he was killed in action in Belgium during World War II, is one of those appearing on the limestone columns.

VIEW FROM SOUTH. The Bartholomew County Courthouse stands behind the memorial for veterans in this photo looking north.

Bartholomew County Memorial for Veterans, Columbus

COLUMBUS—It's a brief letter, one of a number inscribed on sides of limestone columns standing on the Bartholomew County Courthouse square:

26 November 1944

From Daddy to my sweet little darling Emmylou, I know your sweet mother and Grandma will show you a nice Xmas and the way the war news sounds, I am sure that your Daddy will be back next year sometime. So keep your Mother in good spirits.

Love, Daddy

Private First Class Erven Meyer didn't live to see Emmylou the next year. He was killed in action January 7, 1945, in Belgium.

His poignant letter to his daughter is but one of the personal stories reflected in the Bartholomew County Memorial for Veterans, erected on the courthouse lawn and dedicated May 30, 1997, to honor the 170 men and a single woman from the county who died in America's wars during the twentieth century.

The lone woman, incidentally, was Jeanne Lewellen Norbeck, a Columbus native, who served as a test pilot during World War II. She died in a plane crash while flying a military aircraft.

One of the letters on the columns is from the Canadian commanding officer of a Bartholomew County young man, Orville Moyer, killed in World War I. Moyer was one of the men who enlisted in Canadian and British armies before the United States went to war.

The idea for the memorial originated when county commissioners noted the low attendance at a program honoring veterans.

"Some county commissioners were disappointed because so few attended the memorial service and thought something needed to be done to honor these persons who gave their lives before they were forgotten," said Rene Campbell, former executive director of the Columbus Area Visitors Center. "It was a grass roots campaign, although the Cummins founda-

MEMORIAL FOR VETERANS. This memorial on the Bartholomew County Courthouse square consists of twenty-five, forty-foot limestone shafts. The interior walls contain the names of those from the county who died in twentieth-century wars.

IF YOU GO

GETTING THERE: From Interstate 65 south, turn east toward Columbus on Indiana 46 and take the Second Street exit to the courthouse square.

INFORMATION: To inquire about the memorial, the courthouse, and other Columbus sites, call the Columbus Area Visitors Center at (800) 468–6564, go to http://www .columbus.in.us/, or stop at the visitors center at 506 Fifth Street.

tion did pay the architectural fees as they have for many other buildings," she added.

The memorial, costing about $800,000, was built with funds raised during a mid-1990s campaign. It had widespread support. The fund-raisers hoped to sell two thousand bricks at twenty-five dollars each for the Veterans Walk of Honor, but instead more than six thousand were sold.

The memorial is located in a plaza south of the Bartholomew County Courthouse in downtown Columbus. It includes twenty-five, forty-foot limestone columns, which appear to be standing in formation in silent tribute to the dead.

Like many of Columbus's structures, the memorial also is an award winner. Designed by the architectural firm of Thompson and Rose, it won the Boston Society of Architects' Unbuilt Architecture Design Award in 1996.

While you're visiting the memorial, you will also want to inspect the courthouse.

Built in 1874, the French Renaissance structure underwent renovations in 1928, 1953, 1969, and 1998. Some additional interior work has been completed in more recent years. It looks as good as new.

RUGGED TERRAIN. Much of Clifty Falls State Park is hill country with ravines and gorges.

HANOVER CAMPUS. Also nearby to the state park and sitting on the Ohio River is the attractive Hanover College campus

Clifty Falls State Park, Madison

MADISON—It's never too early or out of season to plan trips to some of Indiana's state parks, especially if you're heading south—for instance, to Clifty Falls State Park.

The thirty-one-room motor lodge with its covered walkways was remodeled a few years ago while the forty rooms of the river-view lodge also have been remodeled and upgraded. Guests in the river-view rooms can look out over the Ohio River valley.

The remodeling included a new lobby for the main building, library, gift shop, and indoor swimming pool. They make a classy addition to the state park's inn facilities, but if you're thinking mostly about spellbinding scenery, a chance to walk in the warm sunshine of day or the cool breeze of evening, or in getting close to geological history, these go far beyond the state park's inn.

The park's 1,416 acres includes the Clifty Canyon Nature Preserve, 178 acres located in the canyon acres of the park. Hiking is only permitted on designated trails to protect its geological and ecological nature.

The original park, created in 1920, was half its present size and consisted mainly of the canyon and its waterfalls. The size was doubled with the acquisition of land from the Madison State Hospital in 1965.

The park and surrounding area are survivors of the Ice Age when the waters from the north met the newly formed Ohio River. One result in the park is its waterfalls. There are no man-made efforts to increase either the water flow or height of the falls, so they have a small watershed and are best observed from January through June when there is maximum water runoff.

The Department of Natural Resources estimates that Clifty Falls at one time was more than two hundred feet high. Over the centuries, the falls have cut their way through the bedrock so that now they are two miles north of their original position and the water drop of both Big Clifty and Little Clifty is sixty feet in height.

A third falls, Hoffman Falls, about in the center of the park, is seventy-eight feet. Tunnel Falls is the highest waterfall in the

LIKE PULLING BACK A BLANKET. Fog covered the Ohio River at Clifty Falls State Park this morning. Then, about 9:30 a.m., like a blanket being pulled back from the Indiana side (lower center), the fog receded and a short time later it was gone. This photo was taken from the park's observation tower overlooking the river.

park at eighty-three feet even though it can be almost dry in the autumn.

As you drive or hike around the park you see extremely hilly and rugged country with numerous deep ravines and gorges. Underfoot are shale and limestone rocks that were formed an estimated 425 million years ago.

The park's ten walking trails range in description from easy to very rugged. The "easy" one—Trail 10—is a three-quarter-mile jaunt that starts at the back of the swimming pool parking lot. "Very rugged"—Trail 2—is a three-mile effort.

The park also has the picnic tables and shelter houses, naturalist programs, and playgrounds that you come to expect at Indiana state parks. There are tennis courts near the inn.

One highlight is the observation tower just past the inn on Trail 1 as you enter the park from Indiana 56. It offers a sweeping view of the Ohio River, both up and down stream. The tower is only a short walk from the nature center parking area, and is one of those places where you will want to stay awhile.

IF YOU GO

GETTING THERE: Approaching Madison from the north on U.S. 421, either go west on Indiana 62 to enter the park's north gatehouse, or stay on U.S. 421 into Madison, go west through town on Indiana 56 to enter the south gatehouse.

INFORMATION: The state park telephone number is (812) 273–8885. The fax is (812) 265–6662. The toll-free telephone number for Clifty Inn is (877) 563–4371.

FEES: Park admission fee and inn charges.

HISTORICAL MARKER. This historical marker along Indiana 62 in Madison provides the basic details about "the Madison Hill Incline and Cut."

ABANDONED INCLINE. Somewhat covered by more recent growth, the Madison incline is pictured where it was cut into the cliffs above Madison. Builders created a 5.89 percent grade that allowed railroad cars to be pulled up the incline for a run north to Indianapolis.

Madison and Indianapolis Railroad Incline, Madison

MADISON—The evidence was clear. Madison's leading citizens could tell that what had worked in the early 1800s no longer would allow their city to remain one of the state's leading business and shipping centers in the mid-1800s.

For years, the Ohio River had been the main source of entry into the Indiana Territory and later to the new state as the principal source of navigation and commerce. Madison had grown from a small village to become the largest town in the new state of Indiana in 1816.

The next several decades were even better as the population doubled every ten years. However, it wasn't only the river this time that made Madison's "golden age" possible.

It was a road and the railroad.

The road was completed first. Of course, it wasn't a road in the modern sense of the word, but it did connect Madison to the new state capital of Indianapolis and on to Michigan City at the Indiana-Michigan border. The so-called Michigan Road was constructed between 1831 and 1834.

What made perhaps a greater difference, however, was the Madison and Indianapolis Railroad. It originally was approved in 1832 as part of the state's massive internal improvements plans, which also included the Wabash and Erie Canal. But when the state nearly went belly-up financially in the early 1840s, the costs of building the railroad fell to a newly organized Madison group, the Madison and Indianapolis Railroad Company.

They had gone to work in 1836, completed the incline by 1841, and reached Indianapolis in 1847. Now, the "iron horse" could bring the products of central Indiana down to the river and goods could go north from Madison to the northern part of the state.

The biggest challenge for the railroad, however, lay within a mile of the river city. Just to the north of Madison were high cliffs, some reaching as high as four hundred feet.

What needed to be accomplished was to cut into that cliff to create an "incline" up which a locomotive could either pull or push freight cars. (They did both.) According to the plaque at the site, workers constructed what still is considered the

THE RUEBEN WELLS. This locomotive used on the Madison incline now is on display at the Indianapolis Children's Museum.

steepest standard gauge main railroad track "ascended by wheel-adhesion locomotives in the U. S."—although *Indiana: A New Historical Guide* carefully terms it to be "one of the steepest."

The "Madison Hill Incline and Cut" measures 7,012 feet in length and rises 413 feet to create a 5.89 percent grade. Some half million tons of rock and earth had to be moved in its construction.

Individual railroad cars first were pulled to the top of the incline by horses or oxen and the train then reassembled. Later, locomotives using a rack-and-pinion system were employed. Finally, a fifty-five-ton locomotive, the Reuben Wells, was built that could tow cars to the top without the use of cogs. That's how the railroad operated until 1905.

The line no longer is in use but the incline still can be seen from Indiana 56 just west of downtown Madison. Naturally, no one is going to drive down to the Ohio River to see an abandoned railroad line. As everyone knows, however, Madison has much more year-round to offer the visitor.

IF YOU GO

GETTING THERE: Coming from the north, take U.S. 421 into Madison. The incline can be seen at the bridge on Main Street (Indiana 56) one block west of Cragmont Street just west of where Indiana 7 turns north.

INFORMATION: Call the Madison Area Convention and Visitors Bureau at (800) 559–2956. The Web site is http://visitmadison.org/. Call for specific information about sites, hotels, bed-and-breakfasts, tours, hours, etc.

FEES: None.

HOW IT'S DONE. This equipment is used by the Thomas Family Winery in Madison to produce its wines. That's the wine press to the left. The wine-tasting room serves breads and cheeses but, deliberately, no meals.

NORTH OF TOWN. Madison Vineyards—complete with vineyards—lies just off U.S. 421, north of Madison.

IN DOWNTOWN MADISON. The Thomas Family Winery is located in downtown Madison in an 1855 structure.

Ohio River Wineries, Madison

MADISON—When the Dufour brothers from Switzerland came down the Ohio River in 1802, they stopped in southeastern Indiana Territory at today's Vevay. There they set about doing what they knew best: building terraced vineyards and marketing their wines.

Over time, they became important citizens of Switzerland County and exported wines from what has been called the first commercial vineyards in the United States. (Earlier vineyards established by Thomas Jefferson and others along the East Coast were family ventures, not commercial.)

The Dufour wine-making tradition continues today in thirty-five Indiana wineries, five of them located either along the Ohio River in southeastern Indiana or in the hills that form the Ohio valley, sloping down to the river. A sixth is farther west near New Albany. Of the other five, three are in Madison.

Vineyards and wine making in Indiana have had a recent revival. Indiana was the tenth largest U.S. wine producer in the 1880s, but plant diseases and finally Prohibition about killed the industry. Only since the state legislature's passage of the Small Winery Act in the early 1970s has a rebirth occurred. With about a penny from every bottle sold funding the Indiana Wine Grape Council and research at Purdue University, today several hundred acres of grapes are cultivated—minuscule compared to the thousands of acres in the 1880s.

Obviously, all the Indiana wines now produced do not come from Indiana grapes—only about 30 percent. Others are from grapes imported from New York and the West Coast.

All six southern Indiana wineries welcome visitors to have a taste or two. To the east are the Chateau Pomije Winery at Guilford, set in the heart of the original Dufour wine country but not on the river, and The Ridge Winery, located along the river at Vevay.

Growing its grapes as part of a 550-acre family farm is the Huber Orchard and Winery, located just north of New Albany at Starlight, Indiana. It's quite an operation with a farm market, bakery, cheese factory, petting zoo, and gift shop in addition to the vineyards and winery.

LANTHIER WINERY. The old part of the building at the left was an eighteenth-century fort. It's next door to the railroad station and museum, two blocks from the Lanier state historic site and one hundred yards from the river.

However, it's at Madison—between Chateau to the east and Huber to the west—where the visitor can see three wineries

Only two blocks from the Lanier mansion is the Lanthier Winery. It's in an eighteenth-century fort that has since been added onto. The owners also serve meals upstairs by reservation.

Down the street to the east is the Thomas Family Winery. It is in a rehabilitated carriage house and stable, built around 1855.

Just to the north of Madison off U.S. 421, is Madison Vineyards, where the owners put in their first grape plantings in 1994. Their goal is to have 100 percent estate wines.

One criticism of Indiana wines over the years has been that the red wines are not as satisfying as those from other parts of the world. Purdue's vineyard researchers have been working on that plus other questions such as the best vessels for producing wine—oak or stainless steel—and whether a certain grape has a better flavor if grown in northern or southern Indiana.

Find out for yourself.

IF YOU GO

GETTING THERE: Take U.S. 421 south into Madison.

INFORMATION: Wineries east to west along the river:

Chateau Pomije, 25043 Jacob Road, Guilford 47022. (800) 791–9463. http://www.cpwinery.com/.

The Ridge Winery, 298 Indiana 156, Vevay 47043. (812) 427–3380. http://www.theridgewinery.com/.

Thomas Family Winery, 208 E. Second Street, Madison, 47250. (800) 948–8466. http://www.thomas familywinery.us/.

Lanthier Winery, 123 Mill Street, Madison, 47250. (800) 419–4637. http://www.lanthierwinery.com/.

Madison Vineyards, 1456 East 400N, Madison, 47250. (888) 473–6500. http://www.madisonvineyards.com/.

Huber Orchard, 19816 Huber Road, Starlight, 47106. (800) 345–9463. http://www.huberwinery.com/.

Indiana Wine Grape Council, Purdue, 47907-1160. (800) 832–9463. http://www.indianawines.org/.

FEES: Wine tastings are free.

PEARL/PERLEN, WATER/WASSER.
The intersection of Pearl Street/
Perlen Strasse and Water Street/
Wasser Strasse in Oldenburg. The
English/German street signs honor
the town's German heritage.

MOTHERHOUSE. The main
entrance to the motherhouse—also
showing one of the village's
spires—of Sisters of Saint Frances in
Oldenburg.

Oldenburg

OLDENBURG—If you travel around the state and stop to
check out various places, you know that some can be toured
and enjoyed while you are on foot but only if you more-or-less
work at it. The site might not really be set up for touring and
you may even need to improvise. That's okay and usually there
are reasons why, chiefly that accommodating the tourist isn't
high on the priority list.

For many others, of course, the opposite is true. They
welcome visitors and have organized walking tours, frequently
even offering maps to facilitate your trip.

Such is the case of the Immaculate Conception Convent,
the extensive complex of the Sisters of Saint Francis at Oldenburg. Because of the convent's buildings and other church
structures, Oldenburg has become known as "the village of
spires."

Set in an old German settlement that itself is a tourist center, walking the grounds and visiting the buildings are made
simple tasks through the use of an attractive, color brochure.
One can be picked up at a box outside the complex's Central
Building, facing Main Street/Haupt Strasse. (Oldenburg streets
carry both English and German names and spelling.)

The brochure identifies sixteen stops, all but one in the im-
mediate main complex. The exception is Michaela Farm, three
hundred acres not far away by following Main Street. The farm
was "revitalized" in 1992 to emphasize the merger of agriculture, education, and spirituality.

The Oldenburg Franciscan community was founded in 1851
by Mother Theresa Hackelmeier, who came to Indiana from
Vienna, Austria, at the request of the Reverend Francis Joseph
Rudolf, pastor of Holy Family Parish from 1843 to 1866, to
assist with the settlers coming into southern Indiana, many of
them German Catholics.

Some of them settled on land where William George had
first taken up living in 1817 only a year after Indiana became
a state. What was to become the town of Oldenburg, incorporated in 1869, took on much of the flavor of the German
towns these settlers had known back home. The town was

STOPPING-OFF PLACE. Der Perlen Strasse Pub, near the Sisters of Saint Francis community in Oldenburg, is one of the numerous stopping-off places to visit in the quaint German-like village.

IF YOU GO

GETTING THERE: From Interstate 74 southeast of Indianapolis take the Batesville/Oldenburg exit, Indiana 229, north two miles.

INFORMATION: Call the Sisters of Saint Francis at (812) 934–475, the Web site is http://www.oldenburg franciscans.org/. The Franklin County Convention, Recreation and Visitors Commission telephone number is (866) 647–6555, and the Web site http://www.franklincountyin.com/.

FEES: None.

named after the Dukedom of Oldenburg from which many had come.

The Sisters of Saint Francis community includes one large building that has been added to over the years, first a chapel in 1889, a motherhouse and offices in 1901, and an infirmary in 1959. Extensive remodeling took place in the 1990s. The first two-story convent on the site was destroyed by fire in 1857.

Your stroll—and that's what it needs to be—takes you by Oldenburg Franciscan Center, now a public retreat center, the present cemetery and its Memorial Chapel, the Our Lady of Fatima Shrine and Oldenburg Academy. Formerly a girl's boarding school the academy has been converted into a coed college prep school.

I'm sure I've missed some important structures. There are the powerhouse and the carpenter shop as well as an interesting convent wall along Pearl Street/Perlen Strasse.

This is to say nothing about the rest of Oldenburg.

Our stop included a relaxing time at nearby Der Perlen Strasse Pub, where, of course, a German beer seemed appropriate. And it was.

GETTING THE DAY UNDER WAY.
Only a few visitors were around as
the business day started during the
writer's recent visit to Metamora.
The fourth building from the corner
on the right side of Main Street
is the historic Martindale Hotel
(1838–70).

ORDERING ICE CREAM. A Cincinnati family checks out the menu
at the old-fashioned soda fountain
in Mr. Fudge's Confectionery in
Metamora. Mom recalled "Dad
used to bring me here" and said
she wanted her family to have the
experience.

Metamora

METAMORA—Boat traffic on the canal in Metamora remained idle for one hundred years.

In the mid-1800s, the Whitewater Canal linked Hagerstown
with Cincinnati, passing through Metamora. Whatever success it had was short-lived and within a few years the canal's
towpath had become the rail bed for the White Water Valley
Railroad Company.

Indiana had nearly gone bankrupt attempting to build and
maintain a statewide system of canals. The Department of
Natural Resources estimates the state spent more than $1
million—in 1830s money—building the Whitewater Canal and
keeping its fifty-six locks and seven feeder dams in repair.

It was a century before a portion of the canal at Metamora
was restored, first by private businessmen and later by the
state. Another twenty years or so and other entrepreneurs
began to set up shops in the community along the old canal.
Today, most of central Indiana, if not a wider midwestern
audience, at least knows about Metamora.

While shopping is what draws most of the town's visitors,
the effort at restoring the canal also has appeal. During the
summer months, a canal boat operates, crossing by aqueduct
over Duck Creek, sixteen feet below. (Metamora originally
was called Duck Creek Crossing.) Flood waters destroyed the
aqueduct in 1847 and it was replaced by the present structure. According to the DNR, it is the only remaining covered
wooden aqueduct still in use in the United States.

Locks have been restored, the most recent being a lock next
to U.S. 52 east of Metamora. The mill museum in Metamora
was dedicated by Governor Otis Bowen in 1973.

In peak season now, up to seventy shops, restaurants, historic sites, and bed and breakfasts are open for the thousands
of visitors who come through Metamora. (Shops that are open
usually have a flag flying in front. No flag probably means
it's a private residence of some of the 250 people who live in
Metamora year-round.)

A free newspaper, available in the town, contains a self-
guided tour of a number of Metamora's buildings. The tour

DUCK CREEK AQUEDUCT. This covered aqueduct is believed to be the only one in use in the nation. It replaced one destroyed by flood waters in 1847. The aqueduct is about a city block from the east edge of the Metamora shopping area.

includes an 1845 gristmill, originally opened as a cotton mill, which has been rebuilt twice over the years because of fires. To its east is a classic example of Federal architecture, the two-story Banes House, built of brick in 1840 with a central staircase and fireplaces in each room, later replaced by cast-iron stoves.

While most of these buildings were constructed around the same time, possibly the oldest is the Martindale Hotel building, first built in 1838 as the center of activities for the canal's shipping agent. Later, a wing was added to make it a hotel.

Over the years, we have made a number of trips to Metamora. I have never seen it busier than shortly before Christmas, although I'm told the really busy time is Canal Days in early October, which has "wall to wall" people. On our Christmas trip, we took the Whitewater Valley Railroad down from Connersville. What a great experience—coming, going, shopping, eating!

IF YOU GO

GETTING THERE: Metamora is on U.S. 52, eight miles west of Brookville.

INFORMATION: Call the Merchants Association of Metamora at (765) 647–2109. The Web site is http://www.metamoraindiana.com/OrgMerchAsscn.htm. Between January and March, only a few shops are open. April through Christmas is considered the Metamora season.

FEES: None to visit. Free parking is obtained by entering Metamora off U.S. 52 at either end of the town.

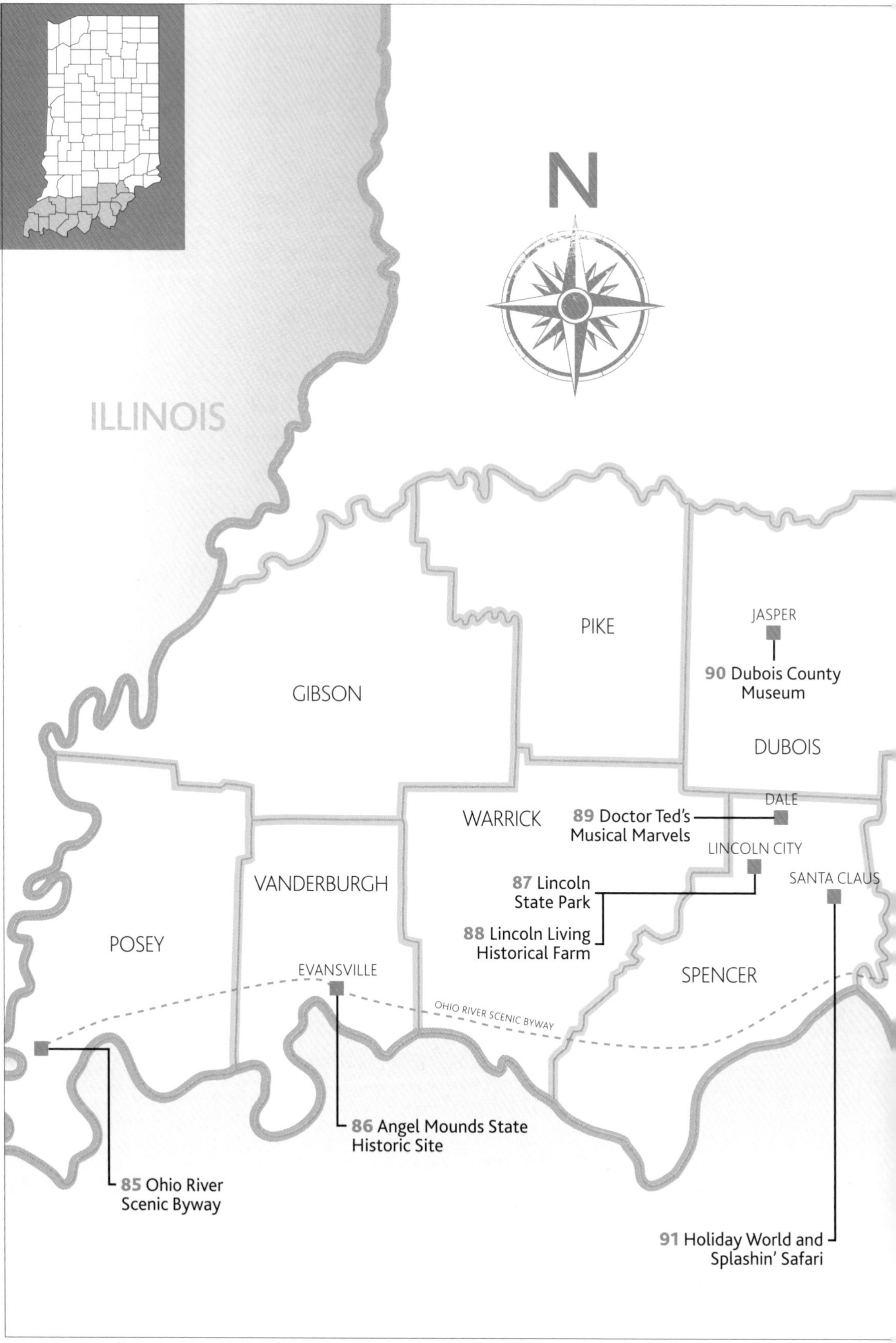

N

ILLINOIS

JASPER

PIKE

GIBSON

90 Dubois County
Museum

DUBOIS

DALE

WARRICK

89 Doctor Ted's
Musical Marvels

LINCOLN CITY

SANTA CLAUS

VANDERBURGH

87 Lincoln
State Park

88 Lincoln Living
Historical Farm

POSEY

SPENCER

EVANSVILLE

OHIO RIVER SCENIC BYWAY

86 Angel Mounds State
Historic Site

85 Ohio River
Scenic Byway

91 Holiday World and
Splashin' Safari

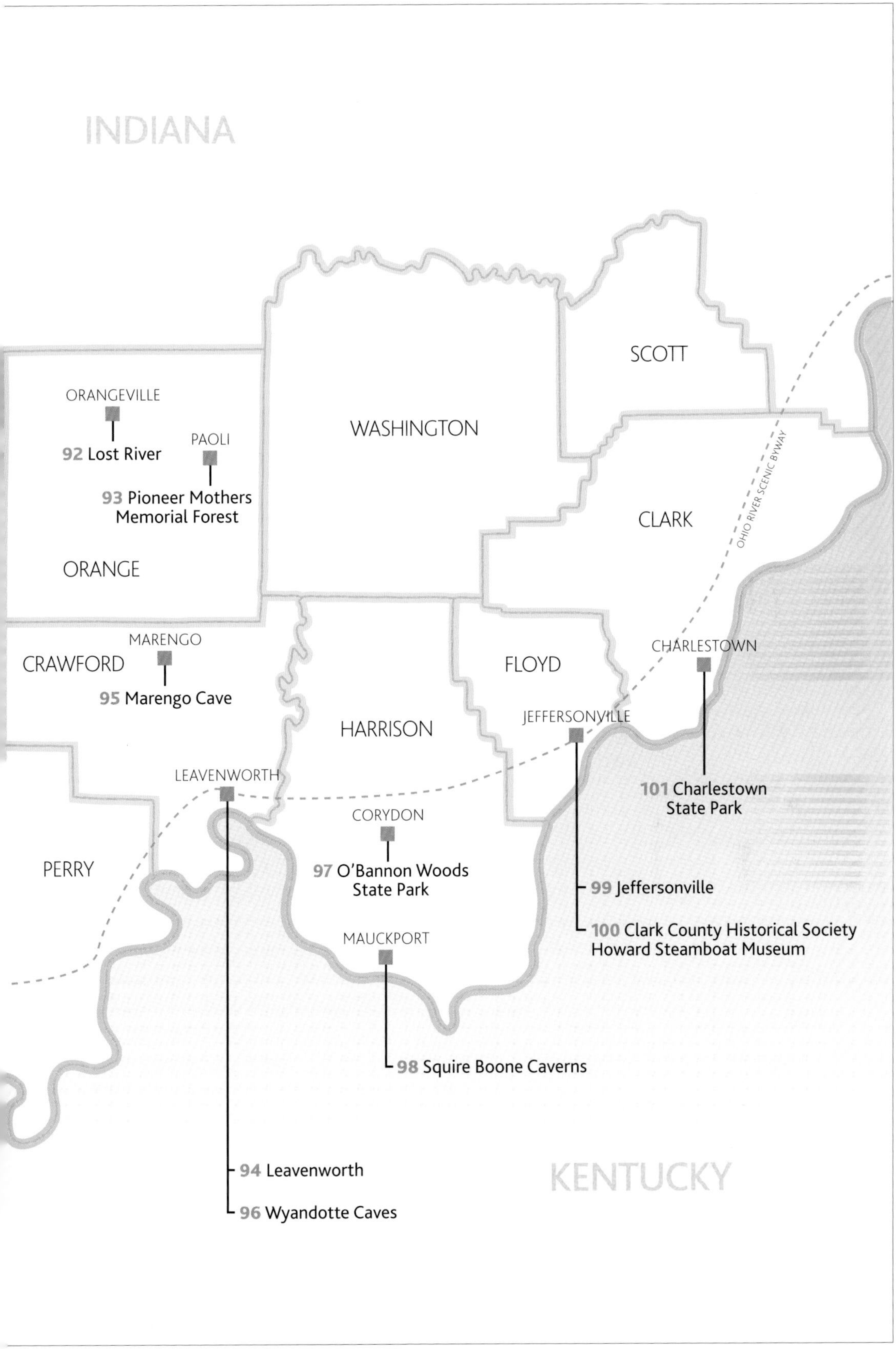

INDIANA

SCOTT

WASHINGTON

ORANGEVILLE

92 Lost River

PAOLI

93 Pioneer Mothers
Memorial Forest

ORANGE

CLARK

OHIO RIVER SCENIC BYWAY

MARENGO

CRAWFORD

95 Marengo Cave

FLOYD

CHARLESTOWN

HARRISON

JEFFERSONVILLE

LEAVENWORTH

101 Charlestown
State Park

PERRY

CORYDON

97 O'Bannon Woods
State Park

MAUCKPORT

99 Jeffersonville

100 Clark County Historical Society
Howard Steamboat Museum

98 Squire Boone Caverns

94 Leavenworth

KENTUCKY

96 Wyandotte Caves

BYWAY SIGN. This sign marks the route of the Ohio River Scenic Byway as it crosses Indiana from Ohio to Illinois.

EVANSVILLE'S SKYLINE. This major city, an exception along the route, can be seen from the Lloyd Expressway, part of the Ohio River Scenic Byway as it approaches the Illinois border in southwestern Indiana.

ILLINOIS BORDER. Indiana's Ohio River Scenic Byway ends at the Wabash River and the state's border with Illinois, west of Evansville.

Ohio River Scenic Byway

My feeling about the Ohio River Scenic Byway reminds me of the old vaudeville joke when the comedian would say, "I came to Indiana as soon as I heard about it." That describes how I feel about the byway: I wanted to travel it as soon as I heard about it.

It didn't work out that way, however. Only recently did I find a full day to actually drive the 297-mile route that sometimes parallels the Ohio.

I say "sometimes," because the truth of the matter is that it is the "scenic byway" not the "river byway"—the Ohio River Scenic Byway.

I also call it a "297-mile route." Literature about the byway describes its length as 302 miles. My speedometer probably is off but 297 miles was my measurement.

It crosses the state from the Ohio to the Illinois border—east to west. However, I started my journey in Evansville, so mine was a trip west to east—from the Illinois to the Ohio border.

Now back to that "scenic byway" point rather than the journey being a "river byway."

When I left Evansville early one morning to drive the few miles west to the Illinois border—so I could then turn back to the east to be certain to drive the entire distance across the state—I did not see the river at all. It wasn't until I reached the attractive small town of Newburgh that, suddenly, I came upon the river. (You're missing a good bet if you don't stop at Newburgh to walk along the river and enjoy the town, plus there's a wonderful overview of the river at the Newburgh Locks and Dam at the junction of Indiana 662 and Indiana 66.)

In every case, sighting the river was a thrill for me. Sometimes, it appears to be almost narrow—sort of a big Wabash River. Other times, especially when I came upon those great, sweeping turns of the river, it is broad and majestic.

Not surprisingly, it is the towns along the river that add so much to enjoyment of the trip. Each one is a gem.

Important, too, for the traveler is the byway's signage. The route uses a highway sign that effectively marks the road all across the state. (I only made one misstep.)

CLOSE ON OCCASION. Sometimes, the Ohio River runs very close to the Ohio River Scenic Byway as it winds its way across the southern part of the state.

The byway, which mostly follows Indiana 56, 62, and 66 across the southern part of Indiana, was designated as a National Scenic Byway in 1996. It passes through thirteen Hoosier counties, traversing the state, west to east, roughly from Evansville to Lawrenceburg. In doing so, it travels through parts of the state rich in prehistoric sites, a panorama of three hundred years of American history and the story of Indiana—archeology, farms, forests, caves, parks, towns, mansions, industry, no less than eight National Historic Register Districts, locks and dams, and variety of architecture.

Would I suggest that anyone do exactly what I did during my trip? In all honestly, probably not. You would be far better off to take two or three days of a long weekend to more or less meander along the byway—stopping where you wished for a more relaxed trip than the one I had during one long day.

Still, I was a happy camper when I arrived back home after my long-anticipated Ohio River Scenic Byway trip.

IF YOU GO

INFORMATION: Brochures about the Ohio River Scenic Byway are available at most Interstate rest stops, county tourism and convention offices, by calling Historic Southern Indiana at (800) 489–4474, or by going to http://www.ohioriverscenicroute.org/.

FEES: None.

RECONSTRUCTED ROUNDHOUSE.
It may have been used by the
Mississippians a thousand years
ago as a "sweat lodge," possibly in
preparation for religious ceremonies.

IN INTERPRETIVE CENTER. This
display is in the interpretive center
at Angel Mounds State Historic Site
near Evansville. The center recently
was enlarged and renovated.

Angel Mounds State Historic Site, Evansville

EVANSVILLE—The idea was straight-forward: The more prominent the Mississippian of nearly one thousand years ago, the taller the mound on which the family lived. At least, that is what archeologists researching Angel Mounds State Historic Site just east of the city conclude.

Excavations of the now 603-acre site along the Ohio River began in the 1930s with Works Progress Administration diggers under the direction of Glenn A. Black.

With prompting and finances provided by Eli Lilly—how many projects did that man aid in Indiana?—the Indiana Historical Society bought the original four hundred-plus acres in 1938. The IHS gave the site to the state in 1965 with excavation rights awarded to Indiana University. Today it is administered as a State Historic Site under the direction of the Department of Natural Resources.

Twenty more acres across the road were a later gift from Elda Clayton Patton Herts. The site contains an early Woodland mound, probably one thousand years older than Angel Mounds, which date back as far as 1100 A.D. Likely intended for burials, it has never been excavated.

The Angel Mounds site is considered one of the best preserved Native American prehistoric settlements in the United States.

The state historic site's history runs something like this: Woodland people settled along the river, possibly as early as 1100 B.C. Then came the Mississippians around 1100 A.D. For whatever reason, they began to leave and were gone by 1450 A.D. Bands of Shawnee, Miami, and probably other groups followed and eventually white settlers arrived.

Where are the Angels in this account? Maybe you made the same mistake I did in assuming it had something to do with one of these earlier cultures. Rather it is the family name of white settlers who farmed there from 1852 to 1899.

On the day I toured Angel Mounds, I was lucky enough to be taken around by Site Manager Mike Linderman in a four-wheel drive. Thank heaven! It was hot, and the walk around the site would have been a long one.

IT'S THE HIGHEST. The tallest of the mounds at Angel Mounds State Historic Site near Evansville is Mound A at forty-four feet. Archaeologists believe the height of each of the mounds was proportionate to the importance of the family living on it.

He pointed out the eleven mounds, which had been inside a one-and-a-half-mile wall the Mississippians built for protection. The tallest—Mound A—is four hundred feet wide, six hundred feet long and forty-four feet high, making it the tenth largest known mound in the United States.

"We are fortunate, although this was a working farm for a hundred years with extensive plowing, because of so much river silt, the mounds themselves had not been greatly damaged," Linderman told me.

Major erosion needed to be stopped and, generally speaking, the site needed big-time maintenance in cleaning out trees, other erosion, poor signage, and rotting steps on Mound A. The interpretive center, erected to house "temporary" exhibits by Lilly in 1971, was totally renovated with permanent exhibits added and was reopened to the public in 2001. Included are reconstructed winter houses, a roundhouse, summerhouses, and a portion of the stockade wall.

IF YOU GO

GETTING THERE: From Interstate 64 take Interstate 164 south at Evansville. Take the Covert Avenue/Indiana 662 exit and follow the signs. The address is 8215 Pollack Ave.

INFORMATION: Call (812) 853–3956, or go to http://www.angelmounds.org/. Open Tuesday through Saturday, 9 a.m. to 5 p.m. and Sunday, 1 p.m. to 5 p.m. Closed Monday. Closed January through mid-March. A visitor's guide for walking tours is available.

FEES: Admission charged.

Lincoln State Park, Lincoln City

ONE OF THE PADDLEBOATS.
Paddleboats can be rented at Lincoln State Park, near Lincoln City in southern Indiana.

THE NATURE CENTER. The nature center at Lincoln State Park is open daily except Tuesday, from 10 a.m. to 2 p.m. Interpretive naturalists present programs at the center as well as other places in the park.

LINCOLN'S SISTER. Tombstones at the Little Pigeon Primitive Baptist Church at Lincoln State Park for Aaron Grigsby and his wife, Sarah Lincoln Grigsby, older sister of Abraham Lincoln.

LINCOLN CITY—Just because it's steeped in tradition and Lincoln lore doesn't mean that things never change, sometimes for the best and sometimes not.

One of the good changes at Lincoln State Park in southern Indiana was the remodeling of the Pine Hills Group Camp to allow individual cottage reservations as well as group camping. The number of cottages to be reserved now ranges from one up to fifteen, probably enough for a large family reunion. The cottages sleep four to sixteen people. They're called "primitive" sleeping cottages with a centralized shower house along with a dining hall, kitchen, restrooms, and play field.

Campgrounds continue to be available—flush toilets, hot water, and showers as well as electricity in the class A spots. If primitive cottages and camping isn't your thing, then other family cabins that sleep six people can be reserved from April through November.

All of this can be done through the Indiana State Parks' Central Reservation System. (See the "If You Go" box.)

Another plus at Lincoln State Park has been the work to improve Weber Lake in the northwest part of the property along with considerable restocking of fish. You can pick up a state fishing license at the park office if you don't have one.

That lake is in addition to the much larger Lake Lincoln near the center of the park, where the nature center, beach (open sunrise to sunset), bathhouse, concessions, boat ramp, fishing pier, and paddleboat, canoe, and rowboat rentals are located.

Hiking trails abound, all easy to moderate and ranging from .8 mile to 3.7 miles. Together, they cover ten miles.

What marks this park particularly is that it lies in the midst of Lincoln country—where young Abraham Lincoln lived from ages seven to twenty-one. Today's visitor at the park is aware of this connection upon viewing the Little Pigeon Primitive Baptist Church, established in 1816, and the tombstones of Lincoln's sister, Sarah Lincoln-Grigsby, and her husband, Aaron Grigsby. She was twenty-one when she died in 1828. A nature preserve in the southern portion of the park is named in her honor.

GENERAL STORE AND BATHHOUSE. Located at Lincoln State Park in southern Indiana in the heart of Lincoln country.

IF YOU GO

GETTING THERE: From Interstate 64, go south on U.S. 231, and then east on Indiana 162 to Lincoln State Park.

INFORMATION: The park's telephone number is (812) 937–4710. The state parks' Central Reservation Systems telephone is (866) 622–6746, or http://www.camp.IN.gov/.

FEES: Park admission charged.

More on Lincoln can be seen across Indiana 162 at the Lincoln Boyhood National Memorial, where Lincoln's beloved mother, Nancy Hanks Lincoln, is buried. It's also the site of the Lincoln farm. Also nearby is the historic Colonel Jones Home. He was the merchant employer of young Abraham Lincoln. Later he was killed fighting for the Union in the Civil War.

The state park was established in 1932 as a memorial to Lincoln's mother. It was constructed largely through the work of the Civilian Conservation Corps, a program to put young men to work during the Great Depression. The CCC built Lake Lincoln, the Lakeside Shelter House, and boat rental building, created hiking trails, and planted thousands of trees.

The result today is a 1,747-acre park of gently rolling forested hills along with the two lakes. I visited once during the warm summer months and, as the state park literature declares, "visitors find a cool repose from the summer sun," in part under those CCC-planted trees.

Lincoln Living Historical Farm, Lincoln City

NINETEENTH-CENTURY FARM HOUSE. Rotted logs in this nineteenth-century farm house have been replaced by the National Park Service with new hand-hewn logs. It stands on the Thomas Lincoln homesite in southern Indiana.

WHAT IT WAS LIKE. An interpreter inside the cabin on the Thomas Lincoln farm explains frontier life in southern Indiana in the early 1800s.

AT THE FARM. This barn, made up from logs from several buildings, on the Thomas Lincoln farm at the Lincoln Boyhood National Memorial is part of the re-creation of a southern Indiana homestead.

LINCOLN CITY—Abraham Lincoln was quoted by one of his first biographers as saying he "never passed through a harder experience than he did in going from Thompson's Ferry" as a young boy to his father's new homesite in what was then Warrick County in southern Indiana in late 1816.

The ferry had carried the Lincoln family from its Kentucky home across the Ohio River into the new state of Indiana. As another biographer, Louis A. Warren, noted, the Lincolns, after crossing the river, at some point left a trail they were following north to hack their way through the woods to what would become the family's homestead.

Hoosiers would do well to remember that Abraham Lincoln spent his formative years, from seven to twenty-one, at this farm in Indiana. What Lincoln has become even two hundred years later—one of the most revered men in the history of the modern world—was very much the direct result of those Indiana years. Lincoln himself said, "There I grew up."

Or, as the National Park Service puts it on its Web site, "His sense of honesty, his belief in the importance of education and learning, his respect for hard work, his compassion for his fellow man, and his moral convictions about right and wrong were all born of this place and this time."

A visit to the Lincoln Living Historical Farm on the grounds of the Lincoln Boyhood National Memorial can give some sense of those years as park interpreters in period clothing perform some of the activities typical for the early 1800s.

The farm is a re-created pioneer homestead that includes a cabin, outbuildings, split-rail fences, farm animals, vegetable and herb gardens, and field crops—much as Thomas Lincoln's farm might have looked following years of work.

The National Park Service's farm was established in 1968, mostly using buildings saved when a power plant was built at Rockport south on the Ohio River and where the Lincolns crossed from Kentucky. The cabin, made up of logs from several buildings, has undergone rehabilitation with rotted and deteriorating logs replaced with new logs hand hewn by park employees.

THE HOMESTEAD. A re-creation of an early-nineteenth-century homestead on the Thomas Lincoln farm at the Lincoln Boyhood National Memorial near Lincoln City gives visitors a sense of pioneer life.

Following the path to the farm from the Lincoln Boyhood National Memorial Visitors Center—certainly an equally important stop—takes the visitor past the grave of Nancy Hanks Lincoln, Abraham's mother who died in 1818 when Lincoln was nine. She had been tending to sick neighbors and probably suffered from the dreaded "milk sickness."

Of course, no interpreters can totally depict the harshness of that early-nineteenth-century pioneer life. Former Superintendent Al Banton is quoted in a park history as saying the survival atmosphere that must have surrounded the struggling Lincoln farm could not be re-created and that visitors could hardly realize the cabin was meant only for sleeping, eating, and few other activities with everything else taking place outdoors.

Still, in the quietness of the moment in the midst of the homestead clearing, it's almost possible to believe a young Abraham Lincoln might come strolling into sight.

IF YOU GO

GETTING THERE: From Interstate 64, go south on U.S. 231, and then east on Indiana 162 to the Lincoln Boyhood National Memorial and the Lincoln Living Historical Farm.

INFORMATION: The memorial and farm are open year-round but interpreters are at the farm only from mid-April through late September. Hours are 8 a.m. to 5 p.m. during summers, central daylight time; close at 4:30 p.m., central standard time, winters. The memorial and farm telephone number is (812) 937–4541. The Web site is http://www.nps .gov/libo/.

FEES: Admission charge includes the memorial and farm.

DUTCH STREET ORGAN. A Dutch street organ is demonstrated by Clara Rust during a tour of Doctor Ted's Musical Marvels.

TOUR GUIDE. Clara Rust demonstrates how air is forced through holes in cardboard books to create music in this Dutch street organ, part of the Doctor Ted's Musical Marvels museum north of Dale in southern Indiana. The organ was manufactured in Rotterdam more than fifty years ago.

AN EARLY ONE. One of the very early Victrolas is part of the musical instruments in the southern Indiana musical museum.

Doctor Ted's Musical Marvels, Dale

DALE—Tour guide Clara Rust explains it this way: Doctor Ted Waflart first was a mechanical engineer, working in Louisville. Then he decided to go into medicine and operated a family practice for more than twenty-five years before he was persuaded to become a physician at Memorial Hospital in nearby Jasper.

Along the way, however, he came across an old pump organ at an antique store in 1973. Because of his background and interest in engineering, he brought the organ home and worked to restore it. In the years that followed, he found musical instruments as he traveled through Europe, at old-time amusement parks, and from classics known about or held by other collectors.

"One thing led to another and then to another and he hasn't quit yet. He is restoring another organ now," the tour guide relates to visitors at Doctor Ted's Musical Marvels, a museum of music in southern Indiana. It features mechanical musical instruments made from the 1800s into the mid-1900s.

The "musical marvels," as tour guides and museum literature explain, "crash their own cymbals, play their own pipes, beat their own drums, all produced by cranking and forcing air through holes that move pulleys and bellows that operate the instrument. The air goes through holes in piano rolls or book music for each fantastic note that's played."

Sometimes the restoration and especially the building of one of the instruments has taken a while. For example, an air-driven reproduction of a Wurlitzer organ from the early 1900s has been in Walfart's museum for three years. It was constructed for him by the Stinson Organ Company of Ohio but it is thought to have taken some twenty years to produce after the project was begun. It's one of the numerous organs in the museum that either can play its original music from a roll or can be played by hand.

Perhaps the highlight of the museum is the Decap Belgian Dance Organ, one of the few still in existence. The "portable" organ was moved from dance hall to dance hall about every six months despite its size: 12 feet high and 24 feet wide with

ALMOST AN ENTIRE BAND. This Decap Belgium Dance Organ was transported from dance hall to dance hall despite its size—twelve feet tall and twenty-four feet wide. It employs a "book" punched for its extensive melodies.

535 pipes. It features two accordions, two saxophones, a snare drum, bass drum, woodblock, tempo block, cymbals, and even a high hat! Literally, it is an orchestra in one instrument. It was located in Sint-Niklaas, Belgium, and shipped to Dr. Ted's. It, too, uses books of longer and different thicknesses to mechanically produce its music.

Said to be Dr. Ted's favorite is a Wurlitzer organ made for the medium-sized merry-go-rounds of the early 1900s. It was crated in storage for thirty years. Today it performs, standing next to three carousel horses to complete the circus feel.

Coming along later was the KT Special, produced in 1925 by the Seeburg Company of Chicago. The nickelodeon, forerunner of the jukebox, primarily was used in bars and dance halls. It plays a ten-tune roll.

Obviously, this is not a museum the visitor hastens through. A tour guide escorts visitors and the average time takes about ninety minutes, depending on how much music you want to hear along the way.

IF YOU GO

GETTING THERE: From Interstate 64 take exit 57 north one mile on U.S. 231 toward Huntingburg to the museum. The address is 11896 South U.S. 231.

INFORMATION: Call (812) 937–4250. The Web site is http://www.drteds.com/. The museum is open year-round for scheduled tours.

FEES: Admission charged.

NEW DUBOIS COUNTY MUSEUM. The museum occupies this former furniture factory building on Jasper's north side, using about 50,000 square feet of the 145,000-square-foot structure.

COUNTY'S ATHLETES. This county athletic history display was the latest large attraction at the Dubois County Museum in Jasper when I visited.

USED IN ATLANTIC TRIP. Trunks such as this one were typically used by immigrants coming to the United States from "the old world" during the nineteenth century. Many Dubois County settlers arrived from Germany.

Dubois County Museum, Jasper

JASPER—I was on my way to Evansville to begin a trek across the southern part of the state following the Ohio River Scenic Byway. While driving through Jasper, I noticed a large sign marking the new Dubois County Museum.

New to me, at least, because when I last visited the museum, it was located some distance away on Main Street, crowded into the historic Gramelspacher-Gutzweiler building.

First things first, however. That meant a German tenderloin sandwich—with cheese and bacon—plus German potatoes and coleslaw at the famous, and rightly so, downtown Schnitzelbank Restaurant.

Although all its artifacts still aren't on display the term "crowded" no longer applies. In 2003 Dubois County Museum Inc. was given a 145,000-square-foot former furniture factory. Now, museum display space is not a problem. The costs for heating and air-conditioning are, of course.

That means the museum's volunteer board of directors is busying targeting every source its members can think of to raise funds. Museum memberships, fund-raisers, renting about 50,000 square feet of space, gifts, and some small grants and county council assistance are the financial mainstays.

But what a museum they have. It took about a year to complete the move and open the doors. New displays have kept coming on line since then. The most recent when I visited was the Cheering Our Champions, a 1,300-square-foot exhibit of county sports memorabilia, history, and records. Prominent among Dubois County athletes are NBA All Star Don Buse, former NBA rookie of the year Paul Hoffman, NFL quarterback Matt Mauck, and another NBA star, Gene Tormohlen.

Some grasp of what it has accomplished in these last few years is the Certificate of Commendation received in 2005 from the American Association of State and Local History for "general excellence." Its evidence abounds as the visitor passes through exhibit after exhibit depicting the many phases of Jasper and Dubois County's fascinating past.

Much of the county's history centers on farming and logging with the resultant furniture-making businesses for which Jasper has been well known over the years.

PLENTY OF ROOM. With far more display space than in the former museum, there's room for this restored double log house in Exhibit Room II of the new museum.

Its history also revolves around its heavy German settlement. How these journeys were made by these hardy immigrants, more often than not crossing the Atlantic in close-quarters packet ships, is another part of the Dubois story told in museum displays and artifacts.

When Jean Hoffman, secretary of the board, was explaining use of the new facility to me, she was standing in the lower-level general purpose room, frequently used as an auditorium. It's but one example of the space available. Large exhibits, such as a sawmill and a threshing machine, now have ample room to be displayed.

While many of the 150 museum volunteers helped in taking out ductwork, etc., as they prepared to move in, they equally appreciated the offices, furniture, and other working materials Kimball International left at the site when it moved to its new facility. "Look at these desks, filing cabinets, office partitions. Think what they would have cost us," Hoffman said during our walk-around.

IF YOU GO

GETTING THERE: U.S. 231 (Newton Street) goes through Jasper. The museum is on the left as you enter town from the north. The address is 2704 Newton Street.

INFORMATION: Call (812) 634–7733. Hours are Tuesday through Saturday 10 a.m. to 2 p.m., Sunday 1 p.m. to 4 p.m., or by appointment. You can also call the Dubois County Tourism Commission at (800) 968–4578, or go to the Web site at http://www.duboiscounty.org/.

FEES: Free admission, but donations accepted.

Holiday World and Splashin' Safari, Santa Claus

VOYAGE'S FIRST DROP. It goes some 154 feet at a 66-degree angle of descent and is the first of three 100-foot-plus drops on the 1.2-mile-long wooden roller coaster at Holiday World and Splashin' Safari in southern Indiana. Note the train reaching the top.

MORE HIS SPEED. Grandpa Conn found the antique car ride more to his speed than the roller coasters. That's grandson Ben Watters at the wheel, accompanied by his brother, Jacob. Imagine what the smiles were like after they rode The Raven fifteen times!

PAT KOCH. Holiday World and Splashin' Safari and Pat Koch are intertwined. Here she poses with grandchildren Leah, who lives in Santa Claus, and Erin and David, who live in Florida. She was making a swoop through the park, checking it out.

SANTA CLAUS—My grandsons, Ben and Jacob Watters, their Mom and Dad, and I spent a pleasant three days recently in southern Indiana in and around Santa Claus, Indiana, including the best part of two days at the theme park, Holiday World and Splashin' Safari.

While the newer roller coaster, The Voyage, commands the most attention these days, Dad's one ride proclaimed it probably too intense for young Ben and Jacob. The wooden coaster, which opened in 2006, has three drops of more than 100 feet, reaches a maximum speed of 67.3 miles per hour, goes through eight tunnels, and is the third highest wooden roller coaster in the world.

But The Raven was different. One ride for the boys followed another and another until the count reached fifteen. The ride opened in 1995, and more than ten years later, it's still rated one of the top five wooden roller coasters in the world. (I can hardly imagine what the ranking will be for Pilgrims Plunge, set to open in 2009—the world's tallest water slide at 135 feet that will go 50 miles an hour down a 45-degree angle.)

Now more about the park. If you've been to Holiday World and Splashin' Safari, you know the drill. Soft drinks are free as are sunscreen and inner tubes at Splashin' Safari.

It consistently is voted the cleanest theme park in the world and friendliest park. Recently, The Voyage was named the number one Wooden Roller Coaster on the Planet while Bakuli was named the best new water ride. *Consumer Digest* has ranked it the number one "Top Value Park" in the country.

In its sixty-first year in 2007, it had more than one million visitors.

The Holiday World themes and rides—Christmas, Fourth of July, Halloween, and Thanksgiving—are only part of the story. Perhaps even more popular is Splashin' Safari, Indiana's largest water park that comes along with the price of admission. Started in 1993, it now perhaps is the major feature of the park, especially during hot summer days. It features eight family water slides.

Recent additions to the water park include Bakuli, a seven-story family water slide ending in a spiraling bowl drop; a sec-

BAKULI'S "BOWL." The bowl finishes the seven-story, family water park ride by dropping tube riders down into the sixty-foot bowl. That comes after a slide in total darkness down six flights. These riders are plunging toward the pool.

ond water wave pool, Bahari and Bahari River; and Kima Bay, with seven water slides and more than one hundred water-play elements.

Also, I'm not sure how frequently in most major theme parks you're going to find the mother of the park's president walking around, checking up on things. Well, Pat Koch was when we were there—as she is most of the time. I'm told you also might just as easily see her cutting up pizza, sweeping one of the sidewalks, or greeting visitors.

The park—the first theme park in the world, opening in 1946—initially was called Santa Claus Land after the town, becoming Holiday World in 1984. It was started by Pat's father-in-law, Louis Koch; further developed by her late husband, Bill; and now is managed by her son, Will.

While you're in Santa Claus, you'll want to go to the nearby Santa Claus Museum. While it's a work in progress, it's certainly worth the several minutes it will take you to drop in and look around.

IF YOU GO

GETTING THERE: From Interstate 64 take exit 63 south on Indiana 162 into Santa Claus.

INFORMATION: Holiday World's telephone number is (877) 463–2645, and Web site is http://www.holidayworld.com/. The park opens at 9:30 a.m. central daylight time daily with differing closing times during the summer and most weekends through mid-October; Splashin' Safari, opens at 10:30 a.m. central daylight time through mid-September. (It's not open some weekends in September because of "buyouts." Check.) For information about other the Spencer County sites, call the visitor bureau at (888) 444–9252, or visit http://www.legendaryplaces.org/.

FEES: A one-price admission covers all activities at the park while a second-day pass is less.

LOST RIVER. Enough water had fallen so the Lost River just south of Orangeville in southern Orange County was above ground.

ON INDIANA 37. Much of the time, this section of the Lost River on Indiana 37 south of Orleans is dry. Enough rain had fallen so the river could be seen above ground.

Lost River, Orangeville

ORANGEVILLE—How do you lose a river? Well, at least one way is what happens to southern Indiana's Lost River: It simply disappears underground from time to time—probably traveling through underground caverns and waterways in the stone formations created hundreds of thousands if not millions of years ago as the various glaciers and Ice Ages of prehistoric times passed. Because of the extensive limestone found in this part of the state, those eons of time had allowed water to find its way through these rock deposits, creating subterranean passageways.

I had heard about the Lost River, mostly from my friend Alan Garinger, Selma naturalist and student of Indiana lands and history. However, nearly nine years elapsed before I had an opportunity to actually see something of this famous river, and that only occurred during a recent trip to see the French Lick Casino and renovated French Lick Springs Hotel.

While making that visit, I asked Rob Denbo, Orange County Convention and Visitors Bureau executive director, if he could point me in the direction of the river. Better than that, he said, and since it was on my way back to Muncie, he would guide me there and so he did.

We turned north off Indiana 150 at 550W—the Ames Chapel United Methodist Church is at the intersection along with a sign "Orangeville 5 miles"—and wound our way about four miles or so before crossing a somewhat rusting orange-painted bridge, one of two in Orange County, according to Denbo. It crosses Lost River.

Then, just a short distance before reaching Orangeville, we came to a place where the river rises above ground. The "rise-pool," it's called, varies in depth and activity according to how much rain has fallen and how low or high the water is.

When I was there, the area recently had received lots of rain—as had much of Indiana—but the pool was not especially active. Compared to some photos I had seen of the pool, the water, however, was high.

Actually, according to *Indiana: A New Historical Guide*, the river really begins its ninety-three-mile journey to the west,

THE "RISE POOL." This spot is south of Orangeville where the Lost River resurfaces after a mostly dry twenty-two-mile stretch. With heavy rains, the water becomes turbulent.

about twenty-two miles usually underground, in Washington County near Smedley's Station.

Even the so-called dry bed of the river, where it crosses about two miles south of Orleans below Indiana 37, contained above-ground water in what almost looked like a drainage ditch. This is one area where the river usually sinks before rising again at the spot we visited south of Orangeville.

While I took photographs, Denbo told me about his long-hoped-for plan to make the rise-pool more of an Orange County tourist attraction. His goal was to put a bridge across the river from the highway to a flat piece of land where he envisioned a picnic area plus playground equipment.

Likely to happen? Given the tightness of county budgets, maybe not. But it could be a pleasant spot to stop for visitors coming and going from the new French Lick Casino and its two renovated hotels and resort facilities.

If you want a really good look at the river, the Lost River Conservation Association offers three tours a year. (See the "If You Go" box for tour information)

IF YOU GO

GETTING THERE: From Indiana 37 south of Bedford into Orange County take Indiana 150 west and go north on 550W—the Ames Chapel United Methodist Church is at the intersection. The rise-pool is just south of Orangeville. Lost River also is crossed on Indiana 37 two miles south of Orleans.

INFORMATION: Call the Orange County Convention and Visitors Bureau at (812) 936–3418 or toll-free at (877) 422–9925. Also use the Web site http://www.orangecountyin .com/. For information on Lost River tours, call (317) 253–6951.

FEES: None.

PATH INTO FOREST. The beginning of the path that leads through the Pioneer Mothers Memorial Forest south of Paoli.

VIRGIN TIMBER. A trail going through part of the eighty-eight acres of the Pioneer Mothers Memorial Forest begins to the left of the photo.

Pioneer Mothers Memorial Forest, Paoli

PAOLI—Lots of people need to be thanked for the preservation of eighty-eight acres of old growth forest that have existed since before the time when the state's first white settlers started migrating into southern Indiana. Today, that area is known as the Pioneer Mothers Memorial Forest and, so far as can be determined, it's the only stand of its size of such forest still left in Indiana.

It's difficult to imagine today, but the U.S. Forest Service tells us that when settlers came into what is now Indiana more than two hundred years ago, the state was covered with more than nineteen million acres of old-growth forest. Walnut trees were forty inches in diameter and frequently grew more than 130 feet high. Oaks, here since before Columbus landed, were "abundant."

So, what happened?

Actually, it's fairly simple. The land was cleared for farming and the trees were used as wood products for just about everything. Over the course of not too many years, the great forests just disappeared.

But not the Pioneer Mothers Memorial Forest. The U.S. Forest Service tells the story.

Joseph and Mary Cox purchased 258 acres southeast of Paoli in 1816, moving to southern Indiana from Tennessee. Because Joseph Cox loved trees, he set aside the eighty-eight-acre tract for future generations. The land stayed in the family through good times and hard times, down through another Joseph Cox who died in 1940.

Heirs sold the property to the Wood-Mosaic Lumber Company of Louisville for $23,000. When word of the sale was announced in the newspapers, the Meridian Club of Paoli convinced the lumber company to delay cutting timber for ninety days and to resell the eighty-eight acres for the purchase price if it could be raised. The U.S. Forest Service kicked in half of the money and the club raised the rest in eighty-nine days. True to its word, the lumber company sold back the virgin timber.

The agreement included that no trees would ever be cut. Because the Indiana Pioneer Mothers Club contributed

FOREST ENTRANCE. This sign marks the Indiana 37 entrance to the Pioneer Mothers Memorial Forest, south of Paoli in southern Indiana.

$5,900 to the cause, the stand of timber, formerly called Cox Woods, was renamed the Pioneer Mothers Memorial Forest.

It was declared a Research Natural Area by the Forest Service in 1944, so no hunting, camping, target-shooting, or plant collecting is allowed. Horses and bikes also are prohibited. The Forest Service maintains a 165-acre "buffer" around the forest to help protect the trees.

Hiking along a trail that cuts through the forest probably is the best way to enjoy seeing this historic forest. The trail goes from a south entry point on Indiana 37 to a north entry point on U.S. 150. A rock-wall memorial, about halfway along the trail, was erected in 1951.

Another interesting part of the story, reported in U.S. Forest Service literature, was the discovery of the site where a Native American village once stood on Lick Creek. Since the area had been undisturbed—except for vandals and souvenir hunters—archaeologists rather easily defined the walls and buildings of the village.

IF YOU GO

GETTING THERE: On Indiana 37 south of Paoli is the Pioneer Mothers Memorial Forest one and one-half miles east of town. That's the location of one trailhead. Another is on U.S. 150, one mile from Paoli.

INFORMATION: Contact the Hoosier National Forest office in Bedford at (812) 275–5987, or go to http://www.fs.fed.us/r9/hoosier.

OVERLOOK RESTAURANT.
Perched high—and safely—above
the Ohio River in New Leavenworth
is the Overlook Restaurant.

Leavenworth

LEAVENWORTH—Old-timers who live near Horseshoe Bend on the Ohio River have seen the worst of times and, more recently, some better ones, too.

Horseshoe Bend is where the Ohio River comes rolling downstream from Louisville and then, at the site of Leavenworth about halfway across the state, makes a horseshoe bend—the sharpest in the river—up into Indiana before turning south again, heading toward Evansville.

Not much of Old Leavenworth, down by the river, is left today and that's part of the worst of times. It was 1937 when the greatest flood in recorded history about wiped out the town. When the waters subsided, 111 homes had been destroyed or damaged, leaving only eight that could be lived in, according to *Indiana: A New Historical Guide*.

So the residents decided to build a New Leavenworth, high up on the bluff overlooking the river. It took time and money and not everyone agreed to move. Plus times were tough all over. The United States was mired in a worldwide depression and this hilly part of the county was poor farming land. The railroads long since had bypassed the area, so there wasn't much business either.

What Leavenworth and the rest of Crawford County did have, though, is southern Indiana scenery that can take your breath away. As good a place as any to enjoy the view of the river is at the Overlook Restaurant. With an expansive deck situated at the edge of the bluff, Overlook diners have a panoramic view of the Ohio River—twenty miles of it coming from the east, moving through the bend and then flowing on to the west.

Actually, you don't have to be out on the deck for a view. The restaurant was constructed so that diners at many tables can see the Ohio, the southern Indiana countryside, and Kentucky across the river.

How popular is the restaurant? It's listed as one of the top ten in *Indiana's Favorite Hometown Restaurants: Where the Local Folks Like to Eat*. According to the restaurant's brochure, "There are seats for 225, which is a lot for a town of 300." The register has the names of guests from all over the world.

LOOKING UPSTREAM. This view from the deck of the Overlook Restaurant looks up the Ohio River. Twenty miles of the Ohio can be seen from the restaurant's deck. That's Kentucky across the river.

Nearby are the Leavenworth Inn, four renovated homes—two of them turn of the century; Annabelle's Gift Shop and Gallery; Annabelle's Arts Center; and Stephenson's General Store and Museum, antiques, crafts, and household items.

Down below, along the river, Old Leavenworth is still there, too. It even has its own restaurant, the Dock Restaurant, which specializes in seafood platters. A few preflood buildings also still stand. Writer Doug Wissing in his *Traveling the Ohio River Scenic Route* describes it as "a place with the air of a slightly raffish yesterday."

Crawford County has more than a river view to offer. Marengo and Wyandotte caves, Patoka Lake, the Harrison-Crawford State Forest, and the Hoosier National Forest are some of the area's other attractions.

If you do go to the Overlook, you should finish off whatever meal you have with homemade pie—and it should be coconut cream. That's the best of times.

IF YOU GO

GETTING THERE: From Interstate 64 take Indiana 66 south for three miles to Indiana 62 and go east one-half mile to the Overlook Restaurant.

INFORMATION: The restaurant's number is (812) 739–4264. The hours are fairly easy to remember. It's open Monday through Thursday 8 a.m. to 8:30 p.m. and Friday through Sunday 8 a.m. to 9 p.m. Closed Christmas Eve and Christmas Day. The menu can be viewed at http://www.theoverlook.com/. The Crawford County Tourism Bureau toll-free number is (888) 846–5397.

FEES: None to look.

FLOWSTONE. This flowstone is an example in Marengo Cave where the rapid flow of water over many years has caused a heavy deposit of calcite along the side of a cave room.

A CAVE ROOM. Some of the formations in one of the Marengo Cave "rooms."

"MIRROR LAKE." The "lake" appears to be a deep body of water but actually measures only a few inches. The illusion comes from the reflection of the cave ceiling in the still water.

Marengo Cave, Marengo

MARENGO—Blanche Hiestand, a fifteen-year-old girl working as a cook at the Marengo Academy, overheard students talking about a hole they had found not far from the school. It was at the bottom of a sinkhole and they planned to check it out.

Blanche, determined to get there before the students, hustled home, conscripted her younger brother, Orris Hiestand, eleven, and set out to be the first to explore the hole. They found the sinkhole, surrounded by trees, not far from the town cemetery. Climbing down to its bottom, they found a small opening in the ground. Lighting candles they had brought from their house, they slithered into the hole and went down and down—and down. The hole got bigger and bigger until finally they found themselves in a large room of a cave. It was September 6, 1883, and they had discovered Marengo Cave.

They kept the news to themselves until the following Sunday when they told Samuel Stewart, who owned the land. He gathered together a group of men and boys who retraced the Hiestands' route and found, according to a cave history, "vast passageways and splendor such as none of them had ever seen before."

At least that's the way the story goes.

The history of the cave, in the intervening 125-plus years, has been a series of exploring new sections of the cave, above and below ground improvements, changes of ownership, and economic ups and downs.

A highlight came in 1984 when the cave was designated a U.S. National Natural Landmark by the Department of the Interior. It called Marengo "a textbook example of a cave in the middle stage of development."

Today, the cave no longer uses the sinkhole entrance the Hiestand children followed to enter the cave. Instead, two other man-made entrances provide easier access to where walking tours into the cave begin.

The Dripstone Trail Tour is seventy minutes and takes visitors by soda straw, stalactite, and stalagmite formations,

WELCOME CENTER. Visitors to Marengo Cave in southern Indiana arrive at and cave tours depart from the welcome center.

including sections called Music Hall, Pulpit Rock—yes, ministers have preached from it, and Penny Ceiling, where you can toss up a penny and it likely will stick to the cave ceiling. (In 1999 there were 90,370 coins removed from the ceiling, totaling $3,855.56.)

The shorter forty-minute Crystal Palace Tour includes huge flowstone formations and a special lighting presentation.

Of course, you can do both as many cave visitors do.

Marengo Cave also operates the nearby Cave County Canoes on the Blue River, which attracts about 30,000 paddlers annually.

In the cave itself, before laws protecting caverns were passed, the cave was damaged by those who wrote graffiti, took rocks, and otherwise despoiled the underground treasure. Thankfully, those days are over. The cave is lighted so the old graffiti doesn't show, and its operators believe that, as cave shows go, it is near pristine condition.

IF YOU GO

GETTING THERE Indiana 64 goes through Marengo. The entrance to the cave is east of the town on the north side of the highway.

INFORMATION: Call toll-free (800) 702–2837 or (812) 365–2705. The Web site is http://www.marengo cave.com/. Summer hours, Memorial Day to Labor Day, are 9 a.m. to 6 p.m.; winter, 9 a.m. to 5 p.m. Closed Thanksgiving Day and Christmas Day.

FEES: Different fees for the tours. Three years and younger, free.

Wyandotte Caves, Leavenworth

ENTER THE CAVE. A Wyandotte Caves tour group enters through a passageway into the southern Indiana cave, which has been known to be used by humans for an estimated three thousand years.

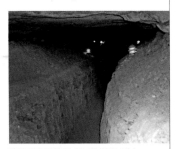

EARLIER THEY CRAWLED. This trenched out passageway allows Wyandotte tourists to stand upright in navigating the cave rather than crawling as earlier cave explorers did.

LODGE MEETINGS. Odd Fellows Lodge members met in this Wyandotte Caves room.

WHICH EXIT? When tourists come to this pile of stones in the Wyandotte Caves, they know only one is the true exit from the cave.

LEAVENWORTH—Early inhabitants of what is today southern Indiana were in Wyandotte Caves thousands of years ago to extract flint and to use the caves for shelter, for food storage, and probably for ceremonies. In more recent times, William Henry Harrison, looking for saltpeter an ingredient in gunpowder, visited the caves early in the nineteenth century. But the present-day use of the caves as a tourist attraction took off in the 1850s when they were opened to the public, making them the fourth-oldest commercial caves in the United States.

The Henry P. Rothrock family had purchased hundreds of acres east of Leavenworth for timber in 1819. When cave explorers found a large new section of the caves, however, the enterprising Rothrocks turned to tourism and charging admission. The family stayed with the business until 1966 when it sold the land to the State of Indiana.

Indiana still owns the property today—part of the O'Bannon Woods State Park—but, with tight budgets, the State leased management of the caves in 2002 to a company that owns, among other caves, nearby Marengo Cave.

Actually, Wyandotte Caves consists of two tour sites—one, a half-hour easier tour through Siberts Cave, owned earlier by another family that competed with the Rothrocks in the tourism business, and the second, in the larger Wyandotte Caves with two longer walking tours through numerous rooms. Siberts has only one set of steps and goes into the cave about a third of a mile. The historic Wyandotte tour is more extensive and has a number of steps.

Wyandotte was designated as a U.S. National Natural Landmark in 1972 by the U.S. Department of the Interior. Its explored length is more than nine miles, consisting primarily of dry upper levels, carved in Mississippian limestone that was deposited by an inland sea more than a million years ago.

As one might imagine, the larger and more accessible rooms of the cave have had various uses over the years. Since Rothrock was a member of the Odd Fellows Lodge, one room hosted lodge meetings and meals.

CRATER LAKE. This room in Wyandotte Caves, near Leavenworth in southern Indiana, is named Crater Lake.

As visitors walk through the caves, they mostly follow passageways of silt left by rivers flowing over the bedrock. In some cases, trenched out passageways have been cut where cave explorers had to crawl.

A critically important room is one with four apparent exits. It's identified by a large pile of stones in its center. However, three are not exits, so far as is known, but instead lead to other caves. When visitors return to the room later in a tour, the guide enjoys asking them to select the only actual exit. (All six on our tour got it right.)

For the more adventurous, "natural" trips through undeveloped sections of Wyandotte are available for groups with advance reservations. These trips take from two to four hours and mounted helmet lights are provided. Yes, you'll crawl—and then crawl some more and scramble, too, over rocks.

Other caves—"wild" or noncommercial—exist in the area but are not open for public tours. Explorers have to fill out daily caving permits with the Department of Natural Resources to explore caves on public property.

IF YOU GO

GETTING THERE: From Interstate 64 take Indiana 66 south and then turn east on Indiana 62. Go about six miles to a turnoff to the north at Wyandotte Caves.

INFORMATION: Call (888) 702–2837, or go to http://www.wyandotte caves.com/. Historic Wyandotte is only open for four months—from May until Labor Day—so that an estimated sixty thousand Indiana bats, an endangered species, can hibernate in the winter. Siberts opens in March and continues through October.

FEES: Admission charged for cave tours.

INSIDE THE PARK. Potato Run Church and its neighboring cemetery are on the grounds of O'Bannon Woods State Park in southern Indiana, west of Corydon.

WAY INTO PARK. A view of the entrance to Indiana's twenty-fourth state park, O'Bannon Woods, in southern Indiana close to the Ohio River.

O'Bannon Woods State Park, Corydon

CORYDON—While he served for years in the halls of Indiana state government in Indianapolis, Frank O'Bannon's heart never was far from southern Indiana, especially his home at Corydon, a combined 175-year-old log cabin and 140-year-old converted barn next to a woods.

Following his death in office as governor, it was not unexpected that a favorite relaxing spot for both Frank and Judy O'Bannon near their home would be named in his honor—O'Bannon Woods State Park, the former Wyandotte Woods State Recreational Area, carved out of the 24,000-acre Harrison-Crawford State Forest.

Indiana's twenty-fourth state park lies less than ten miles west of Corydon. Its 2,000 acres remain basically unchanged from its previous existence as a recreational area except for the difference in name, made in December 2004 and announced by Governor Joe Kernan.

Stephen Sellers, writing in *Outdoor Indiana,* noted that the park actually honors the entire O'Bannon family and its contributions to the state. Frank's grandfather, Lew O'Bannon, published the *Corydon Democrat* as did Frank's father, Robert O'Bannon, and Frank. Lew was a candidate for lieutenant governor, running on an anti-Ku Klux Klan platform, while Robert also was a lawyer and state senator. Frank's widow, Judy, remains active in Indiana public projects.

Converting the recreational area into a state park apparently long had been a goal of the governor, who served two terms as lieutenant governor for Evan Bayh and was in his second term as the state's chief executive when he died in Chicago. He had introduced a bill to make the land a state park some twenty years ago when he was a state senator.

Much of the work at the state park and state forest was completed in the 1930s by the Civilian Conservation Corps.

The park has its own unique features in addition to the customary campsites—nearly three hundred of them—campground for horse riders, picnic shelters, eighty miles of horse and fifteen miles of hiking trails, and, perhaps most interesting

HAY PRESS INSIDE. This large barn houses an old-fashioned hay press. Periodic demonstrations at O'Bannon Woods State Park show how up to 300-pound bales are formed.

for park visitors, a working hay press. It's located in a large barn where hay is fed into the press, turned on the ground level by farm animals, and then, with a thud, a heavy metal press comes slamming down to compact the hay.

On the Sunday afternoon I was there viewing the demonstration, a crowd of fifty or so milled around to watch as a park ranger explained the process and answered questions. Behind the hay press's barn is a representation of an 1830s southern Indiana farmstead. It's staffed by volunteers on holiday weekends.

Another interesting park attraction is the Potato Run Church, an attractive, well-kept building with posted services for Sunday school, worship, and Wednesday Bible study.

Future projects call for building cabins, expanding the horse camp, and perhaps even erecting a lodge. A state-of-the-art family aquatics center opened for swimming in 2007.

IF YOU GO

GETTING THERE: From Interstate 64 go south on Indiana 135, Business Route, into Corydon and then east on Indiana 62 to Indiana 462 into the park.

INFORMATION: When you arrive in Corydon, a good place to start for maps and information is the Harrison County Convention and Visitors Bureau at the corner of Elm and Walnut streets, just behind the old state capitol building. For camping reservations at the state park, go online to http://www.camp.in.gov/, or call (866) 622–6746. The park telephone number is (812) 738–8232.

FEES: Admission charged to enter the park and fees for camping.

Squire Boone Caverns, Mauckport

BREAK TIME. Visitors at Squire Boone Caverns in southern Indiana pause during a tour of the caverns.

MANY, MANY YEARS. Flowstone at Squire Boone Caverns has built up from the flow of water over the centuries.

TOUR GUIDE. Our guide, Trey, relates stories about early exploration of Squire Boone Caverns by Squire and his brother Daniel in the 1790s. A new walnut casket now holds some of what are believed to be Squire Boone's bones, which visitors pass as they near the end of the caverns tour.

MAUCKPORT—We came out of Squire Boone Caverns at its exit. No surprise there, but then we also entered at the exit.

That's because the cavern's management had closed the man-made entrance into the caverns after limestone fell in "room 2." Engineers were checking the safety of the passageway after heavy rains apparently had loosened some of the stone. The entrance was to remain closed while another dugout passageway was considered.

Caverns, incidentally, means a connected system of caves and passageways. The terms "caverns" and "caves" are frequently less precisely and interchangeably used.

The guide for our group was a young Kentucky high school senior, Trey. He seemed to have been doing it for a lifetime, both in terms of knowledge and communication skills.

The deepest point in the caverns for tourists is ninety feet underground. Tour groups in some places walk on heavy steel gratings used for walkways and bridges. At one point, they pass over the twelve-foot waterfall, not far from the caverns' entrance discovered nearly three hundred years ago by the two Boone brothers, Daniel and Squire.

The Boones were on a hunting trip in 1790 in what was then the far West of the new country. Legend has it that, after they crossed the Ohio River, they looked up on a hillside and saw water flowing out of a small opening. They crawled into the entrance in the hillside for about two hundred feet where they encountered a waterfall. In 1804 Squire recalled the area and returned with family members with the idea of using the waterpower for a gristmill to grind corn.

Later cave explorers found that Boone's eight-foot waterfall was followed by yet another and then, finally, a twelve-foot waterfall. That's the one visitors see rushing below the metal grating as they reach this deepest point of the caverns. An estimated million gallons of water flow through the caverns daily, slowly carving away the limestone as it has for millions of years.

The Boones on that first visit weren't finished, however. They found a second entrance into what has become known

VICTIM OF FIRE. Squire Boone's gristmill at the Squire Boone Caverns near Corydon has been destroyed by fire several times. It was last reconstructed in 1975.

as the burial cave. It was on Squire's next trip that, again legend has it, he escaped from Indians by hiding in the burial cave.

At Squire's death, his relatives buried his body in this cave. Searchers in the 1970s found pieces of walnut and twenty-eight human bones that were thought to be Squire's—for example, the skull had an indentation from an Indian tomahawk, so young Trey told us.

A new walnut casket now holds the bones, which visitors pass as they near the end of the tour. There's even a tombstone although, as Trey pointed out, the date of Squire's death is misstated as August 5, 1815, rather than August 15.

The nearby gristmill still uses water as its source of power to turn an eighteen-foot overshot waterwheel. The mill has been destroyed several times by fire.

In addition to the underground tour, a Boone Village has log cabins as shops for hand-dipped candles, cornmeal, baked goods, candy, rocks, and other crafts.

IF YOU GO

GETTING THERE: From Interstate 64 turn south on Indiana 135 to Squire Boone Road, south of Corydon. Go about three miles on a winding, hilly road past the gristmill to the caverns and village.

INFORMATION: The telephone number is (888) 934–1804. The Web site is http://squireboonecaverns .com/. The village is open daily from Memorial Day weekend until Labor Day weekend. Caverns tours are every thirty to forty-five minutes Memorial Day through Labor Day. During the rest of the year, tours leave at 10 a.m., noon, 2 p.m., and 4 p.m. Closed on national holidays and bad weather days in the winter.

FEES: Admission charged for tour as well as a parking fee when the village is open.

THOMAS JEFFERSON. President Thomas Jefferson is depicted in this statue in front of the 1903 Carnegie Library, built in downtown Jeffersonville. Jefferson suggested the original layout for the city.

WHERE IT BEGAN. This statue, at the Falls of the Ohio State Park's Interpretive Center, commemorates the meeting of William Clark, George Rogers Clark's younger brother, with Meriwether Lewis to begin their exploration of the Louisiana Territory.

Jeffersonville

JEFFERSONVILLE—There's something especially captivating about a river town. Maybe it's the slow-moving water and the realization that the river was there long before we were born and will keep on flowing downstream long after we're gone. Maybe it's the vessels on the water. They are something like trains: We wonder where they've been and where they're going. Maybe it's the quiet of the water and the busyness and bustle of activity along the streets leading from the water.

Whatever it is, Indiana towns along the Ohio River to the south and the Wabash River to the west seem imbued with some kind of magical, almost spiritual quality simply because the river is there.

Jeffersonville is a case in point.

If you meander around downtown Jeffersonville or the Falls of the Ohio just west of downtown, you are never far from the Ohio River and its impact on the city's history, commerce, recreation, and future.

Surely, history is there aplenty.

The city was originally laid out in 1802 on a plan suggested by President Thomas Jefferson. The land was part of a huge parcel given to General George Rogers Clark for his Revolutionary War heroics in saving from the British this part of what was to become the new nation.

Later, some of the country's great steamboats were built in Jeffersonville during the 1800s. One stop any tourist wants to make is the Clark County Historical Society Howard Steamboat Museum, a short distance from the river and the business descendant of the steamboat builders, Jeffboat Inc. The twenty-two-room former Howard home is filled with boat-building memorabilia despite a 1971 fire that seriously damaged the structure—plus the 1937 flood that crept up the stairway toward the second floor.

In the downtown itself, a number of historic structures can be viewed. The best guide is the *Jeffersonville Walking Tour* brochure, available at the Clark-Floyd Counties Convention and Tourism Bureau and at other places around town and in neighboring Clarksville. It includes the Riverfront Historic District. Certainly you will want to pause at Jefferson's statue.

2001 REPRESENTATION. What the cabin of George Rogers Clark, overlooking the Ohio River, probably looked like. The original was demolished in 1854.

One stop, of course, has to be Schimpff's Confectionary on Spring Street, where you can see candy being made and, naturally, buy some. Small dining tables are available near an old-fashioned soda fountain.

You'll need a car to see the Falls of the Ohio State Park and its interpretive center, plus going a little farther to the west to a representation of the log cabin home of George Rogers Clark, built in 2001. The original was torn down in 1854.

An added significance of this site is the fact that this is where Clark's brother, William, met Meriwether Lewis in 1803 to start their expedition to explore the Louisiana Purchase.

It's well worth the time spent in a short detour while traveling on Interstate 65 at that point where Indiana and Kentucky meet at the Ohio River. It may be old hat if you live there, but for the rest of us landlocked Hoosiers, the lure of the river is powerful indeed.

IF YOU GO

GETTING THERE: From Interstate 65 at the Ohio River take Exit 0.

INFORMATION: Call the Clark-Floyd Counties Convention and Tourism Bureau (812) 282–6654, or toll-free, (800) 552–3842. The Web site is http://www.sunnysideof louisville.org/. For the Falls of the Ohio, call (812) 280–9970, or go to the Web site at http://www.fallsof theohio.org/. The park is open 6 a.m. to 11 p.m. The interpretive center is open Monday through Saturday 9 a.m. to 5 p.m. and Sunday 1 p.m. to 5 p.m.

FEES: No admission to enter the park. The interpretive center has an admission fee but nothing for children under two years old. No charge for the walking-tour brochure.

HOWARD HOME. The former home of the boat-building Howard family now houses the Clark County Historical Society Howard Steamboat Museum.

INDIANA. The *Indiana* is one of several models in the museum of steamboats built by the Howards during their more than one hundred years of boat building. Most of the models are in the second-floor bedroom of the mansion. A videotape of the second floor is available for those who cannot climb the stairs.

COUNT THIRTEEN. That's how far up the steps the 1937 floodwaters rose in the Howard mansion at Jeffersonville. The water remained in the home for two weeks.

Clark County Historical Society Howard Steamboat Museum, Jeffersonville

JEFFERSONVILLE—"The handsomest residence south of the Alleghenies is that built by Capt. Ed Howard, just back of his shipyard in Jeffersonville," wrote the *Louisville Times* on August 11, 1894.

The *Times* article, typical of the day, was lavish in its praise of the twenty-two-room mansion. The Moorish drawing room was called "the gem of the lower floor" while the upstairs bedrooms, "all named for flowers," were described in awestruck detail. Even the bathroom was commended as having "every appliance known to modern architecture."

Similar to Hillforest, built by another shipbuilder upriver at Aurora, the woods used were its special feature, including rare black walnut, oak, cherry, jasper, and chestnut.

Today, the residence is the site of the Clark County Historical Society Howard Steamboat Museum. No, it doesn't have a real steamboat in it. (The largest display is the shaft of the original paddlewheel from the *Delta Queen*.) But the museum does have artifacts of steamboat days, much of the house restored, and models of some of the country's finest—and fastest—steamboats.

Fast meant everything to the steamboat builders. The "last race of the big side-wheelers" took place on the Ohio River August 19, 1928. The Howards' boat, *America*, finished second to the *Cincinnati*, although *America* was under orders to hold back to let *Cincinnati* win, the historical society reports.

In 1894 the Howards built what is considered one of the fastest steamboats in the world, the *City of Louisville*. The steamer on its record run left Louisville at 3 p. m. and arrived in Cincinnati at the Main Street landing nine hours and forty-two minutes later—and that was after fourteen other stops going upriver!

Spread throughout the mansion are detailed models of some of the Howards' more famous boats. The model of *Indiana*—renamed *America* after a fire and rebuilding—took an estimated 5,200 hours and 34 months to construct. It was built from photos and plans and includes an onboard blacksmith shop, a swing on the hurricane porch for the captain's

CINCINNATI WINS! This is the finish of the 1928 race with the
Cincinnati winning over the Howards' America. That's Louisville in the
background. Two years later, the America lay at the bottom of the river,
destroyed by fire.

IF YOU GO

wife, and a hobbyhorse for the baby. The paddlewheels
contain 1,700 parts and are driven by electric motors.

The mansion has withstood two major catastrophes.
The 1937 flood came up to the thirteenth step of the grand
staircase leading to the second floor. The water stayed
there for about two weeks, according to Ed J. Howard, the
only son of Captain Howard. The second was a 1971 fire.
Evidence of the fire still can be seen in burn marks in the
building.

While the mansion is a treat for the visitor, the story of
the shipyards, just across the street, has its own fascination.

The first James Howard started building boats in 1834.
Over the following decades, the Howard family constructed
about three thousand vessels. During World War II, the U.S.
Navy bought the shipyards to build landing craft (LSTs).
Then, after the war, the shipyards were sold and today Jeffboat Inc. is a manufacturer of inland waterway vessels. It's
the largest shipyard in the nation on an inland river.

GETTING THERE: Southbound on
Interstate 65, take exit 0. You will
be on Market Street facing west.
Go around the block to face east on
Market and go about fifteen blocks.
The museum is on the left. Parking
and the museum entrance are in the
rear.

INFORMATION: Last tour is at
3 p.m. For more information,
call (812) 283–3728, toll-free at
(888)472–0606, or check the Web
site at http://www.steamboat
museum.org/. Hours are Tuesday
through Saturday 10 a.m. to 4 p.m.
and Sunday 1 p.m. to 4 p.m.

FEES: Admission charged, under six,
free; special rates for tour groups.

Charlestown State Park, Charlestown

ONE OF THE TRAILS. This rugged trail at Charlestown State Park starts off easily enough but then descends and climbs as it reaches Fourteenmile Creek.

CHARLESTOWN—Have trouble identifying the third largest state park in Indiana? That might not be too surprising, since it is one of Indiana's more recent assets and has continued expanding its facilities in very recent years.

For most of the 1900s, the park was mostly farmland and pasture. With World War II about to begin for the United States, the federal government built the largest gunpowder plant along the Ohio River, the Indiana Army Ammunition Plant, on 15,000 acres. Neighboring Charlestown, a sleepy little town of less than 1,000, swelled to the tens of thousands.

After the war, Charlestown dropped back to a population of around 5,000, and for nearly fifty years nothing much happened with the plant and its grounds except for jobs during the Korean and Vietnam wars.

That changed in 1995 when the federal government gave Indiana more than 2,000 acres to establish a state park. Other land was purchased from private owners, with the addition of nearly 2,700 more acres in 2004, Charlestown State Park became Indiana's third largest in size. The State opened the park in 1996.

Park visitors are well aware of the area's history. When I drove in, I passed what seemed to be an abandoned rail line, railroad cars, and old, locked buildings, remnants of the ammunition plant.

Although all of the park's territory is not opened to the public, the Department of Natural Resources recently has added parking, a riverbank boardwalk, more picnic areas, restrooms, and a boat ramp, giving access to the Ohio River.

At a park ceremony in late 2004, Governor Joe Kernan called for a master plan for the park, which since has been developed. Actually the park has gone through four phases of facility construction in the last dozen years.

Six hiking trails of more than eight miles are described as being either moderate or rugged. On my trip, I started one of the rugged trails that at one point, "meanders through dense

PARK ENTRANCE. Charlestown State Park, which lies along the Ohio River in southern Indiana, has doubled in size in recent years, making it the third largest state park in Indiana.

forest," as the park's brochure put it. Maybe so, but it rather quickly became more than I thought I could handle in the limited time I had.

Picnic areas, shelters, and playgrounds also are part of the park's features. The park's campground has 132 electric sites and 60 full hookup sites—one of only two Indiana state parks with full hookups. It also has flush toilets, hot water, and showers and can accommodate trailers.

Fourteenmile Creek runs through the state park, emptying into the Ohio River. Fishing includes bass, bluegill, catfish, and other game fish. Electric motor boats are allowed into the Ohio River now and have full access to the river.

One special note about the creek: If it appears that the creek is running north—upstream—that's because the U.S. Army Corps of Engineers is raising the level of the Ohio River, which backs water up into the creek. The valley of the creek is one of the oldest unglaciated—untouched by the long-ago glaciers—stream valleys in Indiana.

IF YOU GO

GETTING THERE: From Interstate 65 go southeast on Indiana 160 to Indiana 403 at Charlestown and then east on Indiana 62 to the park entrance. Another route would be to take Indiana 3 into Charlestown and then Indiana 62 east to the park.

INFORMATION: Call the park office at (812) 256–5600. For camping reservations, go online to http://www.camp.in.gov/, or call (866) 622–6746.

FEES: Admission charged. Shelters also can be reserved.